"Paradise Lost: A Poem Written in Ten Books"

An Authoritative Text of the
1667 First Edition

Medieval & Renaissance Literary Studies

"Paradise Lost:
A Poem Written in Ten Books"

An Authoritative Text
of the 1667 First Edition

————————

Transcribed & edited with commentary by
John T. Shawcross & Michael Lieb

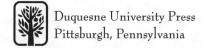
Duquesne University Press
Pittsburgh, Pennsylvania

Published in the United States of America by
DUQUESNE UNIVERSITY PRESS
600 Forbes Avenue
Pittsburgh, Pennsylvania 15282

Library of Congress Cataloging-in-Publication Data

Milton, John, 1608–1674.
    Paradise lost : a poem written in ten books.
      p. cm. — (Medieval & Renaissance literary studies)
    Summary: Vol. 1: "This authoritative text of the first edition of John Milton's Paradise
lost transcribes the original 10-book poem, records its textual problems and numerous differences from the second edition, and discusses in critical commentary the
importance of these issues"—Provided by publisher.
    Summary: Vol. 2: "Essays by ten Miltonists establish the significant differences in
text, context, and effect of the first edition of Paradise lost (1667) from the now standard second edition (1674), examining in particular the original text's relationship
to the literary and theological world it entered in 1667 and thus offering interesting
correctives to our understanding of Milton's thought"—Provided by publisher.
    Includes bibliographical references and indexes.
    ISBN-13: 978-0-8207-0404-3 (set : acid-free paper)
    ISBN-10: 0-8207-0404-0 (set : acid-free paper)
    ISBN-13: 978-0-8207-0392-3 (v. 1 : acid-free paper)
    ISBN-10: 0-8207-0392-3 (v. 1 : acid-free paper)
    [etc.]
    1. Bible. O.T. Genesis—History of Biblical events—Poetry. 2. Adam (Biblical
figure)—Poetry. 3. Eve (Biblical figure)—Poetry. 4. Fall of man—Poetry. 5. Milton,
John, 1608–1674. Paradise lost. 6. Milton, John, 1608–1674—First editions. I.
Shawcross, John T. II. Lieb, Michael, 1940– III. Title.
    PR3560.A2S53 2007
    821'.4—dc22

                                                                              2007025652

Contents

Bibliographic Terms

The following are definitions of the bibliographic terms used here and in the collations and discussions of the copies of the first edition.

edition: a printed text for which the type has been set or has been reset for another edition.

state: a page or pages that have evidence of an alteration in the text or the setting of the text which has occurred during printing.

issue: a text of an edition that has *not* been reset, the edition being issued and often reissued or reprinted (re-pressed) for another issuance.

signature: a gathering of leaves of paper, marked by a letter and/or figure on one or more pages as a guide to binding. *Paradise Lost* is a quarto; that is, it uses a gathering employing four leaves or eight pages, generally "signed" on the first two leaves; e.g., A on the first leaf of the first gathering and A_2 on the second leaf; or G on the first leaf of the seventh gathering and G_2 on the second leaf. Here "r" and "v" will also be used to indicate whether the page is a recto or a verso; e.g., E_3v (although *not* signed) indicates the verso of the third leaf of the fifth gathering.

variant: any change in the text, whether through deliberate or accidental alteration, creating a difference from another occurrence of the same word or form in the same textual position (e.g., "appeer" and "appear"; "Urania" and "*Urania*").

error: any inaccurate form or printed text. Later issues of the first edition of *Paradise Lost* include an errata sheet (single, erratum), which records a few errors that had been recognized.

crux: a variant that may point out an error or deliberate change in a text, or that may be an error; critical examination has not established the validity of either the original or the variant text.

>: a symbol employed to indicate change from one form to another; "ought > aught" indicates that the first spelling has been changed at some point to the second spelling.

∧: subscript indicates a lack of punctuation.

For clarification, a new "edition" means that a text has been reset with or without changes; an "issue" means that a later publication of the text with or without changes but with a new title page has been produced. A "signature" is a gathering of leaves, formed from the folding of a sheet of paper—pages therefore being double the number of leaves, which are set up in coordinate fashion, such as A_1r and A_4v, A_1v and A_4r, A_2r and A_3v, A_2v and A_3r, and so on (that is, pages 1 and 8, 2 and 7, 3 and 6, 4 and 5)—for a quarto as *Paradise Lost* is. A "state" indicates a change made on a page during printing (often changes occur on coordinate leaves). When a specific state has been identified as the first setting, it is (or should be) called "state 1"; when that page evidences changes in the course of printing, it is called "state 2," and so on. (However, Fletcher's assignment of "state 1" or "state 2" is sometimes questionable; see later section, "The First Edition of *Paradise Lost*.")

PREFACE

Despite the many editions of the text of John Milton's *Paradise Lost* as it was published in 1674, this edition represents the only diplomatic text of the epic as it was first published in 1667. To (or authoritative) be sure, several editions claiming to have reproduced the 1667 text have appeared since the nineteenth century. These include items such as an 1873 "facsimile" edition, with a monograph by R[ichard] H[erne] S[hepherd]; a "facsimile" edition by David Masson (1877); the Scolar Press facsimile (1968), actually in two editions; and Harris Francis Fletcher's facsimile published as part of his *John Milton's Complete Poetical Works Reproduced in Photographic Facsimile* (1943–1948). (In addition to these items, there are various e-texts available on the Internet.) Not one of these items, however, can in any way be conceived as the kind of accurate and exhaustive work required to produce an authoritative text of the 1667 edition of *Paradise Lost*. As the only edition of its kind, the text reproduced here seeks to provide access to the first edition of Milton's epic as it was originally published. By making this edition available as an authoritative text, the editors hope to encourage additional research on a work that was, after all, complete and whole unto itself and "worthy t'have not remained so long unsung." With such an objective in mind, a companion volume of essays on the subject of the first edition of *Paradise Lost*, *"Paradise lost: A Poem Written in Ten Books"*: *Essays on the 1667 First Edition*, is likewise the first of its kind. *Nota bene:* The 1667 edition consistently reads "Paradise lost", thus emphasizing what was lost and minimizing the act of loss. Likewise, the running titles print, for example, "Book 3, *Paradise lost*." on versos and "*Paradise lost.* Book 3." on rectos. Line numbers are given in the left margin on versos and in the right margin on rectos. Both of these printing styles are altered to current style.

Although no manuscript of *Paradise Lost* in its entirety has been found as a source for the first edition, the extant manuscript of book 1 (in the hand of an unidentified amanuensis with numerous corrections by various hands) is the copy source for the first edition, as compositor markings make clear, and it thus can offer insights into how the manuscript as a whole was transcribed and the possible differences between manuscript and published text. In addition to taking into account the extant manuscript of book 1 of *Paradise Lost,* the text reproduced here is transcribed from the most authoritative texts, including the text of the 1667 edition (first issue) housed in the collections of the Newberry Library. The transcription, in turn, has been collated with a copy of the 1667 edition (first issue) owned by the British Library. Moreover, all transcriptions have been checked against the facsimiles of Fletcher and the Scolar Press, both of which must be used with care (as noted below). Throughout the present edition, notice has been taken of alterations in the states of given pages or signatures included in the six issues of the poem that are the result of corrections, errors, or non-Miltonic forms. While the second edition sometimes employs one or another state of a page and makes numerous corrections, particularly in orthography and accidentals, it contains its own errors that are correspondingly problematic. Except where indicated, errata are corrected, and all corrections or changes are duly noted in our section "Changes and Lack of Changes Made in the Edited Text," which is part of our full textual discussion that follows the text. In the first edition, there are also errors in line numbers that occur frequently (only sometimes corrected in new states, which may also make incorrect corrections), and these are also noted and corrected. Finally, all textual remarks have been checked against at least one additional copy of each issue of the first edition and one copy of the second edition. However one might attempt to construct a text faithful to the "Miltonic original," no text can be entirely "thorough" or entirely "Miltonic" because the texts as originally published are frequently "non-Miltonic" in such matters as spelling, capitalization, italicization, punctuation, and the like. Furthermore, no copy of any issue of the first edition has been found to be exactly the same as any other copy of any issue.

Some caveats about the Fletcher and Scolar Press facsimiles: To be frank, both are unreliable, and both contain serious errors of omission and transmission. For example, although Fletcher's facsimile edition purports to reproduce the original text as it was published in 1667, his text is drawn from the University of Illinois copy of the 1669 (first issue); that is, the fifth title page issue. His edition, moreover, very often fails to indicate whether specific facsimile pages are from one copy or from another copy. This, along with other errors and omissions, renders Fletcher's edition at once unreliable and even at times unacceptable. In its own way, the Scolar Press edition—or rather two editions—is correspondingly of questionable value. With recourse to an unidentified copy (perhaps the sixth title page issue of 1669) from its own holdings, this edition neglects to identify the states of the text it reproduces, and it ventures to offer "corrected" pages of the text randomly. What results is not a true facsimile of the first issue of the first edition, but a composite of different issues of the first edition. Although we are grateful for all the work that went into both the Fletcher and the Scolar editions, we must also be on guard at all times in any attempt to come to terms with the 1667 edition of *Paradise Lost*.

The 1667 Text and Its Audience

The text of *Paradise Lost* that a 1667 audience would have read poses many problems that a modernized edition of *Paradise Lost* obscures. Not only are there verbal errors, only some of which are corrected in the second edition of 1674, but also difficulties in the mechanics of spelling, punctuation, italicization, and capitalization that may lead to confusion and misreading. Added to this confusion is the visualization of the text on the page. Verbal errors (as well as the errata supplied in the preliminary sheets of issues four through six, and alterations in states of the text) are enumerated below and corrected in the text presented here, as indicated in "Changes and Lack of Changes Made in the Edited Text." While mechanical matters like spelling were not yet codified in the seventeenth century, a reader reading "the sudden blaze / Far round illumin'd hell" (1.665–66) may be disconcerted by the lack of uppercase "Hell"; or in "and fierce with grasped arm's / Clash'd" (1.667–68) by the inaccurate possessive form of "arms." In 8.346 and 706, verbs are capitalized meaninglessly: "his creating hand/ Nothing imperfet or deficient left / Of all that he Created" and "he knows that in the day / Ye Eate thereof, your Eyes . . . shall perfetly be . . . Op'nd and cleer'd." Confusing is the italicization of one noun but not another, as well as a questionable capitalization of that italicized word, in 1.713: "Built like a Temple, where *Pilasters* round / Were set." Regarding these mechanical matters, the copy-text for the first edition (the manuscript of book 1) is frequently not followed. (Not that the manuscript is necessarily correct: it often is not.) For example, the manuscript of book 1 does read "hell" in 1.666, and "arm's" in 1.667, but 1.713 has "Built like a temple, where pilasters round / Were set." This indicates the reproduction of the incompetent text of the manuscript and at the same time the unacceptable alteration of the manuscript.

Milton's long sentences are not always helped by punctuation—for example, 1.192–220, which includes two colons and various commas—but a reader is surely not aided in trying to comprehend all that is being said. The manuscript has a semicolon and a period instead of those two colons, a reading that is thus more easily followed. The punctuation of 1.619–21 in the manuscript (although not all other matters) is repeated in 1667 and is not changed in the second edition: "Thrice he assayd, and thrice in spite of scorn, / Tears such as Angels weep, burst forth: at last/ Words interwove with sighs found out their way." Most modern editions, although seemingly intended for a modern audience, iterate this incompetent punctuation (or in a couple of instances a comma is added after "Tears"—an inadequate change—and other alterations are made). Although the printer Samuel Simmons refers to the reason "why the Poem Rimes not," his expression that "many" were "stumbled" is apt for the text itself.

Looking at the printed page, we pause to make sure that we are reading what goes with what (4.697–703):

Fenc'd up the verdant wall; each beauteous flour,
Iris all hues, Roses, and Gessamin   (wrought
Rear'd high thir flourisht heads between, and
Mosaic; underfoot the Violet,
Crocus, and Hyacinth with rich inlay
Broiderd the ground, more colour'd then with Stone
Of costliest Emblem: other Creature here

Run-over lines, completed either above or below that line, occur frequently because of the size of the page; at times words are run together because of the length of lines: "Thrones, Dominations, Princedoms, Vertues, Pow-" with "(ers," above the line (5.601) or "being,stil" (8.266), causing this wrong and inconsistent spelling of "still." A large decorated first letter of the first word in the first line of each book causes the first three lines to require indentation and frequently overhang; this printing is not reproduced here. One may ask whether such indentation and overhanging in the first three lines may not be interpreted to yield significant meaning for the text.

Further, the poem is long, as Samuel Johnson remarked, and individual books seem to go on and on, but books 7 and 10 in the 1667 edition are very long—1,290 and 1,541 lines, respectively, the next longest being book 8 with 1,189 lines—and perhaps we can entertain the idea that a reader skipped or at best skimmed at least much in those two books, which do not offer pictures of Satan or specifically of the Fall and its aftermath for Adam and Eve.

There is evidence of an educated audience for the poem as presented in 1667, in addition to its source for the aborted translation of Theodore Haak (books 1–3 and part of 4 into German verse, dated ca. 1667–ca. 1680). In a series of letters from John Beale to John Evelyn (now in the British Library) the form, art, and subject of the epic are discussed, but the political concerns, the republicanism and Calvinism perceived in it are the foundation of Beale's enduring impression of it, in the words of Nicholas von Maltzahn.[1] (These

---

1. See Nicholas von Maltzahn, "Laureate, Republican, Calvinist: An Early Response to Milton and *Paradise Lost*," in *Milton Studies*, vol. 29, ed. Albert C. Labriola (Pittsburgh: University of Pittsburgh Press, 1993), 181–98.

letters are dated August 31, September 11, October 16, November 11, November 18, and December 24, 1667.) Letters exchanged between Sir John Hobart and his cousin, dated January 22, January 27, and January 30, 1668, offer favorable comments on the poem.[2] Apparently predating the second edition of *Paradise Lost* is an anonymous manuscript notation in *An Idea of the Perfection of Painting . . . Translated by J. E.* (1668) listing it as one of the "Books of advantage to a Painter . . . ye Paradise lost of Milton." Andrew Marvell, in "Last Instructions to a Painter," reveals many echoes of the poem throughout; the manuscript of Marvell's satire in the James Osborn Collection, Yale University, records its date as "September 1667," and in the Portland manuscripts at the University of Nottingham as "Sept. 4, 1667." Milton's nephew John Phillips includes an appropriation from the poem on page 8 of his *Montelions Predictions; or, The Hogen Mogen Fortuneteller* (1672). The author of *The Transproser Rehears'd; or, The Fifth Act of Mr. Bayes's Play* (1673) attacks Milton's political and religious position by reference to biography, his association with Marvell, and various works including *Paradise Lost*.[3] Rebuttal appeared soon after in 1673 by Marvell, *The Rehearsall Transpros'd: The Second Part* (and reprinted in 1674), which was countered by Parker in *The Reproof to The Rehearsal Transprosed, in a Discourse to Its Author.*

In 1674 two encomiastic poems by S. B. (identified as Samuel Barrow) and A. M. (Andrew Marvell) were printed prefacing the second edition, obviously inspired by the first edition. The first poem emphasizes its "great universe," its inclusiveness of "All things" important to humankind, the War in Heaven, Lucifer and the routing of the rebellious angels, and its dwarfing of epic authors like Homer

---

2. See James M. Rosenheim, "An Early Appreciation of *Paradise Lost*," *Modern Philology* 75 (1978): 280–82.

3. The author has been cited as Richard Leigh and as Samuel Parker, but was probably Samuel Butler, as argued by Paul B. Anderson, "Anonymous Critic of Milton: Richard Leigh? Or Samuel Butler?" *Studies in Philology* 44 (1947): 504–18, and by Nicholas von Maltzahn, "Samuel Butler's Milton," *Studies in Philology* 92 (1995): 482–95.

and Vergil. Interestingly it does *not* cite the Fall and Adam and Eve or the effects of the Fall and ensuing biblical history. As Michael Lieb has shown, S. B. "demonstrates the extent to which Milton's earliest readers were inclined to single out the War in Heaven as an event of paramount importance" (75).[4] In comparison is Marvell's poem which stresses "a rhetorical tradition of praise." Much has been written on Marvell's analysis of the poem and his championing its prosody (which was to receive general disapprobation) against the "tinkling Rhime" of John Dryden's tagging the lines. What is significant for us to observe here is Marvell's change of attitude within his encomium from his "misdoubting" Milton's "Intent / That he would ruine . . . / The sacred Truths to Fable and old Song" to exclaiming "Where couldst thou words of such a compass find? / Whence furnish such a vast expence of minds?"

The difficult text made more difficult for readers by length, by poor printing and composition work, by an unexpected and unpopular literary form did not, apparently, become well known until 1688 with the appearance of the fourth edition. Finally its reputation and influence spread and elicited both positive and negative evaluations of the author and his political and religious positions, but almost universally glowing evaluations of the poem's sublimity. Its author, as Dryden's epigram beneath Milton's frontispiece portrait in the 1688 edition pronounces, joins Homer's loftiness of thought and Vergil's majesty: "The force of nature could no further go."

John T. Shawcross and Michael Lieb

---

4. "S.B.'s '*In Paradisum Amissam*': Sublime Commentary," *Milton Quarterly* 19 (1985): 75.

NOTE ON THE TEXT

The authoritative text reproduced in this edition is a transcription of a copy of 1667[1] owned by the Newberry Library, collated with a copy owned by the British Library (C.14.a.9) and checked against the facsimiles by Fletcher and Scolar Press, which, however, produce a mixture of pages from various issues. Appended are the preliminary leaves first included in the fourth issue, 1668[2], reproduced from a copy owned by the University of Kentucky, including the six-line "The Printer to the Reader." A four-line statement is transcribed from the Huntington Library copy of the fifth issue, 1669[1]. (Please note that the superscripts are *not* footnotes; they refer to the first or the second issue of the text in 1667, 1668, and 1669.)

The states of the variants given for each book of the ten-book epic are as follows, with "state" referring to Fletcher's numbering:

1. Book 1, state 2 of variants given.
2. Book 2, state [2]–3 of variants given.
3. Book 3, state 1 of variants given except for lines 40, 60, 61, 97, 679, 690 (all state 2).
4. Book 4, state 1 of variants given but with line numbers corrected.
5. Book 5, "new" state 1 of variants given for lines 121–203 (Fletcher's state 3); state 2 for remainder of variants.
6. Book 6, no variants.
7. Book 7, state 1 of variants given.
8. Book 8, no variants.
9. Book 9, generally all state 2 of variants given.
10. Book 10, state 1 of variants given except for those at 10.32 and 10.139, where both are state 2.

Paradise lost

A Poem Written in Ten Books

PARADISE LOST

BOOK I.

OF Mans First Disobedience, and
      the Fruit
  Of that Forbidden Tree, whose
      mortal tast
  Brought Death into the World,
      and all our woe,
With loss of *Eden,* till one greater Man
Restore us, and regain the blissful Seat,
Sing Heav'nly Muse, that on the secret top
Of *Oreb,* or of *Sinai,* didst inspire
That Shepherd, who first taught the chosen Seed,
In the Beginning how the Heav'ns and Earth
Rose out of *Chaos:* Or if *Sion* Hill   10
Delight thee more, and *Siloa's* Brook that flow'd
Fast by the Oracle of God; I thence
Invoke thy aid to my adventrous Song,
That with no middle flight intends to soar
Above th' *Aonian* Mount, while it pursues
Things unattempted yet in Prose or Rhime.
And chiefly Thou O Spirit, that dost prefer
Before all Temples th' upright heart and pure,

Instruct me, for Thou know'st; Thou from the first
Wast present, and with mighty wings outspread   20
Dove-like satst brooding on the vast Abyss
And mad'st it pregnant: What in me is dark
Illumine, what is low raise and support;
That to the highth of this great Argument
I may assert Eternal Providence,
And justifie the wayes of God to men.

   Say first, for Heav'n hides nothing from thy view
Nor the deep Tract of Hell, say first what cause
Mov'd our Grand Parents in that happy State,
Favour'd of Heav'n so highly, to fall off   30
From their Creator, and transgress his Will
For one restraint, Lords of the World besides?
Who first seduc'd them to that fowl revolt?
Th' infernal Serpent; he it was, whose guile
Stird up with Envy and Revenge, deceiv'd
The Mother of Mankinde, what time his Pride
Had cast him out from Heav'n, with all his Host
Of Rebel Angels, by whose aid aspiring
To set himself in Glory above his Peers,
He trusted to have equal'd the most High,   40
If he oppos'd; and with ambitious aim
Against the Throne and Monarchy of God
Rais'd impious War in Heav'n and Battel proud
With vain attempt. Him the Almighty Power
Hurld headlong flaming from th' Ethereal Skie
With hideous ruine and combustion down
To bottomless perdition, there to dwell

In Adamantine Chains and penal Fire,
Who durst defie th' Omnipotent to Arms.
Nine times the Space that measures Day and Night   50
To mortal men, he with his horrid crew
Lay vanquisht, rowling in the fiery Gulfe
Confounded though immortal: But his doom
Reserv'd him to more wrath; for now the thought
Both of lost happiness and lasting pain
Torments him; round he throws his baleful eyes
That witness'd huge affliction and dismay
Mixt with obdurate pride and stedfast hate:
At once as far as Angels kenn he views
The dismal Situation waste and wilde,   60
A Dungeon horrible, on all sides round
As one great Furnace flam'd, yet from those flames
No light, but rather darkness visible
Serv'd only to discover sights of woe,
Regions of sorrow, doleful shades, where peace
And rest can never dwell, hope never comes
That comes to all; but torture without end
Still urges, and a fiery Deluge, fed
With ever-burning Sulphur unconsum'd:
Such place Eternal Justice had prepar'd   70
For those rebellious, here their Prison ordain'd
In utter darkness, and their portion set
As far remov'd from God and light of Heav'n
As from the Center thrice to th' utmost Pole.
O how unlike the place from whence they fell!
There the companions of his fall, o'rewhelm'd

With Floods and Whirlwinds of tempestuous fire,
He soon discerns, and weltring by his side
One next himself in power, and next in crime,
Long after known in *Palestine,* and nam'd   80
Bëëlzebub. To whom th' Arch-Enemy,
And thence in Heav'n call'd Satan, with bold words
Breaking the horrid silence thus began.
    If thou beest he; But O how fall'n! how chang'd
From him, who in the happy Realms of Light
Cloth'd with transcendent brightnes didst outshine
Myriads though bright: If he whom mutual league,
United thoughts and counsels, equal hope,
And hazard in the Glorious Enterprize,
Joynd with me once, now misery hath joynd   90
In equal ruin: into what Pit thou seest
From what highth fal'n, so much the stronger provd
He with his Thunder: and till then who knew
The force of those dire Arms? yet not for those
Nor what the Potent Victor in his rage
Can else inflict do I repent or change,
Though chang'd in outward lustre; that fixt mind
And high disdain, from sence of injur'd merit,
That with the mightiest rais'd me to contend,
And to the fierce contention brought along   100
Innumerable force of Spirits arm'd
That durst dislike his reign, and me preferring,
His utmost power with adverse power oppos'd
In dubious Battel on the Plains of Heav'n,
And shook his throne. What though the field be lost?

All is not lost; the unconquerable Will,
And study of revenge, immortal hate,
And courage never to submit or yield:
And what is else not to be overcome?
That Glory never shall his wrath or might   110
Extort from me. To bow and sue for grace
With suppliant knee, and deifie his power
Who from the terrour of this Arm so late
Doubted his Empire, that were low indeed,
That were an ignominy and shame beneath
This downfall; since by Fate the strength of Gods
And this Empyreal substance cannot fail,
Since through experience of this great event
In Arms not worse, in foresight much advanc't,
We may with more successful hope resolve   120
To wage by force or guile eternal Warr
Irreconcileable, to our grand Foe,
Who now triumphs, and in th' excess of joy
Sole reigning holds the Tyranny of Heav'n.
    So spake th' Apostate Angel, though in pain,
Vaunting aloud, but rackt with deep despare:
And him thus answer'd soon his bold Compeer.
    O Prince, O Chief of many Throned Powers,
That led th' imbattelld Seraphim to Warr
Under thy conduct, and in dreadful deeds   130
Fearless, endanger'd Heav'ns perpetual King;
And put to proof his high Supremacy,
Whether upheld by strength, or Chance, or Fate,
Too well I see and rue the dire event,

That with sad overthrow and foul defeat
Hath lost us Heav'n, and all this mighty Host
In horrible destruction laid thus low,
As far as Gods and Heav'nly Essences
Can Perish: for the mind and spirit remains
Invincible, and vigour soon returns,   140
Though all our Glory extinct, and happy state
Here swallow'd up in endless misery.
But what if he our Conquerour, (whom I now
Of force believe Almighty, since no less
Then such could hav orepow'rd such force as ours)
Have left us this our spirit and strength intire
Strongly to suffer and support our pains,
That we may so suffice his vengeful ire,
Or do him mightier service as his thralls
By right of Warr, what e're his business be   150
Here in the heart of Hell to work in Fire,
Or do his Errands in the gloomy Deep;
What can it then avail though yet we feel
Strength undiminisht, or eternal being
To undergo eternal punishment?
Whereto with speedy words th' Arch-fiend reply'd.
    Fall'n Cherube, to be weak is miserable
Doing or Suffering: but of this be sure,
To do aught good never will be our task,
But ever to do ill our sole delight,   160
As being the contrary to his high will
Whom we resist. If then his Providence
Out of our evil seek to bring forth good,

Our labour must be to pervert that end,

And out of good still to find means of evil;

Which oft times may succeed, so as perhaps

Shall grieve him, if I fail not, and disturb

His inmost counsels from their destind aim.

But see the angry Victor hath recall'd

His Ministers of vengeance and pursuit　　　　　　170

Back to the Gates of Heav'n: The Sulphurous Hail

Shot after us in storm, oreblown hath laid

This fiery Surge, that from the Precipice

Of Heav'n receiv'd us falling, and the Thunder,

Wing'd with red Lightning and impetuous rage,

Perhaps hath spent his shafts, and ceases now

To bellow through the vast and boundless Deep.

Let us not slip th' occasion, whether scorn,

Or satiate fury yield it from our Foe.

Seest thou yon dreary Plain, forlorn and wilde,　　　　180

The seat of desolation, voyd of light,

Save what the glimmering of these livid flames

Casts pale and dreadful? Thither let us tend

From off the tossing of these fiery waves,

There rest, if any rest can harbour there,

And reassembling our afflicted Powers,

Consult how we may henceforth most offend

Our Enemy, our own loss how repair,

How overcome this dire Calamity,

What reinforcement we may gain from Hope,　　　　190

If not what resolution from despare.

　　Thus Satan talking to his neerest Mate

With Head up-lift above the wave, and Eyes
That sparkling blaz'd, his other Parts besides
Prone on the Flood, extended long and large
Lay floating many a rood, in bulk as huge
As whom the Fables name of monstrous size,
Titanian, or *Earth-born*, that warr'd on *Jove*,
Briarios or *Typhon*, whom the Den
By ancient *Tarsus* held, or that Sea-beast   200
Leviathan, which God of all his works
Created hugest that swim th' Ocean stream:
Him haply slumbring on th *Norway* foam
The Pilot of some small night-founder'd Skiff,
Deeming some Island, oft, as Sea-men tell,
With fixed Anchor in his skaly rind
Moors by his side under the Lee, while Night
Invests the Sea, and wished Morn delayes:
So stretcht out huge in length the Arch-fiend lay
Chain'd on the burning Lake, nor ever thence   210
Had ris'n or heav'd his head, but that the will
And high permission of all-ruling Heaven
Left him at large to his own dark designs,
That with reiterated crimes he might
Heap on himself damnation, while he sought
Evil to others, and enrag'd might see
How all his malice serv'd but to bring forth
Infinite goodness, grace and mercy shewn
On Man by him seduc't, but on himself
Treble confusion, wrath and vengeance pour'd.   220
Forthwith upright he rears from off the Pool

His mighty Stature; on each hand the flames
Drivn backward slope their pointing spires, & rowld
In billows, leave i'th' midst a horrid Vale.
Then with expanded wings he stears his flight
Aloft, incumbent on the dusky Air
That felt unusual weight, till on dry Land
He lights, if it were Land that ever burn'd
With solid, as the Lake with liquid fire;
And such appear'd in hue, as when the force   230
Of subterranean wind transports a Hill
Torn from *Pelorus*, or the shatter'd side
Of thundring *Ætna*, whose combustible
And fewel'd entrals thence conceiving Fire,
Sublim'd with Mineral fury, aid the Winds,
And leave a singed bottom all involv'd
With stench and smoak: Such resting found the sole
Of unblest feet. Him followed his next Mate,
Both glorying to have scap't the *Stygian* flood
As Gods, and by their own recover'd strength,   240
Not by the sufferance of supernal Power.
    Is this the Region, this the Soil, the Clime,
Said then the lost Arch Angel, this the seat
That we must change for Heav'n, this mournful gloom
For that celestial light? Be it so, since hee
Who now is Sovran can dispose and bid
What shall be right: fardest from him is best
Whom reason hath equald, force hath made supream
Above his equals. Farwel happy Fields
Where Joy for ever dwells: Hail horrours, hail   250

Infernal world, and thou profoundest Hell

Receive they new Possessor: One who brings

A mind not to be chang'd by Place or Time.

The mind is its own place, and in it self

Can make a Heav'n of Hell, a Hell of Heav'n.

What matter where, if I be still the same,

And what I should be, all but less then hee

Whom Thunder hath made greater? Here at least

We shall be free; th' Almighty hath not built

Here for his envy, will not drive us hence: 260

Here we may reign secure, and in my choyce

To reign is worth ambition though in Hell:

Better to reign in Hell, then serve in Heav'n

But wherefore let we then our faithful friends,

Th' associates and copartners of our loss

Lye thus astonisht on th' oblivious Pool,

And call them not to share with us their part

In this unhappy Mansion, or once more

With rallied Arms to try what may be yet

Regaind in Heav'n, or what more lost in Hell?   270

    So *Satan* spake, and him *Bëëlzebub*

Thus answer'd. Leader of those Armies bright,

Which but th' Omnipotent none could have foyld,

If once they hear that voyce, their liveliest pledge

Of hope in fears and dangers, heard so oft

In worst extreams, and on the perilous edge

Of battel when it rag'd, in all assaults

Their surest signal, they will soon resume

New courage and revive, though now they lye

Groveling and prostrate on yon Lake of Fire,   280

As we erewhile, astounded and amaz'd,

No wonder, fall'n such a pernicious highth.

   He scarce had ceas't when the superiour Fiend

Was moving toward the shore; his ponderous shield

Ethereal temper, massy, large and round,

Behind him cast; that broad circumference

Hung on his shoullders like the Moon, whose Orb

Through Optic Glass the *Tuscan* Artist views

At Ev'ning from the top of *Fesole*,

Or in *Valdarno*, to descry new Lands,   290

Rivers or Mountains in her spotty Globe.

His Spear, to equal which the tallest Pine

Hewn on *Norwegian* hills, to be the Mast

Of some great Ammiral, were but a wand,

He walkt with to support uneasie steps

Over the burning Marle, not like those steps

On Heavens Azure, and the torrid Clime

Smote on him sore besides, vaulted with Fire;

Nathless he so endur'd, till on the Beach

Of that inflamed Sea, he stood and call'd   300

His Legions, Angel Forms, who lay intrans't

Thick as Autumnal Leaves that strow the Brooks

In *Vallombrosa*, where th' *Etrurian* shades

High overarch't imbowr; or scatterd sedge

Afloat, when with fierce Winds *Orion* arm'd

Hath vext the Red-Sea Coast, whose waves orethrew

Busiris and his *Memphian* Chivalrie,

VVhile with perfidious hatred they pursu'd

The Sojourners of *Goshen*, who beheld

From the safe shore their floating Carkases   310

And broken Chariot VVheels, so thick bestrown

Abject and lost lay these, covering the Flood,

Under amazement of their hideous change.

He call'd so loud, that all the hollow Deep

Of Hell resounded. Princes, Potentates,

Warriers, the Flowr of Heav'n, once yours, now lost,

If such astonishment as this can sieze

Eternal spirits; or have ye chos'n this place

After the toyl of Battel to repose

Your wearied vertue, for the ease you find   320

To slumber here, as in the Vales of Heav'n?

Or in this abject posture have ye sworn

To adore the Conquerour? who now beholds

Cherube and Seraph rowling in the Flood

With scatter'd Arms and Ensigns, till anon

His swift pursuers from Heav'n Gates discern

Th' advantage, and descending tread us down

Thus drooping, or with linked Thunderbolts

Transfix us to the bottom of this Gulfe.

Awake, arise, or be for ever fall'n.   330

    They heard, and were abasht, and up they sprung

Upon the wing, as when men wont to watch

On duty, sleeping found by whom they dread,

Rouse and bestir themselves ere well awake.

Nor did they not perceave the evil plight

In which they were, or the fierce pains not feel;

Yet to their Generals Voyce they soon obeyd

Innumerable. As when the potent Rod
Of *Amrams* Son in *Egypts* evill day
Wav'd round the Coast, up call'd a pitchy cloud   340
Of *Locusts*, warping on the Eastern Wind,
That ore the Realm of impious *Pharaoh* hung
Like Night, and darken'd all the Land of *Nile:*
So numberless were those bad Angels seen
Hovering on wing under the Cope of Hell
'Twixt upper, nether, and surrounding Fires;
Till, as a signal giv'n, th' uplifted Spear
Of their great Sultan waving to direct
Thir course, in even ballance down they light
On the firm brimstone, and fill all the Plain;   350
A multitude, like which the populous North
Pour'd never from her frozen loyns, to pass
Rhene or the *Danaw*, when her barbarous Sons
Came like a Deluge on the South, and spread
Beneath *Gibraltar* to the *Lybian* sands.
Forthwith from every Squadron and each Band
The Heads and Leaders thither hast where stood
Their great Commander; Godlike shapes and forms
Excelling human, Princely Dignities,
And Powers that earst in Heaven sat on Thrones;   360
Though of their Names in heav'nly Records now
Be no memorial, blotted out and ras'd
By thir Rebellion, from the Books of Life.
Nor had they yet among the Sons of *Eve*
Got them new Names, till wandring ore the Earth,
Through Gods high sufferance for the tryal of man,

By falsities and lyes the greatest part
Of Mankind they corrupted to forsake
God their Creator, and th' invisible
Glory of him, that made them, to transform   370
Oft to the Image of a Brute, adorn'd
With gay Religions full of Pomp and Gold,
And Devils to adore for Deities:
Then were they known to men by various Names,
And various Idols through the Heathen World.
Say, Muse, their Names then known, who first, who last,
Rous'd from thir slumber, on that fiery Couch,
At thir great Emperors call, as next in worth
Came singly where he stood on the bare strand,
While the promiscuous croud stood yet aloof?   380
The chief were those who from the Pit of Hell
Roaming to seek their prey on earth, durst fix
Their Seats long after next the Seat of God,
Their Altars by his Altar, Gods ador'd
Among the Nations round, and durst abide
Jehovah thundring out of *Sion*, thron'd
Between the Cherubim; yea, often plac'd
Within his Sanctuary it self their Shrines,
Abominations; and with cursed things
His holy Rites, and solemn Feasts profan'd,   390
And with their darkness durst affront his light.
First *Moloch*, horrid King besmear'd with blood
Of human sacrifice, and parents tears,
Though for the noyse of Drums and Timbrels loud
Their childrens cries unheard, that past through fire

To his grim Idol. Him the *Ammonite*
Worshipt in *Rabba* and her watry Plain,
In *Argob* and in *Basan*, to the stream
Of utmost *Arnon*. Nor content with such
Audacious neighbourhood, the wisest heart   400
Of *Solomon* he led by fraud to build
His Temple right against the Temple of God
On that opprobrious Hill, and made his Grove
The pleasant Vally of *Hinnom*, *Tophet* thence
And black *Gehenna* call'd, the Type of Hell.
Next *Chemos*, th' obscene dread of *Moabs* Sons,
From *Aroer* to *Nebo*, and the wild
Of Southmost *Abarim*; in *Hesebon*
And *Horonaim*, *Seons* Realm, beyond
The flowry Dale of *Sibma* clad with Vines,   410
And *Eleale* to th' *Asphaltick* Pool.
Peor his other Name, when he entic'd
Israel in *Sittim* on their march from *Nile*
To do him wanton rites, which cost them woe.
Yet thence his lustful Orgies he enlarg'd
Even to that Hill of scandal, by the Grove
Of *Moloch* homicide, lust hard by hate;
Till good *Josiah* drove them thence to Hell.
With these came they, who from the bordring flood
Of old *Euphrates* to the Brook that parts   420
Egypt from *Syrian* ground, had general Names
Of *Baalim* and *Ashtaroth*, those male,
These Feminine. For Spirits when they please
Can either Sex assume, or both; so soft

and uncompounded is their Essence pure,
Not ti'd or manacl'd with joynt or limb,
Nor founded on the brittle strength of bones,
Like cumbrous flesh; but in what shape they choose
Dilated or condens't, bright or obscure,
Can execute their aerie purposes,   430
And works of love or enmity fulfill.
For these the Race of *Israel* oft forsook
Their living strength, and unfrequented left
His righteous Altar, bowing lowly down
To bestial Gods; for which their heads as low
Bow'd down in Battel, sunk before the Spear
Of despicable foes. With these in troop
Came *Astoreth*, whom the *Phœnicians* call'd
Astarte, Queen of Heav'n, with crescent Horns;
To whose bright Image nightly by the Moon   440
Sidonian Virgins paid their Vows and Songs,
In *Sion* also not unsung, where stood
Her Temple on th' offensive Mountain, built
By that uxorious King, whose heart though large,
Beguil'd by fair Idolatresses, fell
To Idols foul. *Thammuz* came next behind,
Whose annual wound in *Lebanon* allur'd
The *Syrian* Damsels to lament his fate
In amorous dittyes all a Summers day,
While smooth *Adonis* from his native Rock   450
Ran purple to the Sea, suppos'd with blood
Of *Thammuz* yearly wounded: the Love-tale
Infected *Sions* daughters with like heat,

Whose wanton passions in the sacred Porch

Ezekiel saw, when by the Vision led

His eye survay'd the dark Idolatries

Of alienated *Judah*. Next came one

Who mourn'd in earnest, when the Captive Ark

Maim'd his brute Image, head and hands lopt off

In his own Temple, on the grunsel edge,   460

Where he fell flat, and sham'd his Worshipers:

Dagon his Name, Sea Monster, upward Man

And downward Fish: yet had his Temple high

Rear'd in *Azotus*, dreaded through the Coast

Of *Palestine*, in *Gath* and *Ascalon*,

And *Accaron* and *Gaza*'s frontier bounds.

Him follow'd *Rimmon*, whose delightful Seat

Was fair *Damascus*, on the fertil Banks

Of *Abbana* and *Pharphar*, lucid streams.

He also against the house of God was bold: 470

A Leper once he lost and gain'd a King,

Ahaz his sottish Conquerour, whom he drew

Gods Altar to disparage and displace

For one of *Syrian* mode, whreon to burn

His odious offrings, and adore the Gods

Whom he had vanquisht. After these appear'd

A crew who under Names of old Renown,

Osiris, Isis, Orus and their Train

With monstrous shapes and sorceries abus'd

Fanatic *Egypt* and her Priests, to seek   480

Thir wandring Gods disguis'd in brutish forms

Rather then human. Nor did *Israel* scape

Th' infection when their borrow'd Gold compos'd
The Calf in *Oreb:* and the Rebel King
Doubl'd that sin in *Bethel* and in *Dan,*
Lik'ning his Maker to the Grazed Ox,
Jehovah, who in one Night when he pass'd
From *Egypt* marching, equal'd with one stroke
Both her first born and all her bleating Gods.
Belial came last, then whom a Spirit more lewd   490
Fell not from Heaven, or more gross to love
Vice for it self: To him no Temple stood
Or Altar smoak'd; yet who more oft then hee
In Temples and at Altars, when the Priest
Turns Atheist, as did *Ely*'s Sons, who fill'd
With lust and violence the house of God.
In Courts and Palaces he also Reigns
And in luxurious Cities, where the noyse
Of riot ascends above thir loftiest Towrs,
And injury and outrage: And when Night   500
Darkens the Streets, then wander forth the Sons
Of *Belial,* flown with insolence and wine.
Witness the Streets of *Sodom,* and that night
In *Gibeah,* when hospitable Dores
Yielded thir Matrons to prevent worse rape.
These were the prime in order and in might;
The rest were long to tell, though far renown'd,
Th' *Ionian* Gods, of *Javans* Issue held
Gods, yet confest later then Heav'n and Earth
Thir boasted Parents; *Titan* Heav'ns first born   510
With his enormous brood, and birthright seis'd

By younger *Saturn*, he from mightier *Jove*
His own and *Rhea*'s Son like measure found;
So *Jove* usurping reign'd: these first in *Creet*
And *Ida* known, thence on the Snowy top
Of cold *Olympus* rul'd the middle Air
Thir highest Heav'n; or on the *Delphian* Cliff,
Or in *Dodona*, and through all the bounds
Of *Doric* Land; or who with *Saturn* old
Fled over *Adria* to th' *Hesperian* Fields,   520
And ore the *Celtic* roam'd the utmost Isles.
All these and more came flocking; but with looks
Down cast and damp, yet such wherein appear'd
Obscure som glimps of joy, to have found thir chief
Not in despair, to have found themselves not lost
In loss it self; which on his count'nance cast
Like doubtful hue: but he his wonted pride
Soon recollecting, with high words, that bore
Semblance of worth not substance, gently rais'd
Their fainted courage, and dispel'd their fears.   530
Then strait commands that at the warlike sound
Of Trumpets loud and Clarions be upreard
His mighty Standard; that proud honour claim'd
Azazel as his right, a Cherube tall:
Who forthwith from the glittering Staff unfurld
Th' Imperial Ensign, which full high advanc't
Shon like a Meteor streaming to the Wind
With Gemms and Golden lustre rich imblaz'd,
Seraphic arms and Trophies: all the while
Sonorous mettal blowing Martial sounds: 540

At which the universal Host upsent
A shout that tore Hells Concave, and beyond
Frighted the Reign of *Chaos* and old Night.
All in a moment through the gloom were seen
Ten thousand Banners rise into the Air
With Orient Colours waving: with them rose
A Forrest huge of Spears: and thronging Helms
Appear'd, and serried Shields in thick array
Of depth immeasurable: Anon they move
In perfect *Phalanx* to the *Dorian* mood   550
Of Flutes and soft Recorders; such as rais'd
To highth of noblest temper Hero's old
Arming to Battel, and in stead of rage
Deliberate valour breath'd, firm and unmov'd
With dread of death to flight or foul retreat,
Nor wanting power to mitigate and swage
With solemn touches, troubl'd thoughts, and chase
Anguish and doubt and fear and sorrow and pain
From mortal or immortal minds. Thus they
Breathing united force with fixed thought   560
Mov'd on in silence to soft Pipes that charm'd
Thir painful steps o're the burnt soyle; and now
Advanc't in view they stand, a horrid Front
Of dreadful length and dazling Arms, in guise
Of Warriers old with order'd Spear and Shield,
Awaiting what command thir mighty Chief
Had to impose: He through the armed Files
Darts his experienc't eye, and soon traverse
The whole Battalion views, thir order due,

Thir visages and stature as of Gods,   570
Thir number last he summs. And now his heart
Distends with pride, and hardning in his strength
Glories: For never since created man,
Met such imbodied force, as nam'd with these
Could merit more then that small infantry
Warr'd on by Cranes: though all the Giant brood
Of *Phlegra* with th' Heroic Race were joyn'd
That fought at *Theb's* and *Ilium,* on each side
Mixt with auxiliar Gods; and what resounds
In Fable or *Romance* of *Uthers* Son   580
Begirt with *British* and *Armoric* Knights;
And all who since, Baptiz'd or Infidel
Jousted in *Aspramont* or *Montalban,*
Damasco, or *Marocco,* or *Trebisond,*
Or whom *Biserta* sent from *Afric* shore
When *Charlemain* with all his Peerage fell
By *Fontarabbia.* Thus far these beyond
Compare of mortal prowess, yet observ'd
Thir dread Commander: he above the rest
In shape and gesture proudly eminent   590
Stood like a Towr; his form had yet not lost
All her Original brightness, nor appear'd
Less then Arch Angel ruind, and th' excess
Of Glory obscur'd: As when the Sun new ris'n
Looks through the Horizontal misty Air
Shorn of his Beams, or from behind the Moon
In dim Eclips disastrous twilight sheds
On half the Nations, and with fear of change

Perplexes Monarchs. Dark'n'd so, yet shon

Above them all th' Arch Angel: but his face   600

Deep scars of Thunder had intrencht, and care

Sat on his faded cheek, but under Browes

Of dauntless courage, and considerate Pride

Waiting revenge: cruel his eyes, but cast

Signs of remorse and passion to behold

The fellows of his crime, the followers rather

(Far other once beheld in bliss) condemn'd

For ever now to have their lot in pain,

Millions of Spirits for his fault amerc't

Of Heav'n, and from Eternal Splendors flung   610

For his revolt, yet faithfull how they stood,

Thir Glory witherd. As when Heavens Fire

Hath scath'd the Forrest Oaks, or Mountain Pines,

With singed top their stately growth though bare

Stands on the blasted Heath. He now prepar'd

To speak; whereat their doubl'd Ranks they bend

From Wing to Wing, and half enclose him round

With all his Peers: attention held them mute.

Thrice he assayd, and thrice in spite of scorn,

Tears such as Angels weep, burst forth: at last   620

Words interwove with sighs found out their way.

  O Myriads of immortal Spirits, O Powers

Matchless, but with th' Almighty, and that strife

Was not inglorious, though th' event was dire,

As this place testifies, and this dire change

Hateful to utter: but what power of mind

Foreseeing or presaging, from the Depth

Of knowledge past or present, could have fear'd,
How such united force of Gods, how such
As stood like these, could ever know repulse?   630
For who can yet beleeve, though after loss,
That all these puissant Legions, whose exile
Hath emptied Heav'n, shall faile to re-ascend
Self-rais'd, and repossess their native seat.
For me, be witness all the Host of Heav'n,
If counsels different, or danger shun'd
By me, have lost our hopes. But he who reigns
Monarch in Heav'n, till then as one secure
Sat on his Throne, upheld by old repute,
Consent or custome, and his Regal State   640
Put forth at full, but still his strength conceal'd,
Which tempted our attempt, and wrought our fall.
Henceforth his might we know, and know our own
So as not either to provoke, or dread
New warr, provok't; our better part remains
To work in close design, by fraud or guile
What force effected not: that he no less
At length from us may find, who overcomes
By force, hath overcome but half his foe.
Space may produce new Worlds; whereof so rife   650
There went a fame in Heav'n that he ere long
Intended to create, and therein plant
A generation, whom his choice regard
Should favour equal to the Sons of Heaven:
Thither, if but to prie, shall be perhaps
Our first eruption, thither or elsewhere:

For this Infernal Pit shall never hold
Cælestial Spirits in Bondage, nor th' Abysse
Long under darkness cover. But these thoughts
Full Counsel must mature: Peace is despaird,   660
For who can think Submission? Warr then, Warr
Open or understood must be resolv'd.

   He spake: and to confirm his words, out-flew
Millions of flaming swords, drawn from the thighs
Of mighty Cherubim; the sudden blaze
Far round illumin'd hell: highly they rag'd
Against the Highest, and fierce with grasped arm's
Clash'd on their sounding shields the din of war,
Hurling defiance toward the vault of Heav'n.

   There stood a Hill not far whose griesly top   670
Belch'd fire and rowling smoak; the rest entire
Shon with a glossie scurff, undoubted sign
That in his womb was hid metallic Ore,
The work of Sulphur. Thither wing'd with speed
A numerous Brigad hasten'd. As when bands
Of Pioners with Spade and Pickaxe arm'd
Forerun the Royal Camp, to trench a Field,
Or cast a Rampart. *Mammon* led them on,
Mammon, the least erected Spirit that fell
From heav'n, for ev'n in heav'n his looks & thoughts   680
Were always downward bent, admiring more
The riches of Heav'ns pavement, trod'n Gold,
Then aught divine or holy else enjoy'd
In vision beatific: by him first
Men also, and by his suggestion taught,

Ransack'd the Center, and with impious hands
Rifl'd the bowels of thir mother Earth
For Treasures better hid. Soon had his crew
Op'nd into the Hill a spacious wound
And dig'd out ribs of Gold. Let none admire   690
That riches grow in Hell; that soyle may best
Deserve the pretious bane. And here let those
Who boast in mortal things, and wondring tell
Of *Babel*, and the works of *Memphian* Kings,
Learn how thir greatest Monuments of Fame,
And Strength and Art are easily outdone
By Spirits reprobate, and in an hour
What in an age they with incessant toyle
And hands innumerable scarce perform.
Nigh on the Plain in many cells prepar'd,   700
That underneath had veins of liquid fire
Sluc'd from the Lake, a second multitude
With wondrous Art founded the massie Ore,
Severing each kinde, and scum'd the Bullion dross:
A third as soon had form'd within the ground
A various mould, and from the boyling cells
By strange conveyance fill'd each hollow nook,
As in an Organ from one blast of wind
To many a row of Pipes the sound-board breaths.
Anon out of the earth a Fabrick huge   710
Rose like an Exhalation, with the sound
Of Dulcet Symphonies and voices sweet,
Built like a Temple, where *Pilasters* round
Were set, and Doric pillars overlaid

With Golden Architrave; nor did there want
Cornice or Freeze, with bossy Sculptures grav'n,
The Roof was fretted Gold. Not *Babilon*,
Nor great *Alcairo* such magnificence
Equal'd in all thir glories, to inshrine
Belus or *Serapis* thir Gods, or seat   720
Thir Kings, when *Ægypt* with *Assyria* strove
In wealth and luxurie. Th' ascending pile
Stood fixt her stately highth, and strait the dores
Op'ning thir brazen foulds discover wide
Within, her ample spaces, o're the smooth
And level pavement: from the arched roof
Pendant by suttle Magic many a row
Of Starry Lamps and blazing Cressets fed
With *Naphtha* and *Asphaltus* yeilded light
As from a sky. The hasty multitude   730
Admiring enter'd, and the work some praise
And some the Architect: his hand was known
In Heav'n by many a Towred structure high,
Where Scepter'd Angels held thir residence,
And sat as Princes, whom the supreme King
Exalted to such power, and gave to rule,
Each in his Hierarchie, the Orders bright.
Nor was his name unheard or unador'd
In ancient *Greece*; and in *Ausonian* land
Men call'd him *Mulciber*; and how he fell   740
From Heav'n, they fabl'd, thrown by angry *Jove*
Sheer o're the Chrystal Battlements: from Morn
To Noon he fell, from Noon to dewy Eve,

A Summers day; and with the setting Sun

Dropt from the Zenith like a falling Star,

On *Lemnos* th' *Ægæan* Ile: thus they relate,

Erring; for he with this rebellious rout

Fell long before; nor aught avail'd him now

To have built in Heav'n high Towrs; nor did he scape

By all his Engins, but was headlong sent   750

With his industrious crew to build in hell.

Mean while the winged Haralds by command

Of Sovran power, with awful Ceremony

And Trumpets sound throughout the Host proclaim

A solemn Councel forthwith to be held

At *Pandæmonium*, the high Capital

Of Satan and his Peers: thir summons call'd

From every Band and squared Regiment

By place or choice the worthiest; they anon

With hunderds and with thousands trooping came   760

Attended: all access was throng'd, the Gates

And Porches wide, but chief the spacious Hall

(Though like a cover'd field, where Champions bold

Wont ride in arm'd, and and at the Soldans chair

Defi'd the best of *Panim* chivalry

To mortal combat or carreer with Lance)

Thick swarm'd, both on the ground and in the air,

Brusht with the hiss of russling wings. As Bees

In spring time, when the Sun with Taurus rides,

Poure forth thir populous youth about the Hive   770

In clusters; they among fresh dews and flowers

Flie to and fro, or on the smoothed Plank,

The suburb of thir Straw-built Cittadel,
New rub'd with Baume, expatiate and confer
Thir State affairs. So thick the aerie crowd
Swarm'd and were straitn'd; till the Signal giv'n,
Behold a wonder! they but now who seemd
In bigness to surpass Earths Giant Sons
Now less then smallest Dwarfs, in narrow room
Throng numberless, like that Pigmean Race   780
Beyond the *Indian* Mount, or Faerie Elves,
Whose midnight Revels, by a Forrest side
Or Fountain some belated Peasant sees,
Or dreams he sees, while over head the Moon
Sits Arbitress, and neerer to the Earth
Wheels her pale course, they on thir mirth & dance
Intent, with jocond Music charm his ear;
At once with joy and fear his heart rebounds.
Thus incorporeal Spirits to smallest forms
Reduc'd thir shapes immense, and were at large,   790
Though without number still amidst the Hall
Of that infernal Court. But far within
And in thir own dimensions like themselves
The great Seraphic Lords and Cherubim
In close recess and secret conclave sat
A thousand Demy-Gods on golden seat's,
Frequent and full. After short silence then
And summons read, the great consult began.

The End of the First Book.

PARADISE LOST

BOOK II.

HIgh on a Throne of Royal State, which far
Outshon the wealth of *Ormus* and of *Ind*,
Or where the gorgeous East with richest hand
Showrs on her Kings *Barbaric* Pearl & Gold,
Satan exalted sat, by merit rais'd
To that bad eminence; and from despair
Thus high uplifted beyond hope, aspires
Beyond thus high, insatiate to pursue
Vain Warr with Heav'n, and by success untaught
His proud imaginations thus displaid.   10
   Powers and Dominions, Deities of Heav'n,
For since no deep within her gulf can hold
Immortal vigor, though opprest and fall'n,
I give not Heav'n for lost. From this descent
Celestial vertues rising, will appear
More glorious and more dread then from no fall,
And trust themselves to fear no second fate:
Mee though just right, and the fixt Laws of Heav'n
Did first create your Leader, next, free choice,
With what besides, in Counsel or in Fight,   20
Hath bin achievd of merit, yet this loss

31

Thus farr at least recover'd, hath much more
Establisht in a safe unenvied Throne
Yeilded with full consent. The happier state
In Heav'n, which follows dignity, might draw
Envy from each inferior; but who here
Will envy whom the highest place exposes
Formost to stand against the Thunderers aime
Your bulwark, and condemns to greatest share
Of endless pain? where there is then no good   30
For which to strive, no strife can grow up there
From Faction; for none sure will claim in hell
Precedence, none, whose portion is so small
Of present pain, that with ambitious mind
Will covet more. With this advantage then
To union, and firm Faith, and firm accord,
More then can be in Heav'n, we now return
To claim our just inheritance of old,
Surer to prosper then prosperity
Could have assur'd us; and by what best way,   40
Whether of open Warr or covert guile,
We now debate; who can advise, may speak.
    He ceas'd, and next him *Moloc*, Scepter'd King
Stood up, the strongest and the fiercest Spirit
That fought in Heav'n; now fiercer by despair:
His trust was with th' Eternal to be deem'd
Equal in strength, and rather then be less
Car'd not to be at all; with that care lost
Went all his fear: of God, or Hell, or worse
He reckd not, and these words thereafter spake.   50

My sentence is for open Warr: Of Wiles,
More unexpert, I boast not: them let those
Contrive who need, or when they need, not now.
For while they sit contriving, shall the rest,
Millions that stand in Arms, and longing wait
The Signal to ascend, sit lingring here
Heav'ns fugitives, and for thir dwelling place
Accept this dark opprobrious Den of shame,
The Prison of his Tyranny who Reigns
By our delay? no, let us rather choose   60
Arm'd with Hell flames and fury all at once
O're Heav'ns high Towrs to force resistless way,
Turning our Tortures into horrid Arms
Against the Torturer; when to meet the noise
Of his Almighty Engin he shall hear
Infernal Thunder, and for Lightning see
Black fire and horror shot with equal rage
Among his Angels; and his Throne it self
Mixt with *Tartarean* Sulphur, and strange fire,
His own invented Torments. But perhaps   70
The way seems difficult and steep to scale
With upright wing against a higher foe.
Let such bethink them, if the sleepy drench
Of that forgetful Lake benumme not still,
That in our proper motion we ascend
Up to our native seat: descent and fall
To us is adverse. Who but felt of late
When the fierce Foe hung on our brok'n Rear
Insulting, and pursu'd us through the Deep,

With what compulsion and laborious flight   80
We sunk thus low? Th' ascent is easie then;
Th' event is fear'd; should we again provoke
Our stronger, some worse way his wrath may find
To our destruction: if there be in Hell
Fear to be worse destroy'd: what can be worse
Then to dwell here, driv'n out from bliss, condemn'd
In this abhorred deep to utter woe;
Where pain of unextinguishable fire
Must exercise us without hope of end
The Vassals of his anger, when the Scourge   90
Inexorably, and the torturing houre
Calls us to Penance? More destroy'd then thus
We should be quite abolisht and expire.
What fear we then? what doubt we to incense
His utmost ire? which to the highth enrag'd,
Will either quite consume us, and reduce
To nothing this essential, happier farr
Then miserable to have eternal being:
Or if our substance be indeed Divine,
And cannot cease to be, we are at worst   100
On this side nothing; and by proof we feel
Our power sufficient to disturb his Heav'n,
And with perpetual inrodes to Allarme,
Though inaccessible, his fatal Throne:
Which if not Victory is yet Revenge.
     He ended frowning, and his look denounc'd
Desperate revenge, and Battel dangerous
To less then Gods. On th' other side up rose

Belial, in act more graceful and humane;
A fairer person lost not Heav'n; he seemd   110
For dignity compos'd and high exploit:
But all was false and hollow; though his Tongue
Dropt Manna, and could make the worse appear
The better reason, to perplex and dash
Maturest Counsels: for his thoughts were low;
To vice industrious, but to Nobler deeds
Timorous and slothful: yet he pleas'd the eare,
And with perswasive accent thus began.
    I should be much for open Warr, O Peers,
As not behind in hate; if what was urg'd   120
Main reason to perswade immediate Warr,
Did not disswade me most, and seem to cast
Ominous conjecture on the whole success:
When he who most excels in fact of Arms,
In what he counsels and in what excels
Mistrustful, grounds his courage on despair
And utter dissolution, as the scope
Of all his aim, after some dire revenge.
First, what Revenge? the Towrs of Heav'n are fill'd
With Armed watch, that render all access   130
Impregnable; oft on the bordering Deep
Encamp thir Legions, or with obscure wing
Scout farr and wide into the Realm of night,
Scorning surprize. Or could we break our way
By force, and at our heels all Hell should rise
With blackest Insurrection, to confound
Heav'ns purest Light, yet our great Enemie

All incorruptible would on his Throne
Sit unpolluted, and th' Ethereal mould
Incapable of stain would soon expel   140
Her mischief, and purge off the baser fire
Victorious. Thus repuls'd, our final hope
Is flat despair: we must exasperate
Th' Almighty Victor to spend all his rage,
And that must end us, that must be our cure,
To be no more; sad cure; for who would loose,
Though full of pain, this intellectual being,
Those thoughts that wander through Eternity,
To perish rather, swallowd up and lost
In the wide womb of uncreated night,   150
Devoid of sense and motion? and who knows,
Let this be good, whether our angry Foe
Can give it, or will ever? how he can
Is doubtful; that he never will is sure.
Will he, so wise, let loose at once his ire,
Belike through impotence, or unaware,
To give his Enemies thir wish, and end
Them in his anger, whom his anger saves
To punish endless? wherefore cease we then?
Say they who counsel Warr, we are decreed,   160
Reserv'd and destin'd to Eternal woe;
Whatever doing, what can we suffer more,
What can we suffer worse? is this then worst,
Thus sitting, thus consulting, thus in Arms?
What when we fled amain, pursu'd and strook
With Heav'ns afflicting Thunder, and besought

The Deep to shelter us? this Hell then seem'd
A refuge from those wounds: or when we lay
Chain'd on the burning Lake? that sure was worse.
What if the breath that kindl'd those grim fires   170
Awak'd should blow them into sevenfold rage
And plunge us in the Flames? or from above
Should intermitted vengeance Arme again
His red right hand to plague us? what if all
Her stores were op'n'd, and this Firmament
Of Hell should spout her Cataracts of Fire,
Impendent horrors, threatning hideous fall
One day upon our heads; while we perhaps
Designing or exhorting glorious Warr,
Caught in a fierie Tempest shall be hurl'd   180
Each on his rock transfixt, the sport and prey
Of racking whirlwinds, or for ever sunk
Under yon boyling Ocean, wrapt in Chains;
There to converse with everlasting groans,
Unrespited, unpitied, unrepreevd,
Ages of hopeless end; this would be worse.
Warr therefore, open or conceal'd, alike
My voice disswades; for what can force or guile
With him, or who deceive his mind, whose eye
Views all things at one view? he from heav'ns highth   190
All these our motions vain, sees and derides;
Not more Almighty to resist our might
Then wise to frustrate all our plots and wiles.
Shall we then live thus vile, the race of Heav'n
Thus trampl'd, thus expell'd to suffer here

Chains & these Torments? better these then worse
By my advice; since fate inevitable
Subdues us, and Omnipotent Decree,
The Victors will. To suffer, as to doe,
Our strength is equal, nor the Law unjust   200
That so ordains: this was at first resolv'd,
If we were wise, against so great a foe
Contending, and so doubtful what might fall.
I laugh, when those who at the Spear are bold
And vent'rous, if that fail them, shrink and fear
What yet they know must follow, to endure
Exile, or ignominy, or bonds, or pain,
The sentence of thir Conquerour: This is now
Our doom; which if we can sustain and bear,
Our Supream Foe in time may much remit   210
His anger, and perhaps thus farr remov'd
Not mind us not offending, satisfi'd
With what is punish't; whence these raging fires
Will slack'n, if his breath stir not thir flames.
Our purer essence then will overcome
Thir noxious vapour, or enur'd not feel,
Or chang'd at length, and to the place conformd
In temper and in nature, will receive
Familiar the fierce heat, and void of pain;
This horror will grow milde, this darkness light,   220
Besides what hope the never-ending flight
Of future days may bring, what chance, what change
Worth waiting, since our present lot appeers
For happy though but ill, for ill not worst,

If we procure not to our selves more woe.

    Thus *Belial* with words cloath'd in reasons garb
Counsel'd ignoble ease, and peaceful sloath,
Not peace: and after him thus *Mammon* spake.

    Either to disinthrone the King of Heav'n
We warr, if warr be best, or to regain   230
Our own right lost: him to unthrone we then
May hope, when everlasting Fate shall yeild
To fickle Chance, and *Chaos* judge the strife:
The former vain to hope argues as vain
The latter: for what place can be for us
Within Heav'ns bound, unless Heav'ns Lord supream
We overpower? Suppose he should relent
And publish Grace to all, on promise made
Of new Subjection; with what eyes could we
Stand in his presence humble, and receive   240
Strict Laws impos'd, to celebrate his Throne
With warbl'd Hymns, and to his Godhead sing
Forc't Halleluiah's; while he Lordly sits
Our envied Sovran, and his Altar breathes
Ambrosial Odours and Ambrosial Flowers,
Our servile offerings. This must be our task
In Heav'n, this our delight; how wearisom
Eternity so spent in worship paid
To whom we hate. Let us not then pursue
By force impossible, by leave obtain'd   250
Unacceptable, though in Heav'n, our state
Of splendid vassalage, but rather seek
Our own good from our selves, and from our own

Live to our selves, though in this vast recess,

Free, and to none accountable, preferring

Hard liberty before the easie yoke

Of servile Pomp. Our greatness will appear

Then most conspicuous, when great things of small,

Useful of hurtful, prosperous of adverse

We can create, and in what place so e're   260

Thrive under evil, and work ease out of pain

Through labour and endurance. This deep world

Of darkness do we dread? How oft amidst

Thick clouds and dark doth Heav'ns all-ruling Sire

Choose to reside, his Glory unobscur'd,

And with the Majesty of darkness round

Covers his Throne; from whence deep thunders roar

Must'ring thir rage, and Heav'n resembles Hell?

As he our Darkness, cannot we his Light

Imitate when we please? This Desart soile   270

Wants not her hidden lustre, Gemms and Gold;

Nor want we skill or art, from whence to raise

Magnificence; and what can Heav'n shew more?

Our torments also may in length of time

Become our Elements, these piercing Fires

As soft as now severe, our temper chang'd

Into their temper; which must needs remove

The sensible of pain. All things invite

To peaceful Counsels, and the settl'd State

Of order, how in safety best we may   280

Compose our present evils, with regard

Of what we are and where, dismissing quite

All thoughts of Warr: ye have what I advise.

   He scarce had finisht, when such murmur filld

Th' Assembly, as when hollow Rocks retain

The sound of blustring winds, which all night long

Had rous'd the Sea, now with hoarse cadence lull

Sea-faring men orewatcht, whose Bark by chance

Or Pinnace anchors in a craggy Bay

After the Tempest: Such applause was heard   290

As *Mammon* ended, and his Sentence pleas'd,

Advising peace: for such another Field

They dreaded worse then Hell: so much the fear

Of Thunder and the Sword of *Michael*

Wrought still within them; and no less desire

To found this nether Empire, which might rise

By pollicy, and long process of time,

In emulation opposite to Heav'n.

Which when *Bëëlzebub* perceiv'd, then whom,

Satan except, none higher sat, with grave   300

Aspect he rose, and in his rising seem'd

A Pillar of State; deep on his Front engraven

Deliberation sat and publick care;

And Princely counsel in his face yet shon,

Majestick though in ruin: sage he stood

With *Atlantean* shoulders fit to bear

The weight of mightiest Monarchies; his look

Drew audience and attention still as Night

Or Summers Noon-tide air, while thus he spake.

   Thrones and imperial Powers, off-spring of heav'n,   310

Ethereal Vertues; or these Titles now

Must we renounce, and changing stile be call'd
Princes of Hell? for so the popular vote
Inclines, here to continue, and build up here
A growing Empire; doubtless; while we dream,
And know not that the King of Heav'n hath doom'd
This place our dungeon, not our safe retreat
Beyond his Potent arm, to live exempt
From Heav'ns high jurisdiction, in new League
Banded against his Throne, but to remaine   320
In strictest bondage, though thus far remov'd,
Under th' inevitable curb, reserv'd
His captive multitude: For he, be sure,
In highth or depth, still first and last will Reign
Sole King, and of his Kingdom loose no part
By our revolt, but over Hell extend
His Empire, and with Iron Scepter rule
Us here, as with his Golden those in Heav'n.
Why sit we then projecting Peace and Warr?
Warr hath determin'd us, and foild with loss   330
Irreparable; tearms of peace yet none
Voutsaf't or sought; for what peace will be giv'n
To us enslav'd, but custody severe,
And stripes, and arbitrary punishment
Inflicted? and what peace can we return,
But to our power hostility and hate,
Untam'd reluctance, and revenge though slow,
Yet ever plotting how the Conquerour least
May reap his conquest, and may least rejoyce
In doing what we most in suffering feel?   340

Nor will occasion want, nor shall we need

With dangerous expedition to invade

Heav'n, whose high walls fear no assault or Siege,

Or ambush from the Deep. What if we find

Some easier enterprize? There is a place

(If ancient and prophetic fame in Heav'n

Err not) another World, the happy seat

Of som new Race call'd *Man*, about this time

To be created like to us, though less

In power and excellence, but favour'd more   350

Of him who rules above; so was his will

Pronounc'd among the Gods, and by an Oath,

That shook Heav'ns whol circumference, confirm'd.

Thither let us bend all our thoughts, to learn

What creatures there inhabit, of what mould,

Or substance, how endu'd, and what thir Power,

And where thir weakness, how attempted best,

By force or suttlety: Though Heav'n be shut,

And Heav'ns high Arbitrator sit secure

In his own strength, this place may lye expos'd   360

The utmost border of his Kingdom, left

To their defence who hold it: here perhaps

Som advantagious act may be achiev'd

By sudden onset, either with Hell fire

To waste his whole Creation, or possess

All as our own, and drive as we were driven,

The punie habitants, or if not drive,

Seduce them to our Party, that thir God

May prove thir foe, and with repenting hand

Abolish his own works. This would surpass   370
Common revenge, and interrupt his joy
In our Confusion, and our Joy upraise
In his disturbance; when his darling Sons
Hurl'd headlong to partake with us, shall curse
Thir frail Originals, and faded bliss,
Faded so soon. Advise if this be worth
Attempting, or to sit in darkness here
Hatching vain Empires. Thus *Bëëlzebub*
Pleaded his devilish Counsel, first devis'd
By *Satan,* and in part propos'd: for whence,   380
But from the Author of all ill could Spring
So deep a malice, to confound the race
Of mankind in one root, and Earth with Hell
To mingle and involve, done all to spite
The great Creatour? But thir spite still serves
His glory to augment. The bold design
Pleas'd highly those infernal States, and joy
Sparkl'd in all thir eyes; with full assent
They vote: whereat his speech he thus renews.
    Well have ye judg'd, well ended long debate,   390
Synod of Gods, and like to what ye are,
Great things resolv'd; which from the lowest deep
Will once more lift us up, in spight of Fatc,
Neerer our ancient Seat; perhaps in view
Of those bright confines, whence with neighbouring Arms
And opportune excursion we may chance
Re-enter Heav'n; or else in some milde Zone
Dwell not unvisited of Heav'ns fair Light

Secure, and at the brightning Orient beam

Purge off this gloom; the soft delicious Air,   400

To heal the scarr of these corrosive Fires

Shall breath her balme. But first whom shall we send

In search of this new world, whom shall we find

Sufficient? who shall tempt with wandring feet

The dark unbottom'd infinite Abyss

And through the palpable obscure find out

His uncouth way, or spread his aerie flight

Upborn with indefatigable wings

Over the vast abrupt, ere he arrive

The happy Ile; what strength, what art can then   410

Suffice, or what evasion bear him safe

Through the strict Senteries and Stations thick

Of Angels watching round? Here he had need

All circumspection, and we now no less

Choice in our suffrage; for on whom we send,

The weight of all and our last hope relies.

    This said, he sat; and expectation held

His look suspence, awaiting who appeer'd

To second, or oppose, or undertake

The perilous attempt: but all sat mute,   420

Pondering the danger with deep thoughts; & each

In others count'nance read his own dismay

Astonisht: none among the choice and prime

Of those Heav'n-warring Champions could be found

So hardie as to proffer or accept

Alone the dreadful voyage; till at last

Satan, whom now transcendent glory rais'd

Above his fellows, with Monarchal pride
Conscious of highest worth, unmov'd thus spake.

   O Progeny of Heav'n, Empyreal Thrones,   430
With reason hath deep silence and demurr
Seis'd us, though undismaid: long is the way
And hard, that out of Hell leads up to Light;
Our prison strong, this huge convex of Fire,
Outrageous to devour, immures us round
Ninefold, and gates of burning Adamant
Barr'd over us prohibit all egress.
These past, if any pass, the void profound
Of unessential Night receives him next
Wide gaping, and with utter loss of being   440
Threatens him, plung'd in that abortive gulf.
If thence he scape into what ever world,
Or unknown Region, what remains him less
Then unknown dangers and as hard escape.
But I should ill become this Throne, O Peers,
And this Imperial Sov'ranty, adorn'd
With splendor, arm'd with power, if aught propos'd
And judg'd of public moment, in the shape
Of difficulty or danger could deterre
Me from attempting. Wherefore do I assume   450
These Royalties, and not refuse to Reign,
Refusing to accept as great a share
Of hazard as of honour, due alike
To him who Reigns, and so much to him due
Of hazard more, as he above the rest
High honourd sits? Go therfore mighty powers,

Terrror of Heav'n, though fall'n; intend at home,
While here shall be our home, what best may ease
The present misery, and render Hell
More tollerable; if there be cure or charm   460
To respite or deceive, or slack the pain
Of this ill Mansion: intermit no watch
Against a wakeful Foe, while I abroad
Through all the coasts of dark destruction seek
Deliverance for us all: this enterprize
None shall partake with me. Thus saying rose
The Monarch, and prevented all reply,
Prudent, least from his resolution rais'd
Others among the chief might offer now
(Certain to be refus'd) what erst they feard;   470
And so refus'd might in opinion stand
His rivals, winning cheap the high repute
Which he through hazard huge must earn. But they
Dreaded not more th' adventure then his voice
Forbidding; and at once with him they rose;
Thir rising all at once was as the sound
Of Thunder heard remote. Towards him they bend
With awful reverence prone; and as a God
Extoll him equal to the highest in Heav'n:
Nor fail'd they to express how much they prais'd,   480
That for the general safety he despis'd
His own: for neither do the Spirits damn'd
Loose all thir vertue; least bad men should boast
Thir specious deeds on earth, which glory excites,
Or close ambition varnisht o're with zeal.

Thus they thir doubtful consultations dark
Ended rejoycing in thir matchless Chief:
As when from mountain tops the dusky clouds
Ascending, while the North wind sleeps, o'respread
Heav'ns chearful face, the lowring Element   490
Scowls ore the dark'nd lantskip Snow, or showre;
If chance the radiant Sun with farewell sweet
Extend his ev'ning beam, the fields revive,
The birds thir notes renew, and bleating herds
Attest thir joy, that hill and valley rings.
O shame to men! Devil with Devil damn'd
Firm concord holds, men onely disagree
Of Creatures rational, though under hope
Of heavenly Grace: and God proclaiming peace,
Yet live in hatred, enmitie, and strife   500
Among themselves, and levie cruel warres,
Wasting the Earth, each other to destroy:
As if (which might induce us to accord)
Man had not hellish foes anow besides,
That day and night for his destruction waite.
    The *Stygian* Councel thus dissolv'd; and forth
In order came the grand infernal Peers,
Midst came thir mighty Paramount, and seemd
Alone th' Antagonist of Heav'n, nor less
Then Hells dread Emperour with pomp Supream,   510
And God-like imitated State; him round
A Globe of fierie Seraphim inclos'd
With bright imblazonrie, and horrent Arms.
Then of thir Session ended they bid cry

With Trumpets regal sound the great result:
Toward the four winds four speedy Cherubim
Put to thir mouths the sounding Alchymie
By Haralds voice explain'd: the hollow Abyss
Heard farr and wide, and all the host of Hell
With deafning shout, return'd them loud acclaim.   520
Thence more at ease thir minds and somwhat rais'd
By false presumptuous hope, the ranged powers
Disband, and wandring, each his several way
Pursues, as inclination or sad choice
Leads him perplext, where he may likeliest find
Truce to his restless thoughts, and entertain
The irksome hours, till his great Chief return.
Part on the Plain, or in the Air sublime
Upon the wing, or in swift race contend,
As at th' Olympian Games or *Pythian* fields;   530
Part curb thir fierie Steeds, or shun the Goal
With rapid wheels, or fronted Brigads form.
As when to warn proud Cities warr appears
Wag'd in the troubl'd Skie, and Armies rush
To Battel in the Clouds, before each Van
Prick forth the Aerie Knights, and couch thir spears
Till thickest Legions close; with feats of Arms
From either end of Heav'n the welkin burns,
Others with vast *Typhæan* rage more fell
Rend up both Rocks and Hills, and ride the Air   540
In whirlwind; Hell scarce holds the wilde uproar.
As when *Alcides* from *Oealia* Crown'd
With conquest, felt th' envenom'd robe, and tore

Through pain up by the roots *Thessalian* Pines,
And *Lichas* from the top of *Oeta* threw
Into th' *Euboic* Sea. Others more milde,
Retreated in a silent valley, sing
With notes Angelical to many a Harp
Thir own Heroic deeds and hapless fall
By doom of Battel; and complain that Fate   550
Free Vertue should enthrall to Force or Chance.
Thir song was partial, but the harmony
(What could it less when Spirits immortal sing?)
Suspended Hell, and took with ravishment
The thronging audience. In discourse more sweet
(For Eloquence the Soul, Song charms the Sense,)
Others apart sat on a Hill retir'd,
In thoughts more elevate, and reason'd high
Of Providence, Foreknowledge, Will, and Fate,
Fixt Fate, free will, foreknowledge absolute,   560
And found no end, in wandring mazes lost.
Of good and evil much they argu'd then,
Of happiness and final misery,
Passion and Apathie, and glory and shame,
Vain wisdom all, and false Philosophie:
Yet with a pleasing sorcerie could charm
Pain for a while or anguish, and excite
Fallacious hope, or arm th' obdured brest
With stubborn patience as with triple steel.
Another part in Squadrons and gross Bands,   570
On bold adventure to discover wide
That dismal world, if any Clime perhaps

Might yeild them easier habitation, bend

Four ways thir flying March, along the Banks

Of four infernal Rivers that disgorge

Into the burning Lake thir baleful streams;

Abhorred *Styx* the flood of deadly hate,

Sad *Acheron* of sorrow, black and deep;

Cocytus, nam'd of lamentation loud

Heard on the ruful stream; fierce *Phlegeton*   580

Whose waves of torrent fire inflame with rage.

Farr off from these a slow and silent stream,

Lethe the River of Oblivion roules

Her watrie Labyrinth, whereof who drinks,

Forthwith his former state and being forgets,

Forgets both joy and grief, pleasure and pain.

Beyond this flood a frozen Continent

Lies dark and wilde, beat with perpetual storms

Of Whirlwind and dire Hail, which on firm land

Thaws not, but gathers heap, and ruin seems   590

Of ancient pile; all else deep snow and ice,

A gulf profound as that *Serbonian* Bog

Betwixt *Damiata* and the mount *Casius* old,

Where Armies whole have sunk: the parching Air

Burns frore, and cold performs th' effect of Fire.

Thither by harpy-footed Furies hail'd,

At certain revolutions all the damn'd

Are brought: and feel by turns the bitter change

Of fierce extreams, extreams by change more fierce,

From Beds of raging Fire to starve in Ice   600

Thir soft Ethereal warmth, and there to pine

Immovable, infixt, and frozen round,

Periods of time, thence hurried back to fire.

They ferry over this *Lethean* Sound

Both to and fro, thir sorrow to augment,

And wish and struggle, as they pass, to reach

The tempting stream, with one small drop to loose

In sweet fortgetfulness all pain and woe,

All in one moment, and so neer the brink;

But fate withstands, and to oppose th' attempt   610

Medusa with *Gorgonian* terror guards

The Ford, and of it self the water flies

All taste of living wight, as once it fled

The lip of *Tantalus*. Thus roving on

In confus'd march forlorn, th' adventrous Bands

With shuddring horror pale, and eyes agast

View'd first thir lamentable lot, and found

Not rest: through many a dark and drearie Vaile

They pass'd, and many a Region dolorous,

O're many a Frozen, many a Fierie Alpe,   620

Rocks, Caves, Lakes, Fens, Bogs, Dens, and shades of death,

A Universe of death, which God by curse

Created evil, for evil only good,

Where all life dies, death lives, and nature breeds,

Perverse, all monstrous, all prodigious things,

Abominable, inutterable, and worse

Then Fables yet have feign'd, or fear conceiv'd,

Gorgons and *Hydra's*, and *Chimera's* dire.

    Mean while the Adversary of God and Man,

Satan with thoughts inflam'd of highest design,   630

Puts on swift wings, and toward the Gates of Hell
Explores his solitary flight; som times
He scours the right hand coast, som times the left,
Now shaves with level wing the Deep, then soares
Up to the fiery concave touring high.
As when farr off at Sea a Fleet descri'd
Hangs in the Clouds, by *Æquinoctial* Winds
Close sailing from *Bengala,* or the Iles
Of *Ternate* and *Tidore,* whence Merchants bring
Thir spicie Drugs: they on the trading Flood   640
Through the wide *Ethiopian* to the Cape
Ply stemming nightly toward the Pole. So seem'd
Farr off the flying Fiend: at last appeer
Hell bounds high reaching to the horrid Roof,
And thrice threefold the Gates; three folds were Brass
Three Iron, three of Adamantine Rock,
Impenitrable, impal'd with circling fire,
Yet unconsum'd. Before the Gates there sat
On either side a formidable shape;
The one seem'd Woman to the waste, and fair,   650
But ended foul in many a scaly fould
Voluminous and vast, a Serpent arm'd
With mortal sting: about her middle round
A cry of Hell Hounds never ceasing bark'd
With wide *Cerberean* mouths full loud, and rung
A hideous Peal: yet, when they list, would creep,
If aught disturb'd thir noyse, into her woomb,
And kennel there, yet there still bark'd and howl'd
Within unseen. Farr less abhorrd then these

Vex'd *Scylla* bathing in the Sea that parts   660
Calabria from the hoarce *Trinacrian* shore:
Nor uglier follow the Night-Hag, when call'd
In secret, riding through the Air she comes
Lur'd with the smell of infant blood, to dance
With *Lapland* Witches, while the labouring Moon
Eclipses at thir charms. The other shape,
If shape it might be call'd that shape had none
Distinguishable in member, joynt, or limb,
Or substance might be call'd that shadow seem'd,
For each seem'd either; black it stood as Night,   670
Fierce as ten Furies, terrible as Hell,
And shook a dreadful Dart; what seem'd his head
The likeness of a Kingly Crown had on.
Satan was now at hand, and from his seat
The Monster moving onward came as fast,
With horrid strides, Hell trembled as he strode.
Th' undaunted Fiend what this might be admir'd,
Admir'd, not fear'd; God and his Son except,
Created thing naught vallu'd he nor shun'd;
And with disdainful look thus first began.   680
    Whence and what art thou, execrable shape,
That dar'st, though grim and terrible, advance
Thy miscreated Front athwart my way
To yonder Gates? through them I mean to pass,
That be assur'd, without leave askt of thee:
Retire, or taste thy folly, and learn by proof,
Hell-born, not to contend with Spirits of Heav'n.
    To whom the Goblin full of wrauth reply'd,

Art thou that Traitor Angel, art thou hee,
Who first broke peace in Heav'n and Faith, till then   690
Unbrok'n, and in proud rebellious Arms
Drew after him the third part of Heav'ns Sons
Conjur'd against the highest, for which both Thou
And they outcast from God, are here condemn'd
To waste Eternal daies in woe and pain?
And reck'n'st thou thy self with Spirits of Heav'n,
Hell-doomd, and breath'st defiance here and scorn,
Where I reign King, and to enrage thee more,
Thy King and Lord? Back to thy punishment,
False fugitive, and to thy speed add wings,   700
Least with a whip of Scorpions I pursue
Thy lingring, or with one stroke of this Dart
Strange horror seise thee, and pangs unfelt before.
    So spake the grieslie terrour, and in shape,
So speaking and so threatning, grew ten fold
More dreadful and deform: on th' other side
Incenc't with indignation *Satan* stood
Unterrifi'd, and like a Comet burn'd,
That fires the length of *Ophiucus* huge
In th' Artick Sky, and from his horrid hair   710
Shakes Pestilence and Warr. Each at the Head
Level'd his deadly aime; thir fatall hands
No second stroke intend, and such a frown
Each cast at th' other, as when two black Clouds
With Heav'ns Artillery fraught, come rattling on
Over the *Caspian*, then stand front to front
Hov'ring a space, till Winds the signal blow

To joyn thir dark Encounter in mid air:
So frownd the mighty Combatants, that Hell
Grew darker at thir frown, so matcht they stood;   720
For never but once more was either like
To meet so great a foe: and now great deeds
Had been achiev'd, whereof all Hell had rung,
Had not the Snakie Sorceress that sat
Fast by Hell Gate, and kept the fatal Key,
Ris'n, and with hideous outcry rush'd between.
      O Father, what intends thy hand, she cry'd,
Against thy only Son? What fury O Son,
Possesses thee to bend that mortal Dart
Against thy Fathers head? and know'st for whom;   730
For him who sits above and laughs the while
At thee ordain'd his drudge, to execute
What e're his wrath, which he calls Justice, bids.
His wrath which one day will destroy ye both.
      She spake, and at her words the hellish Pest
Forbore, then these to her *Satan* return'd:
      So strange thy outcry, and thy words so strange
Thou interposest, that my sudden hand
Prevented spares to tell thee yet by deeds
What it intends; till first I know of thee,   740
What thing thou art, thus double-form'd, and why
In this infernal Vaile first met thou call'st
Me Father, and that Fantasm call'st my Son?
I know thee not, nor ever saw till now
Sight more detestable then him and thee.
      T' whom thus the Portress of Hell Gate reply'd;

Hast thou forgot me then, and do I seem
Now in thine eye so foul, once deemd so fair
In Heav'n, when at th' Assembly, and in sight
Of all the Seraphim with thee combin'd   750
In bold conspiracy against Heav'ns King,
All on a sudden miserable pain
Surpris'd thee, dim thine eyes, and dizzie swumm
In darkness, while thy head flames thick and fast
Threw forth, till on the left side op'ning wide,
Likest to thee in shape and count'nance bright,
Then shining heav'nly fair, a Goddess arm'd
Out of thy head I sprung: amazement seis'd
All th' Host of Heav'n; back they recoild affraid
At first, and call'd me *Sin,* and for a Sign   760
Portentous held me; but familiar grown,
I pleas'd, and with attractive graces won
The most averse, thee chiefly, who full oft
Thy self in me thy perfect image viewing
Becam'st enamour'd, and such joy thou took'st
With me in secret, that my womb conceiv'd
A growing burden. Mean while Warr arose,
And fields were fought in Heav'n; wherein remaind
(For what could else) to our Almighty Foe
Cleer Victory, to our part loss and rout   770
Through all the Empyrean: down they fell
Driv'n headlong from the Pitch of Heaven, down
Into this Deep, and in the general fall
I also; at which time this powerful Key
Into my hand was giv'n, with charge to kccp

These Gates for ever shut, which none can pass
Without my op'ning. Pensive here I sat
Alone, but long I sat not, till my womb
Pregnant by thee, and now excessive grown
Prodigious motion felt and rueful throes.   780
At last this odious offspring whom thou seest
Thine own begotten, breaking violent way
Tore through my entrails, that with fear and pain
Distorted, all my nether shape thus grew
Transform'd: but he my inbred enemie
Forth issu'd, brandishing his fatal Dart
Made to destroy: I fled, and cry'd out *Death*;
Hell trembl'd at the hideous Name, and sigh'd
From all her Caves, and back resounded *Death*.
I fled, but he pursu'd (though more, it seems,   790
Inflam'd with lust then rage) and swifter far,
Me overtook his mother all dismaid,
And in embraces forcible and foule
Ingendring with me, of that rape begot
These yelling Monsters that with ceasless cry
Surround me, as thou sawst, hourly conceiv'd
And hourly born, with sorrow infinite
To me, for when they list into the womb
That bred them they return, and howle and gnaw
My Bowels, their repast; then bursting forth   800
Afresh with conscious terrours vex me round,
That rest or intermission none I find.
Before mine eyes in opposition sits
Grim *Death* my Son and foe, who sets them on,

And me his Parent would full soon devour

For want of other prey, but that he knows

His end with mine involvd; and knows that I

Should prove a bitter Morsel, and his bane,

When ever that shall be; so Fate pronounc'd.

But thou O Father, I forewarn thee, shun   810

His deadly arrow; neither vainly hope

To be invulnerable in those bright Arms,

Though temper'd heav'nly, for that mortal dint,

Save he who reigns above, none can resist.

　　She finish'd, and the suttle Fiend his lore

Soon learnd, now milder, and thus answerd smooth.

Dear Daughter, since thou claim'st me for thy Sire,

And my fair Son here showst me, the dear pledge

Of dalliance had with thee in Heav'n, and joys

Then sweet, now sad to mention, through dire change   820

Befalln us unforeseen, unthought of, know

I come no enemie, but to set free

From out this dark and dismal house of pain,

Both him and thee, and all the heav'nly Host

Of Spirits that in our just pretenses arm'd

Fell with us from on high: from them I go

This uncouth errand sole, and one for all

My self expose, with lonely steps to tread

Th' unfounded deep, & through the void immense

To search with wandring quest a place foretold   830

Should be, and, by concurring signs, ere now

Created vast and round, a place of bliss

In the Pourlieues of Heav'n, and therein plac't

A race of upstart Creatures, to supply
Perhaps our vacant room, though more remov'd,
Least Heav'n surcharg'd with potent multitude
Might hap to move new broiles: Be this or aught
Then this more secret now design'd, I haste
To know, and this once known, shall soon return,
And bring ye to the place where Thou and Death   840
Shall dwell at ease, and up and down unseen
Wing silently the buxom Air, imbalm'd
With odours; there ye shall be fed and fill'd
Immeasurably, all things shall be your prey.
He ceas'd, for both seemd highly pleasd, and Death
Grinnd horrible a gastly smile, to hear
His famine should be fill'd, and blest his mawe
Destin'd to that good hour: no less rejoyc'd
His mother bad, and thus bespake her Sire.
　　The key of this infernal Pit by due,   850
And by command of Heav'ns all-powerful King
I keep, by him forbidden to unlock
These Adamantine Gates; against all force
Death ready stands to interpose his dart,
Fearless to be o'rematcht by living might.
But what ow I to his commands above
Who hates me, and hath hither thrust mc down
Into this gloom of *Tartarus* profound,
To sit in hateful Office here confin'd,
Inhabitant of Heav'n, and heav'nlie-born,   860
Here in perpetual agonie and pain,
With terrors and with clamors compasst round

Of mine own brood, that on my bowels feed:

Thou art my Father, thou my Author, thou

My being gav'st me; whom should I obey

But thee, whom follow? thou wilt bring me soon

To that new world of light and bliss, among

The Gods who live at ease, where I shall Reign

At thy right hand voluptuous, as beseems

Thy daughter and thy darling, without end.   870

    Thus saying, from her side the fatal Key,

Sad instrument of all our woe, she took;

And towards the Gate rouling her bestial train,

Forthwith the huge Porcullis high up drew,

Which but her self not all the *Stygian* powers

Could once have mov'd; then in the key-hole turns

Th' intricate wards, and every Bolt and Bar

Of massie Iron or sollid Rock with ease

Unfast'ns: on a sudden op'n flie

With impetuous recoile and jarring sound   880

Th' infernal dores, and on thir hinges grate

Harsh Thunder, that the lowest bottom shook

Of *Erebus*. She op'nd, but to shut

Excel'd her power; the Gates wide op'n stood,

That with extended wings a Bannerd Host

Under spread Ensigns marching might pass through

With Horse and Chariots rankt in loose array;

So wide they stood, and like a Furnace mouth

Cast forth redounding smoak and ruddy flame.

Before thir eyes in sudden view appear   890

The secrets of the hoarie deep, a dark

Illimitable Ocean without bound,

Without dimension, where length, breadth, and highth,

And time and place are lost; where eldest Night

And *Chaos*, Ancestors of Nature, hold

Eternal *Anarchie*, amidst the noise

Of endless warrs, and by confusion stand.

For hot, cold, moist, and dry, four Champions fierce

Strive here for Maistrie, and to Battel bring

Thir embryon Atoms; they around the flag   900

Of each his faction, in thir several Clanns,

Light-arm'd or heavy, sharp, smooth, swift or slow,

Swarm populous, unnumber'd as the Sands

Of *Barca* or *Cyrene's* torrid soil,

Levied to side with warring Winds, and poise

Thir lighter wings. To whom these most adhere,

Hee rules a moment; *Chaos* Umpire sits,

And by decision more imbroiles the fray

By which he Reigns: next him high Arbiter

Chance governs all. Into this wilde Abyss,   910

The Womb of nature and perhaps her Grave,

Of neither Sea, nor Shore, nor Air, nor Fire,

But all these in thir pregnant causes mixt

Confus'dly, and which thus must ever fight,

Unless th' Almighty Maker them ordain

His dark materials to create more Worlds,

Into this wilde Abyss the warie fiend

Stood on the brink of Hell and look'd a while,

Pondering his Voyage; for no narrow frith

He had to cross. Nor was his eare less peal'd   920

With noises loud and ruinous (to compare

Great things with small) then when *Bellona* storms,

With all her battering Engines bent to rase

Som Capital City, or less then if this frame

Of Heav'n were falling, and these Elements

In mutinie had from her Axle torn

The stedfast Earth. At last his Sail-broad Vannes

He spreads for flight, and in the surging smoak

Uplifted spurns the ground, thence many a League

As in a cloudy Chair ascending rides   930

Audacious, but that seat soon failing, meets

A vast vacuitie: all unawares

Fluttring his pennons vain plumb down he drops

Ten thousand fadom deep, and to this hour

Down had been falling, had not by ill chance

The strong rebuff of som tumultuous cloud

Instinct with Fire and Nitre hurried him

As many miles aloft: that furie stay'd,

Quencht in a Boggie *Syrtis*, neither Sea,

Nor good dry Land: nigh founderd on he fares,   940

Treading the crude consistence, half on foot,

Half flying; behoves him now both Oare and Saile.

As when a Gryfon through the Wilderness

With winged course ore Hill or moarie Dale,

Pursues the *Arimaspian*, who by stelth

Had from his wakeful custody purloind

The guarded Gold: So eagerly the fiend

Ore bog or steep, through strait, rough, dense, or rare,

With head, hands, wings, or feet pursues his way,

And swims or sinks, or wades, or creeps, or flyes: 950
At length a universal hubbub wilde
Of stunning sounds and voices all confus'd
Born through the hollow dark assaults his eare
With loudest vehemence: thither he plyes,
Undaunted to meet there what every power
Or Spirit of the nethermost Abyss
Might in that noise reside, of whom to ask
Which way the neerest coast of darkness lyes
Bordcring on light; when strait behold the Throne
Of *Chaos,* and his dark Pavilion spread   960
Wide on the wasteful Deep; with him Enthron'd
Sat Sable-vested Night, eldest of things,
The consort of his Reign; and by them stood
Orcus and *Ades,* and the dreaded name
Of *Demogorgon;* Rumor next and chance,
And Tumult and Confusion all imbroild,
And Discord with a thousand various mouths.
   T' whom *Satan* turning boldly, thus. Ye Powers
And Spirits of this nethermost Abyss,
Chaos and *ancient Night,* I come no Spie,   970
With purpose to explore or to disturb
The secrets of your Realm, but by constraint
Wandring this darksome desart, as my way
Lies through your spacious Empire up to light,
Alone, and without guide, half lost, I seek
What readiest path leads where your gloomie bounds
Confine with Heav'n; or if som other place
From your Dominion won, th' Ethereal King

Possesses lately, thither to arrive

I travel this profound, direct my course; 980

Directed, no mean recompence it brings

To your behoof, if I that Region lost,

All usurpation thence expell'd, reduce

To her original darkness and your sway

(Which is my present journey) and once more

Erect the Standerd there of *ancient Night*;

Yours be th' advantage all, mine the revenge.

 Thus *Satan*; and him thus the Anarch old

With faultring speech and visage incompos'd

Answer'd. I know thee, stranger, who thou art, 990

That mighty leading Angel, who of late

Made head against Heav'ns King, though overthrown.

I saw and heard, for such a numerous host

Fled not in silence through the frighted deep

With ruin upon ruin, rout on rout,

Confusion worse confounded; and Heav'n Gates

Pourd out by millions her victorious Bands

Pursuing. I upon my Frontieres here

Keep residence; if all I can will serve,

That little which is left so to defend 1000

Encroacht on still through our intestine broiles

Weakning the Scepter of old Night: first Hell

Your dungeon stretching far and wide beneath;

Now lately Heaven and Earth, another World

Hung ore my Realm, link'd in a golden Chain

To that side Heav'n from whence your Legions fell:

If that way be your walk, you have not farr;

So much the neerer danger; goe and speed;
Havock and spoil and ruin are my gain.
    He ceas'd; and *Satan* staid not to reply,   1010
But glad that now his Sea should find a shore,
With fresh alacritie and force renew'd
Springs upward like a Pyramid of fire
Into the wilde expanse, and through the shock
Of fighting Elements, on all sides round
Environ'd wins his way; harder beset
And more endanger'd, then when *Argo* pass'd
Through *Bosporus* betwixt the justling Rocks:
Or when *Ulysses* on the Larbord shunnd
Charybdis and by th' other whirlpool steard.   1020
So he with difficulty and labour hard
Mov'd on, with difficulty and labour hee;
But hee once past, soon after when man fell,
Strange alteration! Sin and Death amain
Following his track, such was the will of Heav'n,
Pav'd after him a broad and beat'n way
Over the dark Abyss, whose boiling Gulf
Tamely endur'd a Bridge of wondrous length
From Hell continu'd reaching th' utmost Orbe
Of this frail World; by which the Spirits perverse   1030
With easie intercourse pass to and fro
To tempt or punish mortals, except whom
God and good Angels guard by special grace.
But now at last the sacred influence
Of light appears, and from the walls of Heav'n
Shoots farr into the bosom of dim Night

A glimmering dawn; here Nature first begins

Her fardest verge, and *Chaos* to retire

As from her outmost works a brok'n foe

With tumult less and with less hostile din,   1040

That *Satan* with less toil, and now with ease

Wafts on the calmer wave by dubious light

And like a weather-beaten Vessel holds

Gladly the Port, though Shrouds and Tackle torn;

Or in the emptier waste, resembling Air,

Weighs his spread wings, at leasure to behold

Farr off th' Empyreal Heav'n, extended wide

In circuit, undetermind square or round,

With Opal Towrs and Battlements adorn'd

Of living Saphire, once his native Seat;   1050

And fast by hanging in a golden Chain

This pendant world, in bigness as a Starr

Of smallest Magnitude close by the Moon.

Thither full fraught with mischievous revenge,

Accurst, and in a cursed hour he hies.   .

    The End of the Second Book

PARADISE
LOST

BOOK III.

HAil holy light, ofspring of Heav'n first-born,
Or of th' Eternal Coeternal beam
May I express thee unblam'd? since God is light,
And never but in unapproached light
Dwelt from Eternitie, dwelt then in thee,
Bright effluence of bright essence increate.
Or hear'st thou rather pure Ethereal stream,
Whose Fountain who shall tell? before the Sun,
Before the Heavens thou wert, and at the voice
Of God, as with a Mantle didst invest   10
The rising world of waters dark and deep,
Won from the void and formless infinite.
Thee I re-visit now with bolder wing,
Escap't the *Stygian* Pool, though long detain'd
In the obscure sojourn, while in my flight
Through utter and through middle darkness borne
With other notes then to th' *Orphean* Lyre
I sung of *Chaos* and *Eternal Night*,
Taught by the heav'nly Muse to venture down
The dark descent, and up to reascend,   20
Though hard and rare: thee I revisit safe,

And feel thy sovran vital Lamp; but thou
Revisit'st not these eyes, that rowle in vain
To find thy piercing ray, and find no dawn;
So thick a drop serene hath quencht thir Orbs,
Or dim suffusion veild. Yet not the more
Cease I to wander where the Muses haunt
Cleer Spring, or shadie Grove, or Sunnie Hill,
Smit with the love of sacred song; but chief
Thee *Sion* and the flowrie Brooks beneath   30
That wash thy hallowd feet, and warbling flow,
Nightly I visit: nor somtimes forget
Those other two equal'd with me in Fate,
So were I equal'd with them in renown,
Blind *Thamyris* and blind *Mæonides*,
And *Tiresias* and *Phineus* Prophets old.
Then feed on thoughts, that voluntarie move
Harmonious numbers; as the wakeful Bird
Sings darkling, and in shadiest Covert hid
Tunes her nocturnal Note. Thus with the Year   40
Seasons return, but not to me returns
Day, or the sweet approach of Ev'n or Morn,
Or sight of vernal bloom, or Summers Rose,
Or flocks, or herds, or human face divine;
But cloud in stead, and ever-during dark
Surrounds me, from the chearful waies of men
Cut off, and for the Book of knowledg fair
Presented with a Universal blanc
Of Natures works to mee expung'd and ras'd,
And wisdome at one entrance quite shut out.   50

So much the rather thou Celestial light
Shine inward, and the mind through all her powers
Irradiate, there plant eyes, all mist from thence
Purge and disperse, that I may see and tell
Of things invisible to mortal sight.
   Now had the Almighty Father from above,
From the pure Empyrean where he sits
High Thron'd above all highth, bent down his eye,
His own works and their works at once to view:
About him all the Sanctities of Heaven   60
Stood thick as Starrs, and from his sight receiv'd
Beatitude past utterance; on his right
The radiant image of his Glory sat,
His onely Son; On Earth he first beheld
Our two first Parents, yet the onely two
Of mankind, in the happie Garden plac't,
Reaping immortal fruits of joy and love,
Uninterrupted joy, unrivald love
In blissful solitude; he then survey'd
Hell and the Gulf between, and *Satan* there   70
Coasting the wall of Heav'n on this side Night
In the dun Air sublime, and ready now
To stoop with wearied wings, and willing feet
On the bare outside of this World, that seem'd
Firm land imbosom'd without Firmament,
Uncertain which, in Ocean or in Air.
Him God beholding from his prospect high,
Wherein past, present, future he beholds,
Thus to his onely Son foreseeing spake.

Onely begotten Son, seest thou what rage   80
Transports our adversarie, whom no bounds
Prescrib'd, no barrs of Hell, not all the chains
Heapt on him there, nor yet the main Abyss
Wide interrupt can hold; so bent he seems
On desperat revenge, that shall redound
Upon his own rebellious head. And now
Through all restraint broke loose he wings his way
Not farr off Heav'n, in the Precincts of light,
Directly towards the new created World,
And Man there plac't, with purpose to assay   90
If him by force he can destroy, or worse,
By som false guile pervert; and shall pervert;
For man will heark'n to his glozing lyes,
And easily trangress the sole Command,
Sole pledge of his obedience: So will fall
Hee and his faithless Progenie: whose fault?
Whose but his own? ingrate, he had of mee
All he could have; I made him just and right,
Sufficient to have stood, though free to fall.
Such I created all th' Ethereal Powers   100
And Spirits, both them who stood & them who faild;
Freely they stood who stood, and fell who fell.
Not free, what proof could they have givn sincere
Of tru allegiance, constant Faith or Love,
Where onely what they needs must do, appeard,
Not what they would? what praise could they receive?
What pleasure I from such obedience paid,
When Will and Reason (Reason also is choice)

Useless and vain, of freedom both despoild,

Made passive both, had servd necessitie,   110

Not mee. They therefore as to right belongd,

So were created, nor can justly accuse

Thir maker, or thir making, or thir Fate;

As if Predestination over-rul'd

Thir will, dispos'd by absolute Decree

Or high foreknowledge; they themselves decreed

Thir own revolt, not I: if I foreknew,

Foreknowledge had no influence on their fault,

Which had no less prov'd certain unforeknown.

So without least impulse or shadow of Fate,   120

Or aught by me immutablie foreseen,

They trespass, Authors to themselves in all

Both what they judge and what they choose; for so

I formd them free, and free they must remain,

Till they enthrall themselves: I else must change

Thir nature, and revoke the high Decree

Unchangeable, Eternal, which ordain'd

Thir freedom, they themselves ordain'd thir fall.

The first sort by thir own suggestion fell,

Self-tempted, self-deprav'd: Man falls deceiv'd   130

By the other first: Man therefore shall find grace,

The other none: in Mercy and Justice both,

Through Heav'n and Earth, so shall my glorie excel,

But Mercy first and last shall brightest shine.

    Thus while God spake, ambrosial fragrance fill'd

All Heav'n, and in the blessed Spirits elect

Sense of new joy ineffable diffus'd:

Beyond compare the Son of God was seen
Most glorious, in him all his Father shon
Substantially express'd, and in his face 140
Divine compassion visibly appeerd,
Love without end, and without measure Grace,
Which uttering thus he to his Father spake.

   O Father, gracious was that word which clos'd
Thy sovran sentence, that Man should find grace;
For which both Heav'n and Earth shall high extoll
Thy praises, with th' innumerable sound
Of Hymns and sacred Songs, wherewith thy Throne
Encompass'd shall resound thee ever blest.
For should Man finally be lost, should Man 150
Thy creature late so lov'd, thy youngest Son
Fall circumvented thus by fraud, though joynd
With his own folly? that be from thee farr,
That farr be from thee, Father, who art Judge
Of all things made, and judgest onely right.
Or shall the Adversarie thus obtain
His end, and frustrate thine, shall he fulfill
His malice, and thy goodness bring to naught,
Or proud return though to his heavier doom,
Yet with revenge accomplish't and to Hell 160
Draw after him the whole Race of mankind,
By him corrupted? or wilt thou thy self
Abolish thy Creation, and unmake,
For him, what for thy glorie thou hast made?
So should thy goodness and thy greatness both
Be questiond and blaspheam'd without defence.

To whom the great Creatour thus replyd.
O Son, in whom my Soul hath chief delight,
Son of my bosom, Son who art alone
My word, my wisdom, and effectual might,   170
All hast thou spok'n as my thoughts are, all
As my Eternal purpose hath decreed:
Man shall not quite be lost, but sav'd who will,
Yet not of will in him, but grace in me
Freely voutsaft; once more I will renew
His lapsed powers, though forfeit and enthrall'd
By sin to foul exorbitant desires;
Upheld by me, yet once more he shall stand
On even ground against his mortal foe,
By me upheld, that he may know how frail   180
His fall'n condition is, and to me ow
All his deliv'rance, and to none but me.
Some I have chosen of peculiar grace
Elect above the rest; so is my will:
The rest shall hear me call, and oft be warnd
Thir sinful state, and to appease betimes
Th' incensed Deitie, while offerd grace
Invites; for I will cleer thir senses dark,
What may suffice, and soft'n stonie hearts
To pray, repent, and bring obedience due.   190
To prayer, repentance, and obedience due,
Though but endevord with sincere intent,
Mine eare shall not be slow, mine eye not shut.
And I will place within them as a guide
My Umpire *Conscience*, whom if they will hear,

Light after light well us'd they shall attain,

And to the end persisting, safe arrive.

This my long sufferance and my day of grace

They who neglect and scorn, shall never taste;

But hard be hard'nd, blind be blinded more,   200

That they may stumble on, and deeper fall;

And none but such from mercy I exclude.

But yet all is not don; Man disobeying,

Disloyal breaks his fealtie, and sinns

Against the high Supremacie of Heav'n,

Affecting God-head, and so loosing all,

To expiate his Treason hath naught left,

But to destruction sacred and devote,

He with his whole posteritie must die,

Die hee or Justice must; unless for him   210

Som other able, and as willing, pay

The rigid satisfaction, death for death.

Say Heav'nly Powers, where shall we find such love,

Which of ye will be mortal to redeem

Mans mortal crime, and just th' unjust to save,

Dwels in all Heaven charitie so deare?

   He ask'd, but all the Heav'nly Quire stood mute,

And silence was in Heav'n: on mans behalf

Patron or Intercessor none appeerd,

Much less that durst upon his own head draw   220

The deadly forfeiture, and ransom set.

And now without redemption all mankind

Must have bin lost, adjudg'd to Death and Hell

By doom severe, had not the Son of God,

In whom the fulness dwels of love divine,
His dearest mediation thus renewd.

   Father, thy word is past, man shall find grace;
And shall grace not find means, that finds her way,
The speediest of thy winged messengers,
To visit all thy creatures, and to all   230
Comes unprevented, unimplor'd, unsought,
Happie for man, so coming; he her aide
Can never seek, once dead in sins and lost;
Attonement for himself or offering meet,
Indebted and undon, hath none to bring:
Behold mee then, mee for him, life for life
I offer, on mee let thine anger fall;
Account mee man; I for his sake will leave
Thy bosom, and this glorie next to thee
Freely put off, and for him lastly die   240
Well pleas'd, on me let Death wreck all his rage;
Under his gloomie power I shall not long
Lie vanquisht; thou hast givn me to possess
Life in my self for ever, by thee I live,
Though now to Death I yeild, and am his due
All that of me can die, yet that debt paid,
Thou wilt not leave me in the loathsom grave
His prey, nor suffer my unspotted Soule
For ever with corruption there to dwell;
But I shall rise Victorious, and subdue   250
My Vanquisher, spoild of his vanted spoile;
Death his deaths wound shall then receive, & stoop
Inglorious, of his mortall sting disarm'd.

I through the ample Air in Triumph high
Shall lead Hell Captive maugre Hell, and show
The powers of darkness bound. Thou at the sight
Pleas'd, out of Heaven shalt look down and smile,
While by thee rais'd I ruin all my foes,
Death last, and with his Carcass glut the Grave:
Then with the multitude of my redeemd   260
Shall enter Heaven long absent, and returne,
Father, to see thy face, wherein no cloud
Of anger shall remain, but peace assur'd,
And reconcilement; wrauth shall be no more
Thenceforth, but in thy presence Joy entire.

   HIs words here ended, but his meek aspect
Silent yet spake, and breath'd immortal love
To mortal men, above which only shon
Filial obedience: as a sacrifice
Glad to be offer'd, he attends the will   270
Of his great Father. Admiration seis'd
All Heav'n, what this might mean, & whither tend
Wondring; but soon th' Almighty thus reply'd:

   O thou in Heav'n and Earth the only peace
Found out for mankind under wrauth, O thou
My sole complacence! well thou know'st how dear,
To me are all my works, nor Man the least
Though last created, that for him I spare
Thee from my bosom and right hand, to save,
By loosing thee a while, the whole Race lost.   280
Thou therefore whom thou only canst redeeme,
Thir Nature also to thy Nature joyne;

And be thy self Man among men on Earth,
Made flesh, when time shall be, of Virgin seed,
By wondrous birth: Be thou in *Adams* room
The Head of all mankind, though *Adams* Son.
As in him perish all men, so in thee
As from a second root shall be restor'd,
As many as are restor'd, without thee none.
His crime makes guiltie all his Sons, thy merit   290
Imputed shall absolve them who renounce
Thir own both righteous and unrighteous deeds,
And live in thee transplanted, and from thee
Receive new life. So Man, as is most just,
Shall satisfie for Man, be judg'd and die,
And dying rise, and rising with him raise
His Brethren, ransomd with his own dear life.
So Heav'nly love shal outdoo Hellish hate,
Giving to death, and dying to redeeme,
So dearly to redeem what Hellish hate   300
So easily destroy'd, and still destroyes
In those who, when they may, accept not grace.
Nor shalt thou by descending to assume
Mans Nature, less'n or degrade thine owne.
Because thou hast, though Thron'd in highest bliss
Equal to God, and equally enjoying
God-like fruition, quitted all to save
A World from utter loss, and hast been found
By Merit more then Birthright Son of God,
Found worthiest to be so by being Good,   310
Farr more then Great or High; because in thee

Love hath abounded more then Glory abounds,

Therefore thy Humiliation shall exalt

With thee thy Manhood also to this Throne;

Here shalt thou sit incarnate, here shalt Reigne

Both God and Man, Son both of God and Man,

Anointed universal King; all Power

I give thee, reign for ever, and assume

Thy Merits; under thee as Head Supream

Thrones, Princedoms, Powers, Dominions I reduce: 320

All knees to thee shall bow, of them that bide

In Heaven, or Earth, or under Earth in Hell;

When thou attended gloriously from Heav'n

Shalt in the Skie appeer, and from thee send

The summoning Arch-Angels to proclaime

Thy dread Tribunal: forthwith from all Windes

The living, and forthwith the cited dead

Of all past Ages to the general Doom

Shall hast'n, such a peal shall rouse thir sleep.

Then all thy Saints assembl'd, thou shalt judge   330

Bad men and Angels, they arraignd shall sink

Beneath thy Sentence; Hell, her numbers full,

Thenceforth shall be for ever shut. Mean while

The World shall burn, and from her ashes spring

New Heav'n and Earth, wherein the just shall dwell

And after all thir tribulations long

See golden days, fruitful of golden deeds,

With Joy and Love triumphing, and fair Truth.

Then thou thy regal Scepter shalt lay by,

For regal Scepter then no more shall need,   340

God shall be All in All. But all ye Gods,
Adore him, who to compass all this dies,
Adore the Son, and honour him as mee.
  No sooner had th' Almighty ceas't, but all
The multitude of Angels with a shout
Loud as from numbers without number, sweet
As from blest voices, uttering joy, Heav'n rung
With Jubilee, and loud Hosanna's fill'd
Th' eternal Regions: lowly reverent
Towards either Throne thy bow, & to the ground   350
With solemn adoration down they cast
Thir Crowns inwove with Amarant and Gold,
Immortal Amarant, a Flour which once
In Paradise, fast by the Tree of Life
Began to bloom, but soon for mans offence
To Heav'n remov'd where first it grew, there grows,
And flours aloft shading the Fount of Life,
And where the river of Bliss through midst of Heavn
Rowls o're *Elisian* Flours her Amber stream;
With these that never fade the Spirits Elect   360
Bind thir resplendent locks inwreath'd with beams,
Now in loose Garlands thick thrown off, the bright
Pavement that like a Sea of Jasper shon
Impurpl'd with Celestial Roses smil'd.
Then Crown'd again thir gold'n Harps they took,
Harps ever tun'd, that glittering by their side
Like Quivers hung, and with Præamble sweet
Of charming symphonie they introduce
Thir sacred Song, and waken raptures high;

No voice exempt, no voice but well could joine   370
Melodious part, such concord is in Heav'n.
    Thee Father first thy sung Omnipotent,
Immutable, Immortal, Infinite,
Eternal King; thee Author of all being,
Fountain of Light, thy self invisible
Amidst the glorious brightness where thou sit'st
Thron'd inaccessible, but when thou shad'st
The full blaze of thy beams, and through a cloud
Drawn round about thee like a radiant Shrine,
Dark with excessive bright thy skirts appeer,   380
Yet dazle Heav'n, that brightest Seraphim
Approach not, but with both wings veil thir eyes.
Thee next they sang of all Creation first,
Begotten Son, Divine Similitude,
In whose conspicuous count'nance, without cloud
Made visible, th' Almighty Father shines,
Whom else no Creature can behold; on thee
Impresst the effulgence of his Glorie abides,
Transfus'd on thee his ample Spirit rests.
Hee Heav'n of Heavens and all the Powers therein   390
By thee created, and by thee threw down
Th' aspiring Dominations: thou that day
Thy Fathers dreadful Thunder didst not spare,
Nor stop thy flaming Chariot wheels, that shook
Heav'ns everlasting Frame, while o're the necks
Thou drov'st of warring Angels disarraid.
Back from pursuit thy Powers with loud acclaime
Thee only extold, Son of thy Fathers might,

To execute fierce vengeance on his foes,

Not so on Man; him through their malice fall'n,   400

Father of Mercie and Grace, thou didst not doome

So strictly, but much more to pitie encline:

No sooner did thy dear and onely Son

Perceive thee purpos'd not to doom frail Man

So strictly, but much more to pitie enclin'd,

He to appease thy wrauth, and end the strife

Of Mercy and Justice in thy face discern'd,

Regardless of the Bliss wherein hee sat

Second to thee, offerd himself to die

For mans offence. O unexampl'd love,   410

Love no where to be found less then Divine!

Hail Son of God, Saviour of Men, thy Name

Shall be the copious matter of my Song

Henceforth, and never shall my Harp thy praise

Forget, nor from thy Fathers praise disjoine.

   Thus they in Heav'n, above the starry Sphear,

Thir happie hours in joy and hymning spent.

Mean while upon the firm opacous Globe

Of this round World, whose first convex divides

The luminous inferior Orbs, enclos'd   420

From *Chaos* and th' inroad of Darkness old,

Satan alighted walks: a Globe farr off

It seem'd, now seems a boundless Continent

Dark, waste, and wild, under the frown of Night

Starless expos'd, and ever-threatning storms

Of *Chaos* blustring round, inclement skie;

Save on that side which from the wall of Heav'n

Though distant farr som small reflection gaines
Of glimmering air less vext with tempest loud:
Here walk'd the Fiend at large in spacious field.   430
As when a Vultur on *Imaus* bred,
Whose snowie ridge the roving *Tartar* bounds,
Dislodging from a Region scarce of prey
To gorge the flesh of Lambs or yeanling Kids
On Hills where Flocks are fed, flies toward the Springs
Of *Ganges* or *Hydaspes, Indian* streams;
But in his way lights on the barren plaines
Of *Sericana*, where *Chineses* drive
With Sails and Wind thir canie Waggons light:
So on this windie Sea of Land, the Fiend   440
Walk'd up and down alone bent on his prey,
Alone, for other Creature in this place
Living or liveless to be found was none,
None yet, but store hereafter from the earth
Up hither like Aereal vapours flew
Of all things transitorie and vain, when Sin
With vanity had filld the works of men:
Both all things vain, and all who in vain things
Built thir fond hopes of Glorie or lasting fame,
Or happiness in this or th' other life;   450
All who have thir reward on Earth, the fruits
Of painful Superstition and blind Zeal,
Naught seeking but the praise of men, here find
Fit retribution, emptie as thir deeds;
All th' unaccomplisht works of Natures hand,
Abortive, monstrous, or unkindly mixt,

Dissolvd on earth, fleet hither, and in vain,

Till final dissolution, wander here,

Not in the neighbouring Moon, as some have dreamd;

Those argent Fields more likely habitants,   460

Translated Saints, or middle Spirits hold

Betwixt th' Angelical and Human kinde:

Hither of ill-joynd Sons and Daughters born

First from the ancient World those Giants came

With many a vain exploit, though then renownd:

The builders next of *Babel* on the Plain

Of *Sennaar*, and still with vain designe

New *Babels*, had they wherewithall, would build:

Others came single; hee who to be deemd

A God, leap'd fondly into *Ætna* flames,   470

Empedocles, and hee who to enjoy

Plato's *Elysium*, leap'd into the Sea,

Cleombrotus, and many more too long,

Embryo's and Idiots, Eremits and Friers

White, Black and Grey, with all thir trumperie.

Here Pilgrims roam, that stray'd so farr to seek

In *Golgotha* him dead, who lives in Heav'n;

And they who to be sure of Paradise

Dying put on the weeds of *Dominic*,

Or in *Franciscan* think to pass disguis'd;   480

They pass the Planets seven, and pass the sixt,

And that Crystalline Sphear whose ballance weighs

The Trepidation talkt, and that first mov'd;

And now Saint *Peter* at Heav'ns Wicket seems

To wait them with his Keys, and now at foot

Of Heav'ns ascent they lift thir Feet, when loe
A violent cross wind from either Coast
Blows them transverse ten thousand Leagues awry
Into the devious Air; then might ye see
Cowles, Hoods and Habits with thir wearers tost 490
And flutterd into Raggs, then Reliques, Beads,
Indulgences, Dispenses, Pardons, Bulls,
The sport of Winds: all these upwhirld aloft
Fly o're the backside of the World farr off
Into a *Limbo* large and broad, since calld
The Paradise of Fools, to few unknown
Long after, now unpeopl'd, and untrod;
All this dark Globe the Fiend found as he pass'd,
And long he wanderd, till at last a gleame
Of dawning light turnd thither-ward in haste 500
His travell'd steps; farr distant hee descries
Ascending by degrees magnificent
Up to the wall of Heaven a Structure high,
At top whereof, but farr more rich appeerd
The work as of a Kingly Palace Gate
With Frontispice of Diamond and Gold
Imbellisht, thick with sparkling orient Gemmes
The Portal shon, inimitable on Earth
By Model, or by shading Pencil drawn.
The Stairs were such as whereon *Jacob* saw 510
Angels ascending and descending, bands
Of Guardians bright, when he from *Esau* fled
To *Padan-Aram* in the field of *Luz*,
Dreaming by night under the open Skie,

And waking cri'd, This is the Gate of Heav'n.

Each Stair mysteriously was meant, nor stood

There alwaies, but drawn up to Heav'n somtimes

Viewless, and underneath a bright Sea flow'd

Of Jasper, or of liquid Pearle, whereon

Who after came from Earth, sayling arriv'd,   520

Wafted by Angels, or flew o're the Lake

Rapt in a Chariot drawn by fiery Steeds.

The Stairs were then let down, whether to dare

The Fiend by easie ascent, or aggravate

His sad exclusion from the dores of Bliss.

Direct against which op'nd from beneath,

Just o're the blissful seat of Paradise,

A passage down to th' Earth, a passage wide,

Wider by farr then that of after-times

Over Mount *Sion*, and, though that were large,   530

Over the *Promis'd Land* to God so dear,

By which, to visit oft those happy Tribes,

On high behests his Angels to and fro

Pass'd frequent, and his eye with choice regard

From *Paneas* the fount of *Jordans* flood

To *Bëersaba*, where the *Holy Land*

Borders on *Ægypt* and the *Arabian* shoare;

So wide the op'ning seemd, where bounds were set

To darkness, such as bound the Ocean wave.

Satan from hence now on the lower stair   540

That scal'd by steps of Gold to Heav'n Gate

Looks down with wonder at the sudden view

Of all this World at once. As when a Scout

Through dark and desart wayes with peril gone
All night; at last by break of chearful dawne
Obtains the brow of some high-climbing Hill,
Which to his eye discovers unaware
The goodly prospect of some forein land
First-seen, or some renownd Metropolis
With glistering Spires and Pinnacles adornd,   550
Which now the Rising Sun guilds with his beams.
Such wonder seis'd, though after Heaven seen,
The Spirit maligne, but much more envy seis'd
At sight of all this World beheld so faire.
Round he surveys, and well might, where he stood
So high above the circling Canopie
Of Nights extended shade; from Eastern Point
Of *Libra* to the fleecie Starr that bears
Andromeda farr off *Atlantick* Seas
Beyond th' *Horizon*; then from Pole to Pole   560
He views in bredth, and without longer pause
Down right into the Worlds first Region throws
His flight precipitant, and windes with ease
Through the pure marble Air his oblique way
Amongst innumerable Starrs, that shon
Stars distant, but nigh hand seemd other Worlds,
Or other Worlds they seemd, or happy Iles,
Like those *Hesperian* Gardens fam'd of old,
Fortunate Fields, and Groves and flourie Vales,
Thrice happy Iles, but who dwelt happy there   570
He stayd not to enquire: above them all
The golden Sun in splendor likest Heaven

Allur'd his eye: Thither his course he bends
Through the calm Firmament; but up or downe
By center, or eccentric, hard to tell,
Or Longitude, where the great Luminarie
Aloof the vulgar Constellations thick,
That from his Lordly eye keep distance due,
Dispenses Light from farr; they as they move
Thir Starry dance in numbers that compute   580
Days, months, and years, towards his all-chearing Lamp
Turn swift their various motions, or are turnd
By his Magnetic beam, that gently warms
The Univers, and to each inward part
With gentle penetration, though unseen,
Shoots invisible vertue even to the deep:
So wondrously was set his Station bright.
There lands the Fiend, a spot like which perhaps
Astronomer in the Sun's lucent Orbe
Through his glaz'd Optic Tube yet never saw.   590
The place he found beyond expression bright,
Compar'd with aught on Earth, Metal or Stone;
Not all parts like, but all alike informd
With radiant light, as glowing Iron with fire;
If mettal, part seemd Gold, part Silver cleer;
If stone, Carbuncle most or Chrysolite,
Rubie or Topaz, to the Twelve that shon
In *Aarons* Brest-plate, and a stone besides
Imagind rather oft then elsewhere seen,
That stone, or like to that which here below   600
Philosophers in vain so long have sought,

In vain, though by thir powerful Art they binde
Volatil *Hermes*, and call up unbound
In various shapes old *Proteus* from the Sea,
Draind through a Limbec to his Native forme.
What wonder then if fields and regions here
Breathe forth *Elixir* pure, and Rivers run
Potable Gold, when with one vertuous touch
Th' Arch-chimic Sun so farr from us remote
Produces with Terrestrial Humor mixt   610
Here in the dark so many precious things
Of colour glorious and effect so rare?
Here matter new to gaze the Devil met
Undazl'd, farr and wide his eye commands,
For sight no obstacle found here, nor shade,
But all Sun-shine, as when his Beams at Noon
Culminate from th' *Æquator*, as they now
Shot upward still direct, whence no way round
Shadow from body opaque can fall, and the Aire,
No where so cleer, sharp'nd his visual ray   620
To objects distant farr, whereby he soon
Saw within kenn a glorious Angel stand,
The same whom *John* saw also in the Sun:
His back was turnd, but not his brightness hid;
Of beaming sunnie Raies, a golden tiar
Circl'd his Head, nor less his Locks behind
Illustrious on his Shoulders fledge with wings
Lay waving round; on som great charge imploy'd
Hee seemd, or fixt in cogitation deep.
Glad was the Spirit impure; as now in hope   630

To find who might direct his wandring flight
To Paradise the happie seat of Man,
His journies end and our beginning woe.
But first he casts to change his proper shape,
Which else might work him danger or delay:
And now a stripling Cherube he appeers,
Not of the prime, yet such as in his face
Youth smil'd Celestial, and to every Limb
Sutable grace diffus'd, so well he feignd;
Under a Coronet his flowing haire   640
In curles on either cheek plaid, wings he wore
Of many a colourd plume sprinkl'd with Gold,
His habit fit for speed succinct, and held
Before his decent steps a Silver wand.
He drew not nigh unheard, the Angel bright,
Ere he drew nigh, his radiant visage turnd,
Admonisht by his eare, and strait was known
Th' Arch-Angel *Uriel*, one of the seav'n
Who in Gods presence, neerest to his Throne
Stand ready at command, and are his Eyes   650
That run through all the Heav'ns, or down to th' Earth
Bear his swift errands over moist and dry,
O're Sea and Land: him *Satan* thus accostes.
   Uriel, for thou of those seav'n Spirits that stand
In sight of Gods high Throne, gloriously bright,
The first art wont his great authentic will
Interpreter through highest Heav'n to bring,
Where all his Sons thy Embassie attend;
And here art likeliest by supream decree

Like honour to obtain, and as his Eye   660
To visit oft his new Creation round;
Unspeakable desire to see, and know
All these his wondrous works, but chiefly Man,
His chief delight and favour, him for whom
All these his works so wondrous he ordaind,
Hath brought me from the Quires of Cherubim
Alone thus wandring. Brightest Seraph tell
In which of all these shining Orbes hath Man
His fixed seat, or fixed seat hath none,
But all these shining Orbes his choice to dwell;   670
That I may find him, and with secret gaze,
Or open admiration him behold
On whom the great Creator hath bestowd
Worlds, and on whom hath all these graces powrd;
That both in him and all things, as is meet,
The Universal Maker we may praise;
Who justly hath drivn out his Rebell Foes
To deepest Hell, and to repair that loss
Created this new happie Race of Men
To serve him better: wise are all his wayes.   680
    So spake the false dissembler unperceivd;
For neither Man nor Angel can discern
Hypocrisie, the only evil that walks
Invisible, except to God alone,
By his permissive will, through Heav'n and Earth:
And oft though wisdom wake, suspicion sleeps
At wisdoms Gate, and to simplicitie
Resigns her charge, while goodness thinks no ill

Where no ill seems: Which now for once beguil'd
Uriel, though Regent of the Sun, and held   690
The sharpest sighted Spirit of all in Heav'n;
Who to the fraudulent Impostor foule
In his uprightness answer thus returnd.
Faire Angel, thy desire which tends to know
The works of God, thereby to glorifie
The great Work-Maister, leads to no excess
That reaches blame, but rather merits praise
The more it seems excess, that led thee hither
From thy Empyreal Mansion thus alone,
To witness with thine eyes what some perhaps   700
Contented with report heare onely in heav'n:
for wonderful indeed are all his works,
Pleasant to know, and worthiest to be all
Had in remembrance alwayes with delight;
But what created mind can comprehend
Thir number, or the wisdom infinite
That brought them forth, but hid thir causes deep.
I saw when at his Word the formless Mass,
This worlds material mould, came to a heap:
Confusion heard his voice, and wilde uproar   710
Stood rul'd, stood vast infinitude confin'd;
Till at his sccond bidding darkness fled,
Light shon, and order from disorder sprung:
Swift to thir several Quarters hasted then
The cumbrous Elements, Earth, Flood, Aire, Fire,
And this Ethereal quintessence of Heav'n
Flew upward, spirited with various forms,

That rowld orbicular, and turnd to Starrs

Numberless, as thou seest, and how they move;

Each had his place appointed, each his course,   720

The rest in circuit walles this Universe.

Look downward on that Globe whose hither side

With light from hence, though but reflected, shines;

That place is Earth the seat of Man, that light

His day, which else as th' other Hemisphere

Night would invade, but there the neighbouring Moon

(So call that oppiste fair Starr) her aide

Timely interposes, and her monthly round

Still ending, still renewing through mid Heav'n,

With borrowd light her countenance triform   730

Hence fills and empties to enlighten the Earth,

And in her pale dominion checks the night.

That spot to which I point is *Paradise*,

Adams abode, those loftie shades his Bowre.

Thy way thou canst not miss, me mine requires.

 Thus said, he turnd, and *Satan* bowing low,

As to superior Spirits is wont in Heav'n,

Where honour due and reverence none neglects,

Took leave, and toward the coast of Earth beneath,

Down from th' Ecliptic, sped with hop'd success,   740

Throws his steep flight in many an Aerie wheele,

Nor staid, till on *Niphates* top he lights.

       The End of the Third Book.

PARADISE
LOST

BOOK IV.

O For that warning voice, which he who saw
Th' *Apocalyps*, heard cry in Heaven aloud,
Then when the Dragon, put to second rout,
Came furious down to be reveng'd on men,
Wo to the inhabitants on Earth! that now,
While time was, our first Parents had bin warnd
The coming of thir secret foe, and scap'd
Haply so scap'd his mortal snare; for now
Satan, now first inflam'd with rage, came down,
The Tempter ere th' Accuser of man-kind,   10
To wreck on innocent frail man his loss
Of that first Battel, and his flight to Hell:
Yet not rejoycing in his speed, though bold,
Far off and fearless, nor with cause to boast,
Begins his dire attempt, which nigh the birth
Now rowling, boiles in his tumultuous brest,
And like a devillish Engine back recoiles
Upon himself; horror and doubt distract
His troubl'd thoughts, and from the bottom stirr
The Hell within him, for within him Hell   20
He brings, and round about him, nor from Hell

One step no more then from himself can fly

By change of place: Now conscience wakes despair

That slumberd, wakes the bitter memorie

Of what he was, what is, and what must be

Worse; of worse deeds worse sufferings must ensue.

Sometimes towards *Eden* which now in his view

Lay pleasant, his grievd look he fixes sad,

Sometimes towards Heav'n and the full-blazing Sun,

Which now sat high in his Meridian Towre: 30

Then much revolving, thus in sighs began.

   O thou that with surpassing Glory crownd,

Look'st from thy sole Dominion like the God

Of this new World; at whose sight all the Starrs

Hide thir diminisht heads; to thee I call,

But with no friendly voice, and add thy name

O Sun, to tell thee how I hate thy beams

That bring to my remembrance from what state

I fell, how glorious once above thy Spheare;

Till Pride and worse Ambition threw me down   40

Warring in Heav'n against Heav'ns matchless King:

Ah wherefore! he deservd no such return

From me, whom he created what I was

In that bright eminence, and with his good

Upbraided none; nor was his service hard.

What could be less then to afford him praise,

The easiest recompence, and pay him thanks,

How due! yet all his good prov'd ill in me,

And wrought but malice; lifted up so high

I sdeind subjection, and thought one step higher   50

Would set me highest, and in a moment quit

The debt immense of endless gratitude,

So burthensome, still paying, still to ow;

Forgetful what from him I still receivd,

And understood not that a grateful mind

By owing owes not, but still pays, at once

Indebted and dischargd; what burden then?

O had his powerful Destiny ordaind

Me some inferiour Angel, I had stood

Then happie; no unbounded hope had rais'd   60

Ambition. Yet why not? som other Power

As great might have aspir'd, and me though mean

Drawn to his part; but other Powers as great

Fell not, but stand unshak'n, from within

Or from without, to all temptations arm'd.

Hadst thou the same free Will and Power to stand?

Thou hadst: whom hast thou then or what to accuse,

But Heav'ns free Love dealt equally to all?

Be then his Love accurst, since love or hate,

To me alike, it deals eternal woe.   70

Nay curs'd be thou; since against his thy will

Chose freely what it now so justly rues.

Me miserable! which way shall I flie

Infinite wrauth, and infinite despaire?

Which way I flie is Hell; my self am Hell;

And in the lowest deep a lower deep

Still threatning to devour me opens wide,

To which the Hell I suffer seems a Heav'n.

O then at last relent: is there no place

Left for Repentance, none for Pardon left?   80
None left but by submission; and that word
Disdain forbids me, and my dread of shame
Among the Spirits beneath, whom I seduc'd
With other promises and other vaunts
Then to submit, boasting I could subdue
Th' Omnipotent. Ay me, they little know
How dearly I abide that boast so vaine,
Under what torments inwardly I groane:
While they adore me on the Throne of Hell,
With Diadem and Scepter high advanc't   90
The lower still I fall, onely supream
In miserie; such joy Ambition findes.
But say I could repent and could obtaine
By Act of Grace my former state; how soon
Would highth recal high thoughts, how soon unsay
What feign'd submission swore: ease would recant
Vows made in pain, as violent and void.
For never can true reconcilement grow
Where wounds of deadly hate have peirc'd so deep:
Which would but lead me to a worse relapse,   100
And heavier fall: so should I purchase deare
Short intermission bought with double smart.
This knows my punisher; therefore as farr
From granting hee, as I from begging peace:
All hope excluded thus, behold in stead
Of us out-cast, exil'd, his new delight,
Mankind created, and for him this World.
So farwel Hope, and with Hope farwel Fear,

Farwel Remorse: all Good to me is lost;
Evil be thou my Good; by thee at least   110
Divided Empire with Heav'ns King I hold
By thee, and more then half perhaps will reigne;
As Man ere long, and this new World shall know.
    Thus while he spake, each passion dimm'd his face
Thrice chang'd with pale, ire, envie and despair,
Which marrd his borrow'd visage, and betraid
Him counterfet, if any eye beheld.
For heav'nly mindes from such distempers foule
Are ever cleer. Whreof hee soon aware,
Each perturbation smooth'd with outward calme,   120
Artificer of fraud; and was the first
That practisd falshood under saintly shew,
Deep malice to conceale, couch't with revenge:
Yet not anough had practisd to deceive
Uriel once warnd; whose eye pursu'd him down
The way he went, and on th' *Assyrian* mount
Saw him disfigur'd, more then could befall
Spirit of happie sort: his gestures fierce
He markd and mad demeanour, then alone,
As he suppos'd, all unobserv'd, unseen.   130
So on he fares, and to the border comes
Of *Eden*, where delicious Paradisc,
Now nearer, Crowns with her enclosure green,
As with a rural mound the champain head
Of a steep wilderness, whose hairie sides
With thicket overgorwn, grottesque and wilde,
Access deni'd; and over head up grew

Insuperable highth of loftiest shade,

Cedar, and Pine, and Firr, and branching Palm,

A Silvan Scene, and as the ranks ascend   140

Shade above shade, a woodie Theatre

Of stateliest view. Yet higher then thir tops

The verdurous wall of Paradise up sprung:

Which to our general Sire gave prospect large

Into his neather Empire neighbouring round.

And higher then that Wall a circling row

Of goodliest Trees loaden with fairest Fruit,

Blossoms and Fruits at once of golden hue

Appeerd, with gay enameld colours mixt:

On which the Sun more glad impress'd his beams   150

Then in fair Evening Cloud, or humid Bow,

When God hath showrd the earth; so lovely seemd

That Lantskip: And of pure now purer aire

Meets his approach, and to the heart inspires

Vernal delight and joy, able to drive

All sadness but despair: now gentle gales

Fanning thir odoriferous wings dispense

Native perfumes, and whisper whence they stole

Those balmie spoiles. As when to them who saile

Beyond the *Cape of Hope*, and now are past   160

Mozambic, off at Sea North-East windes blow

Sabean Odours from the spicie shoare

Of *Arabie* the blest, with such delay

Well pleas'd they slack thir course, and many a League

Cheard with the grateful smell old Ocean smiles.

So entertaind those odorous sweets the Fiend

Who came thir bane, though with them better pleas'd
Then *Asmodeus* with the fishie fume,
That drove him, though enamourd, from the Spouse
Of *Tobits* Son, and with a vengeance sent   170
From *Media* post to *Ægypt*, there fast bound.
    Now to th' ascent of that steep savage Hill
Satan had journied on, pensive and slow;
But further way found none, so thick entwin'd,
As one continu'd brake, the undergrowth
Of shrubs and tangling bushes had perplext
All path of Man or Beast that past that way:
One Gate there onely was, and that look'd East
On th' other side: which when th' arch-fellon saw
Due entrance he disdaind, and in contempt,   180
At one slight bound high overleap'd all bound
Of Hill or highest Wall, and sheer within
Lights on his feet. As when a prowling Wolfe,
Whom hunger drives to seek new haunt for prey,
Watching where Shepherds pen thir Flocks at eeve
In hurdl'd Cotes amid the field secure,
Leaps o're the fence with ease into the Fould:
Or as a Thief bent to unhoord the cash
Of some rich Burgher, whose substantial dores,
Cross-barrd and bolted fast, fear no assault,   190
In at the window climbes, or o're the tiles;
So clomb this first grand Thief into Gods Fould:
So since into his Church lewd Hirelings climbe.
Thence up he flew, and on the Tree of Life,
The middle Tree and highest there that grew,

Sat like a Cormorant; yet not true Life

Thereby regaind, but sat devising Death

To them who liv'd; nor on the vertue thought

Of that life-giving Plant, but only us'd

For prospect, what well us'd had bin the pledge   200

Of immortalitie. So little knows

Any, but God alone, to value right

The good before him, but perverts best things

To worst abuse, or to thir meanest use.

Beneath him with new wonder now he views

To all delight of human sense expos'd

In narrow room Natures whole wealth, yea more,

A Heaven on Earth: for blissful Paradise

Of God the Garden was, by him in the East

Of *Eden* planted; *Eden* stretchd her Line   210

From *Auran* Eastward to the Royal Towrs

Of great *Seleucia,* built by *Grecian* Kings,

Or where the Sons of *Eden* long before

Dwelt in *Telassar:* in this pleasant soile

His farr more pleasant Garden God ordaind;

Out of the fertil ground he caus'd to grow

All Trees of noblest kind for sight, smell, taste;

And all amid them stood the Tree of Life,

High eminent, blooming Ambrosial Fruit

Of vegetable Gold; and next to Life   220

Our Death the Tree of Knowledge grew fast by,

Knowledge of Good bought dear by knowing ill.

Southward through *Eden* went a River large,

Nor chang'd his course, but through the shaggie hill

Pass'd underneath ingulft, for God had thrown
That Mountain as his Garden mould high rais'd
Upon the rapid current, which through veins
Of porous Earth with kindly thirst up drawn,
Rose a fresh Fountain, and with many a rill
Waterd the Garden; thence united fell   230
Down the steep glade, and met the neather Flood,
Which from his darksom passage now appeers,
And now divided into four main Streams,
Runs divers, wandring many a famous Realme
And Country whreof here needs no account,
But rather to tell how, if Art could tell,
How from that Saphire Fount the crisped Brooks,
Rowling on Orient Pearl and sands of Gold,
With mazie error under pendant shades
Ran Nectar, visiting each plant, and fed   240
Flours worthy of Paradise which not nice Art
In Beds and curious Knots, but Nature boon
Powrd forth profuse on Hill and Dale and Plaine,
Both where the morning Sun first warmly smote
The open field, and where the unpierc't shade
Imbround the noontide Bowrs: Thus was this place,
A happy rural seat of various view;
Groves whose rich Trees wept odorous Gumms and Balme,
Others whose fruit burnisht with Golden Rinde
Hung amiable, *Hesperian* Fables true,   250
If true, here onely, and of delicious taste:
Betwixt them Lawns, or level Downs, and Flocks
Grasing the tender herb, were interpos'd,

Or palmie hilloc, or the flourie lap
Of som irriguous Valley spread her store,
Flours of all hue, and without Thorn the Rose:
Another side, umbrageous Grots and Caves
Of coole recess, o're which the mantling Vine
Layes forth her purple Grape, and gently creeps
Luxuriant; mean while murmuring waters fall   260
Down the slope hills, disperst, or in a Lake,
That to the fringed Bank with Myrtle crownd,
Her chrystall mirror holds, unite thir streams.
The Birds thir quire apply; aires, vernal aires,
Breathing the smell of field and grove, attune
The trembling leaves, while Universal *Pan*
Knit with the *Graces* and the *Hours* in dance
Led on th' Eternal Spring. Not that faire field
Of *Enna*, where *Proserpin* gathring flours
Her self a fairer Floure by gloomie *Dis*   270
Was gatherd, which cost *Ceres* all that pain
To seek her through the world; nor that sweet Grove
Of *Daphne* by *Orontes*, and th' inspir'd
Castalian Spring might with this Paradise
Of *Eden* strive; nor that *Nyseian* Ile
Girt with the River *Triton*, where old *Cham*,
Whom Gentiles *Ammon* call and *Libyan Jove*,
Hid *Amalthea* and her Florid Son
Young *Bacchus* from his Stepdame *Rhea's* eye;
Nor where *Abassin* Kings thir issue Guard,   280
Mount *Amara*, though this by som suppos'd
True Paradise under the *Ethiop* Line

By *Nilus* head, enclos'd with shining Rock,
A whole dayes journey high, but wide remote
From this *Assyrian* Garden, where the Fiend
Saw undelighted all delight, all kind
Of living Creatures new to sight and strange:
Two of far nobler shape erect and tall,
Godlike erect, with native Honour clad
In naked Majestie seemd Lords of all,   290
And worthie seemd, for in thir looks Divine
The image of thir glorious Maker shon,
Truth, Wisdome, Sanctitude severe and pure,
Severe, but in true filial freedom plac't;
Whence true autoritie in men; though both
Not equal, as thir sex not equal seemd;
For contemplation hee and valour formd,
For softness shee and sweet attractive Grace,
Hee for God only, shee for God in him:
His fair large Front and Eye sublime declar'd   300
Absolute rule; and Hyacinthin Locks
Round from his parted forelock manly hung
Clustring, but not beneath his shoulders broad:
Shee as a vail down to the slender waste
Her unadorned golden tresses wore
Dissheveld, but in wanton ringlets wav'd
As the Vine curles her tendrils, which impli'd
Subjection, but requir'd with gentle sway,
And by her yeilded, by him best receivd,
Yeilded with coy submission, modest pride,   310
And sweet reluctant amorous delay.

Nor those mysterious parts were then conceald,

Then was not guiltie shame, dishonest shame

Of natures works, honor dishonorable,

Sin-bred, how have ye troubl'd all mankind

With shews instead, meer shews of seeming pure,

And banisht from mans life his happiest life,

Simplicitie and spotless innocence.

So passd they naked on, nor shund the sight

Of God or Angel, for they thought no ill: 320

So hand in hand they passd, the lovliest pair

That ever since in loves imbraces met,

Adam the goodliest man of men since borne

His Sons, the fairest of her Daughters *Eve*.

Under a tuft of shade that on a green

Stood whispering soft, by a fresh Fountain side

They sat them down, and after no more toil

Of thir sweet Gardning labour then suffic'd

To recommend coole *Zephyr*, and made ease

More easie, wholsom thirst and appetite   330

More grateful, to thir Supper Fruits they fell,

Nectarine Fruits which the compliant boughes

Yeilded them, side-long as they sat recline

On the soft downie Bank damaskt with flours:

The savourie pulp they chew, and in the rinde

Still as they thirsted scoop the brimming stream;

Nor gentle purpose, nor endearing smiles

Wanted, nor youthful dalliance as beseems

Fair couple, linkt in happie nuptial League,

Alone as they. About them frisking playd   340

All Beasts of th' Earth, since wilde, and of all chase
In Wood or Wilderness, Forrest or Den;
Sporting the Lion rampd, and in his paw
Dandl'd the Kid; Bears, Tygers, Ounces, Pards
Gambold before them, th' unwieldy Elephant
To make them mirth us'd all his might, & wreathd
His Lithe Proboscis; close the Serpent sly
Insinuating, wove with Gordian twine
His breaded train, and of his fatal guile
Gave proof unheeded; others on the grass   350
Coucht, and now fild with pasture gazing sat,
Or Bedward ruminating: for the Sun
Declin'd was hasting now with prone carreer
To th' Ocean Iles, and in th' ascending Scale
Of Heav'n the Starrs that usher Evening rose:
When *Satan* still in gaze, as first he stood,
Scarce thus at length faild speech recoverd sad.
    O Hell! what doe mine eyes with grief behold,
Into our room of bliss thus high advanc't
Creatures of other mould, earth-born perhaps,   360
Not Spirits, yet to heav'nly Spirits bright
Little inferior; whom my thoughts pursue
With wonder, and could love, so lively shines
In them Divine resemblance, and such grace
The hand that formd them on thir shape hath pourd.
Ah gentle pair, yee little think how nigh
Your change approaches, when all these delights
Will vanish and deliver ye to woe,
More woe, the more your taste is now of joy;

Happie, but for so happie ill secur'd   370
Long to continue, and this high seat your Heav'n
Ill fenc't for Heav'n to keep out such a foe
As now is enterd; yet no purpos'd foe
To you whom I could pittie thus forlorne
Though I unpittied: League with you I seek,
And mutual amitie so streight, so close,
That I with you must dwell, or you with me
Henceforth; my dwelling haply may not please
Like this fair Paradise, your sense, yet such
Accept your Makers work; he gave it me,   380
Which I as freely give; Hell shall unfould,
To entertain you two, her widest Gates,
And send forth all her Kings; there will be room,
Not like these narrow limits, to receive
Your numerous ofspring; if no better place,
Thank him who puts me loath to this revenge
On you who wrong me not for him who wrongd.
And should I at your harmless innocence
Melt, as I doe, yet public reason just,
Honour and Empire with revenge enlarg'd,   390
By conquering this new World, compels me now
To do what else though damnd I should abhorre.
   So spake the Fiend, and with necessitie,
The Tyrants plea, excus'd his devilish deeds.
Then from his loftie stand on that high Tree
Down he alights among the sportful Herd
Of those fourfooted kindes, himself now one,
Now other, as thir shape servd best his end

Neerer to view his prey, and unespi'd

To mark what of thir state he more might learn   400

By word or action markt: about them round

A Lion now he stalkes with fierie glare,

Then as a Tiger, who by chance hath spi'd

In some Purlieu two gentle Fawnes at play,

Strait couches close, then rising changes oft

His couchant watch, as one who chose his ground

Whence rushing he might surest seise them both

Grip't in each paw: when *Adam* first of men

To first of women *Eve* thus moving speech,

Turnd him all eare to heare new utterance flow.   410

    Sole partner and sole part of all these joyes,

Dearer thy self then all; needs must the Power

That made us, and for us this ample World

Be infinitly good, and of his good

As liberal and free as infinite,

That rais'd us from the dust and plac't us here

In all this happiness, who at his hand

Have nothing merited, nor can performe

Aught whereof hee hath need, hee who requires

From us no other service then to keep   420

This one, this easie charge, of all the Trees

In Paradise that beare delicious fruit

So various, not to taste that onely Tree

Of knowledge, planted by the Tree of Life,

So neer grows Death to Life, what ere Death is,

Som dreadful thing no doubt; for well thou knowst

God hath pronounc't it death to taste that Tree,

The only sign of our obedience left
Among so many signes of power and rule
Conferrd upon us, and Dominion giv'n   430
Over all other Creatures that possesse
Earth, Aire, and Sea. Then let us not think hard
One easie prohibition, who enjoy
Free leave so large to all things else, and choice
Unlimited of manifold delights:
But let us ever praise him, and extoll
His bountie, following our delightful task
To prune these growing Plasnts, & tend these Flours,
Which were it toilsom, yet with thee were sweet.
 To whom thus *Eve* repli'd. O thou for whom   440
And from whom I was formd flesh of thy flesh,
And without whom am to no end, my Guide
And Head, what thou hast said is just and right.
For wee to him indeed all praises owe,
And daily thanks, I chiefly who enjoy
So farr the happier Lot, enjoying thee
Preeminent by so much odds, while thou
Like consort to thy self canst no where find.
That day I oft remember, when from sleep
I first awak't, and found my self repos'd   450
Under a shade on flours, much wondring where
And what I was, whence thither brought, and how.
Not distant far from thence a murmuring sound
Of waters issu'd from a Cave and spread
Into a liquid Plain, then stood unmov'd
Pure as th' expanse of Heav'n; I thither went

With unexperienc't thought, and laid me downe
On the green bank, to look into the cleer
Smooth Lake, that to me seemd another Skie.
As I bent down to look, just opposite,   460
A Shape within the watry gleam appeerd
Bending to look on me, I started back,
It started back, but pleasd I soon returnd,
Pleas'd it returnd as soon with answering looks
Of sympathie and love, there I had fixt
Mine eyes till now, and pin'd with vain desire,
Had not a voice thus warnd me, What thou seest,
What there thou seest fair Creature is thy self,
With thee it came and goes: but follow me,
And I will bring thee where no shadow staies   470
Thy coming, and thy soft imbraces, hee
Whose image thou art, him thou shall enjoy
Inseparablie thine, to him shalt beare
Multitudes like thy self, and thence be call'd
Mother of human Race: what could I doe,
But follow strait, invisibly thus led?
Till I espi'd thee, fair indeed and tall,
Under a Platan, yet methought less faire,
Less winning soft, less amiablie milde,
Then that smooth watry image; back I turnd,   480
Thou following cryd'st aloud, Return fair *Eve*,
Whom fli'st thou? whom thou fli'st, of him thou art,
His flesh, his bone; to give thee being I lent
Out of my side to thee, neerest my heart
Substantial Life, to have thee by my side

Henceforth an individual solace dear;

Part of my Soul I seek thee, and thee claim

My other half: with that thy gentle hand

Seisd mine, I yeilded, and from that time see

How beauty is excelld by manly grace   490

And wisdom, which alone is truly fair.

   So spake our general Mother, and with eyes

Of conjugal attraction unreprov'd,

And meek surrender, half imbracing leand

On our first Father, half her swelling Breast

Naked met his under the flowing Gold

Of her loose tresses hid: he in delight

Both of her Beauty and submissive Charms

Smil'd with superior Love, as *Jupiter*

On *Juno* smiles, when he impregns the Clouds   500

That shed *May* Flowers; and press'd her Matron lip

With kisses pure: aside the Devil turnd

For envie, yet with jealous leer maligne

Ey'd them askance, and to himself thus plaind.

 Sight hateful, sight tormenting! thus these two

Imparadis't in one anothers arms

The happier *Eden*, shall enjoy thir fill

Of bliss on bliss, while I to Hell am thrust,

Where neither joy nor love, but fierce desire,

Among our other torments not the least,   510

Still unfulfill'd with pain of longing pines;

Yet let me not forget what I have gain'd

From thir own mouths; all is not theirs it seems:

One fatal Tree there stands of Knowledge call'd,

Forbidden them to taste: Knowledge forbidd'n?
Suspicious, reasonless. Why should thir Lord
Envie them that? can it be sin to know,
Can it be death? and do they onely stand
By Ignorance, is that thir happie state,
The proof of thir obedience and thir faith?   520
O fair foundation laid whereon to build
Thir ruine! Hence I will excite thir minds
With more desire to know, and to reject
Envious commands, invented with designe
To keep them low whom knowledge might exalt
Equal with Gods; aspiring to be such,
They taste and die: what likelier can ensue?
But first with narrow search I must walk round
This Garden, and no corner leave unspi'd;
A chance but chance may lead where I may meet   530
Some wandring Spirit of Heav'n, by Fountain side,
Or in thick shade retir'd, from him to draw
What further would be learnt. Live while ye may,
Yet happie pair; enjoy, till I return,
Short pleasures, for long woes are to succeed.
      So saying, his proud step he scornful turn'd,
but with sly circumspection, and began
Through wood, through wastc, o'rc hil, o're dale his roam.
Mean while in utmost Longitude, where Heav'n
With Earth and Ocean meets, the setting Sun   540
Slowly descended, and with right aspect
Against the eastern Gate of Paradise
Leveld his eevning Rayes: it was a Rock

Of Alablaster, pil'd up to the Clouds,
Conspicuous farr, winding with one ascent
Accessible from Earth, one entrance high;
The rest was craggie cliff, that overhung
Still as it rose, impossible to climbe.
Betwixt these rockie Pillars *Gabriel* sat
Chief of th' Angelic Guards, awaiting night;   550
About him exercis'd Heroic Games
Th' unarmed Youth of Heav'n, but nigh at hand
Celestial Armourie, Shields, Helmes, and Speares
Hung high with Diamond flaming, and with Gold.
Thither came *Uriel*, gliding through the Eeven
On a Sun beam, swift as a shooting Starr
In *Autumn* thwarts the night, when vapors fir'd
Impress the Air, and shews the Mariner
From what point of his Compass to beware
Impetuous winds: he thus began in haste.   560
    Gabriel, to thee thy cours by Lot hath giv'n
Charge and strict watch that to this happie place
No evil thing approach or enter in;
This day at highth of Noon came to my Spheare
A Spirit, zealous, as he seem'd, to know
More of th' Almighties works, and chiefly Man
Gods latest Image: I decrib'd his way
Bent all on speed, and markt his Aerie Gate;
But in the Mount that lies from *Eden* North,
Where he first lighted, soon discernd his looks   570
Alien from Heav'n, with passions foul obscur'd:
Mine eye pursu'd him still, but under shade

Lost sight of him; one of the banisht crew
I fear, hath ventur'd from the deep, to raise
New troubles; him thy care must be to find.
　　To whom the winged Warriour thus returnd:
Uriel, no wonder if thy perfet sight,
Amid the Suns bright circle where thou sitst,
See farr and wide: in at this Gate none pass
The vigilance here plac't, but such as come　　　　　　　　580
Well known from Heav'n; and since Meridian hour
No Creature thence: if Spirit of other sort,
So minded, have oreleapt these earthie bounds
On purpose, hard thou knowst it to exclude
Spiritual substance with corporeal barr.
But if within the circuit of these walks
In whatsoever shape he lurk, of whom
Though telst, by morrow dawning I shall know.
　　So promi's'd hee, and *Uriel* to his charge
Returnd on the at bright beam, whose point now raisd　　590
Bore him slope downward to the Sun now fall'n
Beneath th' *Azores*; whither the prime Orb,
Incredible how swift, had thither rowl'd
Diurnal, or this less volubil Earth
By shorter flight to th' East, had left him there
Arraying with reflected Purple and Gold
The Clouds that on his Western Throne attend:
Now came still Eevning on, and Twilight gray
Had in her sober Liverie all things clad;
Silence accompanied, for Beast and Bird,　　　　　　　　600
They to thir grassie Couch, these to thir Nests

Were slunk, all but the wakeful Nightingale;
She all night long her amorous descant sung;
Silence was pleas'd: now glow'd the Firmament
With living Saphirs: *Hesperus* that led
The starrie Host, rode brightest, till the Moon
Rising in clouded Majestie, at length
Apparent Queen unvaild her peerless light,
And o're the dark her Silver Mantle threw.
    When *Adam* thus to *Eve:* Fair Consort, th' hour   610
Of night, and all things now retir'd to rest
Mind us of like repose, since God hath set
Labour and rest, as day and night to men
Successive, and the timely dew of sleep
Now falling with soft slumbrous weight inclines
Our eye-lids; other Creatures all day long
Rove idle unimploid, and less need rest;
Man hath his daily work of body or mind
Appointed, which declares his Dignitie,
And the regard of Heav'n on all his waies;   620
While other Animals unactive range,
And of thir doings God takes no account.
To morrow ere fresh Morning streak the East
With first approach of light, we must be ris'n,
And at our pleasant labour, to reform
Yon flourie Arbors, yonder Allies green,
Our walk at noon, with branches overgrown,
That mock our scant manuring, and require
More hands then ours to lop thir wanton growth:
Those Blossoms also, and those dropping Gumms,   630

That lie bestrowne unsightly and unsmooth,
Ask riddace, if we mean to tread with ease;
Mean while, as Nature wills, Night bids us rest.
　　To whom thus *Eve* with perfet beauty adornd.
My Author and Disposer, what thou bidst
Unargu'd I obey; so God ordains,
God is thy Law, thou mine: to know no more
Is womans happiest knowledge and her praise.
With thee conversing I forget all time,
All seaons and thir change, all please alike.   640
Sweet is the breath of morn, her rising sweet,
With charm of earliest Birds; pleasant the Sun
When first on this delightful Land he spreads
His orient Beams, on herb, tree, fruit, and flour,
Glistring with dew; fragrant the fertil earth
After soft showers; and sweet the coming on
Of grateful Eevning milde, then silent Night
With this her solemn Bird and this fair Moon,
And these the Gemms of Heav'n, her starrie train:
But neither breath of Morn when she ascends   650
With charm of earliest Birds, nor rising Sun
On this delightful land, nor herb, fruit, floure,
Glistring with dew, nor fragrance after showers,
Nor grateful Evening mild, nor silent Night
With this her solemn Bird, nor walk by Moon,
Or glittering Starr-light without thee is sweet.
But wherfore all night long shine these, for whom
This glorious sight, when sleep hath shut all eyes?
　　To whom our general Ancestor repli'd.

Daughter of God and Man, accomplisht *Eve*,   660

Those have thir course to finish, round the Earth,

By morrow Eevning, and from Land to Land

In order, though to Nations yet unborn,

Ministring light prepar'd, they set and rise;

Least total darkness should by Night regaine

Her old possession, and extinguish life

In Nature and all things, which these soft fires

Not only enlighten, but with kindly heate

Of various influence foment and warme,

Temper or nourish, or in part shed down   670

Thir stellar vertue on all kinds that grow

On Earth, made hereby apter to receive

Perfection from the Suns more potent Ray.

These then, though unbeheld in deep of night,

Shine not in vain, nor think, though men were none,

That heav'n would want spectators, God want praise;

Millions of spiritual Creatures walk the Earth

Unseen, both when we wake, and when we sleep:

All thse with ceasless praise his works behold

Both day and night: how often from the steep   680

Of echoing Hill or Thicket have we heard

Celestial voices to the midnight air,

Sole, or responsive each to others note

Singing thir great Creator: oft in bands

While they keep watch, or nightly rounding walk

With Heav'nly touch of instrumental sounds

In full harmonic number joind, thir songs

Divide the night, and lift our thoughts to Heaven.

Thus talkiing hand in hand alone they pass'd

On to thir blissful Bower; it was a place   690

Chos'n by the sovran Planter, when he fram'd

All things to mans delightful use; the roofe

Of thickest covert was inwoven shade

Laurel and Mirtle, and what higher grew

Of firm and fragrant leaf; on either side

Acanthus, and each odorous bushie shrub

Fenc'd up the verdant wall; each beauteous flour,

Iris all hues, Roses, and Gessamin

Rear'd high thir flourisht heads between, and wrought

Mosaic; underfoot the Violet,   700

Crocus, and Hyacinth with rich inlay

Broiderd the ground, more colour'd then with stone

Of costliest Emblem: other Creature here

Beast, Bird, Insect, or Worm durst enter none;

Such was thir awe of man. In shadier Bower

More sacred and sequesterd, though but feignd,

Pan or *Silvanus* never slept, nor Nymph,

Nor *Faunus* haunted. Here in close recess

With Flowers, Garlands, and sweet-smelling Herbs

Espoused *Eve* deckt first her Nuptial Bed,   710

And heav'nly Quires the Hymenæan sung,

What day the genial Angel to our Sire

Brought her in naked beauty more adorn'd,

More lovely then *Pandora,* whom the Gods

Endowd with all thir gifts, and O too like

In sad event, when to the unwiser Son

Of *Japhet* brought by *Hermes,* she ensnar'd

Mankind with her faire looks, to be aveng'd
On him who had stole *Joves* authentic fire.

    Thus at thir shadie Lodge arriv'd, both stood,   720
Both turnd, and under op'n Skie ador'd
The God that made both Skie, Air, Earth & Heav'n
Which they beheld, the Moons resplendent Globe
And starrie Pole: Thou also mad'st the Night,
Maker Omnipotent, and thou the Day,
Which we in our appointed work imployd
Have finisht happie in our mutual help
And mutual love, the Crown of all our bliss
Ordain'd by thee, and this delicious place
For us too large, where thy abundance wants   730
Partakers, and uncropt falls to the ground.
But thou hast promis'd from us two a Race
To fill the Earth, who shall with us extoll
Thy goodness infinite, both when we wake,
And when we seek, as now, thy gift of sleep.

    This said unanimous, and other Rites
Observing none, but adoration pure
Which God likes best, into thir inmost bower
Handed they went; and eas'd the putting off
These troublesom disguises which wee wear,   740
Strait side by side were laid, nor turnd I weene
Adam from his fair Spouse, nor *Eve* the Rites
Mysterious of connubial Love refus'd:
Whatever Hypocrites austerely talk
Of puritie and place and innocence,
Defaming as impure what God declares

Pure, and commands to som, leaves free to all.
Our Makes bids increase, who bids abstain
But our Destroyer, foe to God and Man?
Haile wedded Love, mysterious Law, true sourse   750
Of human ofspring, sole proprietie,
In Paradise of all things common else.
By thee adulterous lust was driv'n from men
Among the betial herds to raunge, by thee
Founded in Reason, Loyal, Just, and Pure,
Relations dear, and all the Charities
Of Father, Son, and Brother first were known.
Farr be it, that I should write thee sin or blame,
Or think thee unbefitting holiest place,
Perpetual Fountain of Domestic sweets,   760
Whose Bed is undefil'd and chast pronounc't,
Present, or past, as Saints and Patriarchs us'd.
Here Love his golden shafts imploies, here lights
His constant Lamp, and waves his purple wings,
Reigns herc and revels; not in the bought smile
Of Harlots, loveless, joyless, unindeard,
Casual fruition, nor in Court Amurs
Mixt Dance, or wanton Mask, or Midnight Bal,
Or Serenate, which the starv'd Lover sings
To his proud fair, best quitted with disdain.   770
These lulld by Nightingales imbraceing slept,
And on thir naked limbs the flourie roof
Showrd Roses, which the Morn repair'd. Sleep on,
Blest pair; and O yet happiest if ye seek
No happier state, and know to know no more.

Now had night measur'd with her shaddowie Cone
Half way up Hill this vast Sublunar Vault,
And from thir Ivorie Port the Cherubim
Forth issuing at th'accustomd hour stood armd
To thir night watches in warlike Parade,   780
When *Gabriel* to his next in power thus spake.
   Uzziel, half these draw off, and coast the South
With strictest watch; these other wheel the North,
Our circuit meets full West. As flame they part
Half wheeling to the Shield, half to the Spear.
From these, two strong and suttle Spirits he calld
That neer him stood, and gave them thus in charge.
   Ithuriel and *Zephon*, with wingd speed
Search through this Garden, leav unsearcht no nook,
But chiefly where those two fair Creatures Lodge,   790
Now laid perhaps asleep secure of harme.
This Eevning from the Sun's decline arriv'd
Who tells of som infernal Spirit seen
Hitherward bent (who could have thought?) escap'd
The barrs of Hell, on errand bad no doubt:
Such where ye find, seise fast, and hither bring.
 So saying, on he led his radiant Files,
Daz'ling the Moon; these to the Bower direct
In search of whom they sought: him there they found
Squat like a Toad, close at the eare of *Eve*;   800
Assaying by his Devilish art to reach
The Organs of her Fancie, and with them forge
Illusions as he list, Phantasms and Dreams,
Or if, inspiring venom, he might taint

Th' animal Spirits that from pure blood arise
Like gentle breaths from Rivers pure, thence raise
At least distemperd, discontented thoughts,
Vain hopes, vain aimes, inordinate desires
Blown up with high conceits ingendring pride.
Him thus intent *Ithuriel* with his Spear   810
Touch'd lightly; for no falshood can endure
Touch of Celestial temper, but returns
Of force to its own likeness: up he starts
Discoverd and surpriz'd. As when a spark
Lights on a heap of nitrous Powder, laid
Fit for the Tun som Magazin to store
Against a rumord Warr, the Smuttie graine
With sudden blaze diffus'd, inflames the Aire:
So started up in his own shape the Fiend.
Back stept those two fair Angels half amaz'd   820
So sudden to behold the grieslie King;
Yet thus, unmovd with fear, accost him soon.
    Which of those rebell Spirits adjudg'd to Hell
Com'st thou, escap'd thy prison, and transform'd,
Why satst thou like an enemie in waite
Here watching at the head of these that sleep?
    Know ye not then said *Satan*, filld with scorn,
Know ye not me? ye knew mc once no mate
For you, there sitting where ye durst not soare;
Not to know mee argues your selves unknown,   830
The lowest of your throng; or if ye know,
Why ask ye, and superfluous begin
Your message, like to end as much in vain?

To whom thus *Zephon*, answering scorn with scorn.

Think not, revolted Spirit, thy shape the same,

Or undiminisht brightness, to be known

As when thou stoodst in Heav'n upright and pure;

That Glorie then, when thou no more wast good,

Departed from thee, and thou resembl'st now

Thy sin and place of doom obscure and foule.   840

But come, for thou, be sure, shalt give account

To him who sent us, whose charge is to keep

This place inviolable, and these from harm.

   So spake the Cherube, and his grave rebuke

Severe in youthful beautie, added grace

Invincible: abasht the Devil stood,

And felt how awful goodness is, and saw

Vertue in her shape how lovly, saw, and pin'd

His loss; but chiefly to find here observd

His lustre visibly impar'd; yet seemd   850

Undaunted. If I must contend, said he,

Best with the best, the Sender not the sent,

Or all at once; more glorie will be wonn,

Or less be lost. Thy fear, said *Zephon* bold,

Will save us trial what the least can doe

Single against thee wicked, and thence weak.

   The Fiend repli'd not, overcome with rage;

But like a proud Steed reind, went hautie on,

Chaumping his iron curb: to strive or flie

He held it vain; awe from above had quelld   860

His heart, not else dismai'd. Now drew they nigh

The western point, where those half-rounding guards

Just met, & closing stood in squadron joind
Awaiting next command. To whom thir Chief
Gabriel from the Front thus calld aloud.

O friends, I hear the tread of nimble feet
Hasting this way, and now by glimps discerne
Ithuriel and *Zephon* through the shade,
And with them comes a third of Regal port,
But faded splendor wan; who by his gate   870
And fierce demeanour seems the Prince of Hell,
Not likely to part hence without contest;
Stand firm, for in his look defiance lours.

He scarce had ended, when those two approachd
And brief related whom they brought, wher found,
How busied, in what form and posture coucht.

To whom with stern regard thus *Gabriel* spake.
Why hast thou, *Satan*, broke the bounds prescrib'd
To thy transgressions, and disturbed the charge
Of others, who approve not to transgress   880
By thy example, but have power and right
To question thy bold entrance on this place;
Imploi'd it seems to violate sleep, and those
Whose dwelling God hath planted here in bliss?

To whom thus *Satan* with contemptuous brow.
Gabriel, thou hadst in Heav'n th' esteem of wise,
And such I held thee; but this question askt
Puts me in doubt. Lives ther who loves his pain?
Who would not, finding way, break loose from Hell,
Though thither doomd? Thou wouldst thy self, no doubt,   890
And boldly venture to whatever place

Farthest from pain, where thou mightst hope to change

Torment with ease, & soonest recompence

Dole with delight, which in this place I sought;

To thee no reason; who knowst only good,

But evil hast not tri'd: and wilt object

His will who bound us? let him surer barr

His Iron Gates, if he intends our stay

In that dark durance: thus much what was askt.

The rest is true, they found me where they say;   900

But that implies not violence or harme.

    Thus hee in scorn. The warlike Angel mov'd,

Disdainfully half smiling thus repli'd.

O loss of one in Heav'n to judge of wise,

Since *Satan* fell, whom follie overthrew,

And now returns him from his prison scap't,

Gravely in doubt whether to hold them wise

Or not, who ask what boldness brought him hither

Unlicenc't from his bounds in Hell prescrib'd;

So wise he judges it to fly from pain   910

However, and to scape his punishment.

So judge thou still, presumptuous, till the wrauth,

Which thou incurr'st by flying, meet thy flight

Seavenfold, and scourge that wisdom back to Hell,

Which taught thee yet no better, that no pain

Can equal anger infinite provok't.

But wherefore thou alone? wherefore with thee

Came not all Hell broke loose? is pain to them

Less pain, less to be fled, or thou then they

Less hardie to endure? courageous Chief,   920

The first in flight from pain, had'st thou alleg'd
To thy deserted host this cause of flight,
Thou surely hadst not come sole fugitive.
　　To which the Fiend thus answerd frowning stern.
Not that I less endure, or shrink from pain,
Insulting Angel, well thou knowst I stood
Thy fiercest, when in Battel to thy aide
The blasting volied Thunder made all speed
And seconded thy else not dreaded Spear.
But still thy words at random, as before,   930
Argue thy inexperience what behooves
From hard assaies and ill successes past
A faithful Leader, not to hazard all
Through wayes of danger by himself untri'd.
I therefore, I alone first undertook
To wing the desolate Abyss, and spie
This new created World, whereof in Hell
Fame is not silent, here in hope to find
Better abode, and my afflicted Powers
To settle here on Earth, or in mid Aire;   940
Though for possession put to try once more
What thou and thy gay Legions dare against;
Whose easier business were to serve thir Lord
High up in Heav'n, with songs to hymne his Throne,
And practis'd distances to cringe, not fight,
　　To whom the warriour Angel soon repli'd.
To say and strait unsay, pretending first
Wise to flie pain, professing next the Spie,
Argues no Leader, but a lyar trac't,

Satan, and couldst thou faithful add? O name,   950
O sacred name of faithfulness profan'd!
Faithful to whom? to thy rebellious crew?
Armie of Fiends, fit body to fit head;
Was this your discipline and faith ingag'd,
Your military obedience, to dissolve
Allegeance to th' acknowledg'd Power supream?
And thou sly hypocrite, who now wouldst seem
Patron of liberty, who more then thou
Once fawn'd, and cring'd, and servilly ador'd
Heav'ns awful Monarch? wherefore but in hope   960
To dispossess him, and thy self to reigne?
But mark what I arreede thee now, avant;
Flie thither whence thou fledst: if from this houre
Within these hallowd limits thou appeer,
Back to th' infernal pit I drag thee chaind,
And Seale thee so, as henceforth not to scorne
The facil gates of hell to slightly barrd.
     So threatn'd hee, but *Satan* to no threats
Gave heed, but waxing more in rage repli'd.
     Then when I am thy captive talk of chaines,   970
Proud limitarie Cherube, but ere then
Farr heavier load thy self expect to feel
From my prevailing arme, though Heavens King
Ride on thy wings, and thou with thy Compeers,
Us'd to the yoak, draw'st his triumphant wheels
In progress through the rode of Heav'n Star-pav'd.
 While thus he spake, th' Angelic Squadron bright
Turnd fierie red, sharpning in mooned hornes

Thir Phalanx, and began to hemm him round
With ported Spears, as thick as when a field   980
Of *Ceres* ripe for harvest waving bends
Her bearded Grove of ears, which way the wind
Swayes them; the careful Plowman doubting stands
Least on the threshing floore his hopeful sheaves
Prove chaff. On th' other side *Satan* allarm'd
Collecting all his might dilated stood,
Like *Teneriff* or *Atlas* unremov'd:
His stature reacht the Skie, and on his Crest
Sat horror Plum'd; nor wanted in his graspe
What seemd both Spear and Shield: now dreadful deeds   990
Might have ensu'd, nor onely Paradise
In this commotion, but the Starrie Cope
Of Heav'n perhaps, or all the Elements
At least had gon to rack, disturbd and torne
With violence of this conflict, had not soon
Th' Eternal to prevent such horrid fray
Hung forth in Heav'n his golden Scales, yet seen
Betwixt *Astrea* and the *Scorpion* signe,
Wherein all things created first he weighd,
The pendulous round Earth with ballanc't Aire   1000
In counterpoise, now ponders all events,
Battels and Realms: in these he put two weights
The sequel each of parting and of fight;
The latter quick up flew, and kickt the beam;
Which *Gabriel* spying, thus bespake the Fiend.
    Satan, I know thy strength, and thou knowst mine,
Neither our own but giv'n; what follie then

To boast what Arms can doe, since thine no more

Then Heav'n permits, nor mine, though doubld now

To trample thee as mire: for proof look up,   1010

And read thy Lot in yon celestial Sign

Where thou art weigh'd, & shown how light, how weak,

If thou resist. The Fiend lookt up and knew

His mounted scale aloft: nor more; but fled

Murmuring, and with him fled the shades of night.

The End of the Fourth Book.

PARADISE
LOST

BOOK V.

NOw Morn her rosie steps in th' Eastern Clime
Advancing, sow'd the Earth with Orient Pearle,
When *Adam* wak't, so customd, for his sleep
Was Aerie light, from pure digestion bred,
And temperat vapors bland, which th' only sound
Of leaves and fuming rills, *Aurora*'s fan,
Lightly dispers'd, and the shrill Matin Song
Of Birds on every bough; so much the more
His wonder was to find unwak'nd *Eve*
With Tresses discompos'd, and glowing Cheek,   10
As through unquiet rest: he on his side
Leaning half-rais'd, with looks of cordial Love
Hung over her enamour'd, and beheld
Beautie, which whether waking or asleep,
Shot forth peculiar Graces; then with voice
Milde, as when *Zephyrus* on *Flora* breathes,
Her hand soft touching, whisperd thus. Awake
My fairest, my espous'd, my latest found,
Heav'ns last best gift, my ever new delight,
Awake, the morning shines, and the fresh field   20
Calls us, we lose the prime, to mark how spring

Our tended Plants, how blows the Citron Grove,
What drops the Myrrhe, & what the balmie Reed,
How Nature paints her colours, how the Bee
Sits on the Bloom extracting liquid sweet.
     Such whispering wak'd her, but with startl'd eye
On *Adam*, whom imbracing, thus she spake.
     O Sole in whom my thoughts find all repose,
My Glorie, my Perfection, glad I see
Thy face, and Morn return'd, for I this Night,   30
Such night till this I never pass'd, have dream'd,
If dream'd, not as I oft am wont, of thee,
Works of day pass't, or morrows next designe,
But of offence and trouble, which my mind
Knew never till this irksom night; methought
Close at mine ear one call'd me forth to walk
With gentle voice, I thought it thine; it said,
Why sleepst thou *Eve?* now is the pleasant time,
The cool, the silent, save where silence yields
To the night-warbling Bird, that now awake   40
Tunes sweetest his love-labor'd song; now reignes
Full Orb'd the Moon, and with more pleasing light
Shadowie sets off the face of things; in vain,
If none regard; Heav'n wakes with all his eyes,
Whom to behold but thee, Natures desire,
In whose sight all things joy, with ravishment
Attracted by thy beauty still to gaze.
I rose as at thy call, but found thee not;
To find thee I directed then my walk;
And on, methought, alone I pass'd through ways   50

That brought me on a sudden to the Tree
Of interdicted Knowledge: fair it seem'd,
Much fairer to my Fancie then by day:
And as I wondring lookt, beside it stood
One shap'd & wing'd like one of those from Heav'n
By us oft seen; his dewie locks distill'd
Ambrosia; on that Tree he also gaz'd;
And O fair Plant, said he, with fruit surcharg'd,
Deigns none to ease thy load and taste thy sweet,
Nor God, nor Man; is Knowledge so despis'd?   60
Or envie, or what reserve forbids to taste?
Forbid who will, none shall from me withhold
Longer thy offerd good, why else set here?
This said he paus'd not, but with ventrous Arme
He pluckt, he tasted; mee damp horror chil'd
At such bold words voucht with a deed so bold:
but he thus overjoy'd, O Fruit Divine,
Sweet of thy self, but much more sweet thus cropt,
Forbidd'n here, it seems, as oncly fit
For Gods, yet able to make Gods of Men: 70
And why not Gods of Men, since good, the more
Communicated, more abundant growes,
The Author not impair'd, but honourd more?
Here, happic Creature, fair Angelic *Eve*,
Partake thou also; happie though thou art,
Happier thou mayst be, worthier canst not be:
Taste this, and be henceforth among the Gods
Thy self a Goddess, not to Earth confind,
But somtimes in the Air, as wee, somtimes

Ascend to Heav'n, by merit thine, and see   80
What life the Gods live there, and such live thou.
So saying, he drew nigh, and to me held,
Even to my mouth of that same fruit held part
Which he had pluckt; the pleasant savourie smell
So quick'nd appetite, that I, methought,
Could not but taste. Forthwith up to the Clouds
With him I flew, and underneath beheld
The Earth outstretcht immense, a prospect wide
And various: wondring at my flight and change
To this high exaltation; suddenly   90
My Guide was gon, and I, me thought, sunk down,
And fell asleep; but O how glad I wak'd
To find this but a dream! Thus *Eve* her Night
Related, and thus *Adam* answerd sad.

    Best Image of my self and dearer half,
The trouble of thy thoughts this night in sleep
Affects me equally; nor can I like
This uncouth dream, of evil sprung I fear;
Yet evil whence? in thee can harbour none,
Created pure. But know that in the Soule   100
Are many lesser Faculties that serve
Reason as chief; among these Fansie next
Her office holds; of all external things,
Which the five watchful Senses represent,
She forms Imaginations, Aerie shapes,
Which Reason joyning or disjoyning, frames
All what we affirm or what deny, and call
Our knowledge or opinion; then retires

Into her private Cell when Nature rests.

Oft in her absence mimic Fansie wakes   110

To imitate her; but misjoyning shapes,

Wilde work produces oft, and most in dreams,

Ill matching words and deeds long past or late.

Som such resemblances methinks I find

Of our last Eevnings talk, in this thy dream,

But with addition strange; yet be not sad.

Evil into the mind of God or Man

May come and go, so unapprov'd, and leave

No spot or blame behind: Which gives me hope

That what in sleep thou didst abhorr to dream,   120

Waking thou never wilt consent to do.

Be not disheart'nd then, nor cloud those looks

That wont to be more chearful and serene

Then when fair Morning first smiles on the World,

And let us to our fresh imployments rise

Among the Groves, the Fountains, and the Flours

That open now thir choicest bosom'd smells

Reservd from night, and kept for thee in store.

   So cheard he his fair Spouse, and she was cheard,

But silently a gentle tear let fall   130

From either eye, and wip'd them with her haire;

Two other precious drops that ready stood,

Each in thir chrystal sluce, hee ere they fell

Kiss'd as the gracious signs of sweet remorse

And pious awe, that feard to have offended.

   So all was cleard, and to the Field they haste.

But first from under shadie arborous roof,

Soon as they forth were come to open sight
Of day-spring, and the Sun, who scarce up risen
With wheels yet hov'ring o're the Ocean brim,   140
Shot paralel to the earth his dewie ray,
Discovering in wide Lantskip all the East
Of Paradise and *Edens* happie Plains,
Lowly they bow'd adoring, and began
Thir Orisons, each Morning duly paid
In various style, for neither various style
Nor holy rapture wanted they to praise
Thir Maker, in fit strains pronounc't or sung
Unmeditated, such prompt eloquence
Flowd from thir lips, in Prose or numerous Verse,   150
More tuneable then needed Lute or Harp
To add more sweetness, and they thus began.
   These are thy glorious works, Parent of good,
Almightie, thine this universal Frame,
Thus wondrous fair; thy self how wondrous then!
Unspeakable, who sitst above these Heavens
To us invisible or dimly seen
In these thy lowest works, yet these declare
Thy goodness beyond thought, and Power Divine:
Speak yee who best can tell, ye Sons of light,   160
Angels, for yee behold him, and with songs
And choral symphonies, Day without Night,
Circle his Throne rejoycing, yee in Heav'n,
On Earth joyn all yee Creatures to extoll
Him first, him last, him midst, and without end.
Fairest of Starrs, last in the train of Night,

If better thou belong not to the dawn,
Sure pledge of day, that crownst the smiling Morn
With thy bright Circlet, praise him in thy Spheare
While day arises, that sweet hour of Prime.   170
Thou Sun, of this great World both Eye and Soule,
Acknowledge him thy Greater, sound his praise
In thy eternal course, both when thou climb'st,
And when high Noon hast gaind, & when thou fallst.
Moon, that now meetst the orient Sun, now fli'st
With the fixt Starrs, fixt in thir Orb that flies,
And yee five other wandering Fires that move
In mystic Dance not without Song, resound
His praise, who out of Darkness call'd up Light.
Aire, and ye Elements the eldest birth   180
Of Natures Womb, that in quaternion run
Perpetual Circle, multiform; and mix
And nourish all things, let your ceasless change
Varie to our great Maker still new praise.
Ye Mists and Exhalations that now rise
From Hill or steaming Lake, duskie or grey,
Till the Sun paint your fleecie skirts with Gold,
In honour to the Worlds great Author rise,
Whether to deck with Clouds the uncolourd skie,
Or wet the thirstie Earth with falling showers,   190
Rising or falling still advance his praise.
His praise ye Winds, that from four Quarters blow,
Breathe soft or loud; and wave your tops, ye Pines,
With every Plant, in sign of Worship wave.
Fountains and yee, that warble, as ye flow,

Melodious murmurs, warbling tune his praise.

Joyn voices all ye living Souls, ye Birds,

That singing up to Heaven Gate ascend,

Bear on your wings and in your notes his praise;

Yee that in Waters glide, and yee that walk   200

The Earth, and stately tread, or lowly creep;

Witness if I be silent, Morn or Eeven,

To Hill, or Valley, Fountain, or fresh shade

Made vocal by my Song, and taught his praise.

Hail universal Lord, be bouteous still

To give us onely good; and if the night

Have gathered aught of evil or conceald,

Disperse it, as now light dispels the dark.

    So pray'd they innocent, and to thir thoughts

Firm peace recoverd soon and wonted calm.   210

On to thir mornings rural work they haste

Among sweet dewes and flours; where any row

Of Fruit-trees overwoodie reachd too farr

Thir pamperd boughes, and needed hands to check

Fruitless imbraces: or they led the Vine

To wed her Elm; she spous'd about him twines

Her mariageable arms, and with her brings

Her dowr th' adopted Clusters, to adorn

His barren leaves. Them thus imploid beheld

With pittie Heav'ns high King, and to him call'd   220

Raphael, the sociable Spirit, that deign'd

To travel with *Tobias*, and secur'd

His marriage with the seaventimes-wedded Maid.

    Raphael, said hee, thou hear'st what stir on Earth

Satan from Hell scap't through the darksom Gulf
Hath raisd in Paradise, and how disturbd
This night the human pair, how he designes
In them at once to ruin all mankind.
Go therefore, half this day as friend with friend
Converse with *Adam*, in what Bowre or shade   230
Thou find'st him from the heat of Noon retir'd,
To respit his day-labour with repast,
Or with repose; and such discourse bring on,
As may advise him of his happie state,
Happiness in his power left free to will,
Left to his own free Will, his Will though free,
Yet mutable; whence warne him to beware
He swerve not too secure: tell him withall
His danger, and from whom, what enemie
Late falln himself from Heav'n, is plotting now   240
The fall of others from like state of bliss;
By violence, no, for that shall be withstood,
But by deceit and lies; this let him know,
Least wilfully transgressing he pretend
Surprisal, unadmonisht, unforewarnd.
　　So spake th' Eternal Father, and fulfilld
All Justice: nor delaid the winged Saint
After his charge receivd; but from among
Thousand Celestial Ardors, where he stood
Vaild with his gorgeous wings, up springing light   250
Flew through the midst of Heav'n; th' angelic Quires
On each hand parting, to his speed gave way
Through all th' Empyreal road; till at the Gate

Of Heav'n arriv'd, the gate self-opend wide

On golden Hinges turning, as by work

Divine the sov'ran Architect had fram'd.

From hence, no cloud, or, to obstruct his sight,

Starr interpos'd, however small he sees,

Not unconform to other shining Globes,

Earth and the Gard'n of God, with Cedars crownd   260

Above all Hills. As when by night the Glass

Of *Galileo*, less assur'd, observes

Imagind Lands and Regions in the Moon:

Or Pilot from amidst the *Cyclades*

Delos or *Samos* first appeering kenns

A cloudy spot. Down thither prone in flight

He speeds, and through the vast Ethereal Skie

Sailes between worlds & worlds, with steddie wing

Now on the polar windes, then with quick Fann

Winnows the buxom Air; till within soare   270

Of Towring Eagles, to all the Fowles he seems

A *Phænix*, gaz'd by all, as that sole Bird

When to enshrine his reliques in the Sun's

Bright Temple, to *Ægyptian Theb*'s he flies.

At once on th' Eastern cliff of Paradise

He lights, and to his proper shape returns

A Seraph wingd; six wings he wore, to shade

His lineaments Divine; the pair that clad

Each shoulder broad, came mantling o're his brest

With regal Ornament; the middle pair   280

Girt like a Starrie Zone his waste, and round

Skirted his loines and thighes with downie Gold

And colours dipt in Heav'n; the third his feet
Shaddowd from either heele with featherd maile
Skie-tinctur'd grain. Like *Maia's* son he stood,
And shook his Plumes, that Heav'nly fragance filld
The circuit wide. Strait knew him all the Bands
Of Angels under watch; and to his state,
And to his message high in honour rise;
For on som message high they guessd him bound.   290
Thir glittering Tents he passd, and now is come
Into the blissful field, through Groves of Myrrhe,
And flouring Odours, Cassia, Nard, and Balme;
A Wilderness of sweets; for Nature here
Wantond as in her prime, and plaid at will
Her Virgin Fancies, pouring forth more sweet,
Wilde above rule or Art; enormous bliss.
Him through the spicie Forrest onward com
Adam discernd, as in the dore he sat
Of his coole Bowre, while now the mounted Sun   300
Shot down direct his fervid Raies to warme
Earths inmost womb, more warmth then *Adam* needs;
And *Eve* within, due at her hour prepar'd
For dinner savourie fruits, of taste to please
True appeite, and not disrelish thirst
Of nectarous draughts between, from milkie stream,
Berrie or Grape: to whom thus *Adam* call'd.
    Haste hither *Eve*, and worth thy sight behold
Eastward among those Trees, what glorious shape
Comes this way moving; seems another Morn   310
Ris'n on mid-noon; som great behest from Heav'n

To us perhaps he brings, and will voutsafe

This day to be our Guest. But goe with speed,

And what thy stores contain, bring forth and poure

Abundance, fit to honour and receive

Our Heav'nly stranger; well we may afford

Our givers thir own gifts, and large bestow

From large bestowd, where Nature multiplies

Her fertil growth, and by disburd'ning grows

More fruitful, which instructs us not to spare.   320

    To whom thus *Eve. Adam*, earths hallowd mould,

Of God inspir'd, small store will serve, where store,

All seasons, ripe for use hangs on the stalk;

Save what by frugal storing firmness gains

To nourish, and superfluous moist consumes:

But I will haste and from each bough and break,

Each Plant & juiciest Gourd will pluck such choice

To entertain our Angel guest, as hee

Beholding shall confess that here on Earth

God hath dispenst his bounties as in Heav'n.   330

    So saying, with dispatchful looks in haste

She turns, on hospitable thoughts intent

What choice to chuse for delicacie best,

What order, so contriv'd as not to mix

Tastes, not well joynd, inelegant, but bring

Taste after taste upheld with kindliest change,

Bestirs her then, and from each tender stalk

Whatever Earth all-bearing Mother yeilds

In *India* East or West, or middle shoare

In *Pontus* or the *Punic* Coast, or where   340

Alcinous reign'd, fruit of all kindes, in coate,
Rough, or smooth rin'd, or bearded husk, or shell
She gathers, Tribute large, and on the board
Heaps with unsparing hand; for drink the Grape
She crushes, inoffensive moust, and meathes
From many a berrie, and from sweet kernels prest
She tempers dulcet creams, nor these to hold
Wants her fit vessels pure, then strews the ground
With Rose and Odours from the shrub unfum'd.
Mean while our Primitive great Sire, to meet   350
His god-like Guest, walks forth, without more train
Accompani'd then with his own compleat
Perfections, in himself was all his state,
More solemn then the tedious pomp that waits
On Princes, when thir rich Retinue long
Of Horses led, and Grooms besmeard with Gold
Dazles the croud, and sets them all agape.
Neerer his presence *Adam* though not awd,
Yet with submiss approach and reverence meek,
As to a superior Nature, bowing low,   360
Thus said. Native of Heav'n, for other place
None can then Heav'n such glorious shape contain;
Since by descending from the Thrones above,
Those happie places thou hast deignd a while
To want, and honour these, voutsafe with us
Two onely, who yet by sov'ran gift possess
This spacious ground, in yonder shadie Bowre
To rest, and what the Garden choicest bears
To sit and taste, till this meridian heat

Be over, and the Sun more coole decline.   370

    Whom thus the Angelic Vertue answerd milde.

Adam, I therefore came, nor art thou such

Created, or such place hast here to dwell,

As may not oft invite, though Spirits of Heav'n

To visit thee; lead on then where thy Bowre

Oreshades; for these mid-hours, till Eevning rise

I have at will. So to the Silvan Lodge

They came, that like *Pomona*'s Arbour smil'd

With flourets deck't and fragrant smells; but *Eve*

Undeckt, save with her self more lovely fair   380

Then Wood-Nymph, or the fairest Goddess feign'd

Of three that in Mount *Ida* naked strove,

Stood to entertain her guest from Heav'n; no vaile

Shee needed, Vertue-proof, no thought infirme

Alterd her cheek. On whom the Angel *Haile*

Bestowd, the holy salutation us'd

Long after to blest *Marie*, second *Eve*.

    Haile Mother of Mankind, whose fruitful Womb

Shall fill the World more numerous with thy Sons

Then with these various fruits the Trees of God   390

Have heap'd this Table. Rais'd of grassie terf

Thir Table was, and mossie seats had round,

And on her ample Square from side to side

All *Autumn* pil'd, though *Spring* and *Autumn* here

Danc'd hand in hand. A while discourse they hold;

No fear lest Dinner coole; when thus began

Our Authour. Heav'nly stranger, please to taste

These bounties which our Nourisher, from whom

All perfet good unmeasur'd out, descends,

To us for food and for delight hath caus'd   400

The Earth to yeild; unsavourie food perhaps

To spiritual Natures; only this I know,

That one Celestial Father gives to all.

   To whom the Angel. Therefore what he gives

(Whose praise be ever sung) to man in part

Spiritual, may of purest Spirits be found

No ingrateful food: and food alike those pure

Intelligential substances require

As doth your Rational; and both contain

Within them every lower facultie   410

Of sense, whereby they hear, see, smell, touch, taste,

Tasting concoct, digest, assimilate,

And corporeal to incorporeal turn.

For know, whatever was created, needs

To be sustaind and fed; of Elements

The grosser feeds the purer, earth the sea,

Earth and the Sea feed Air, the Air those Fires

Ethereal, and as lowest first the Moon;

Whence in her visage round those spots, unpurg'd

Vapours not yet into her substance turnd.   420

Nor doth the Moon no nourishment exhale

From her moist Continent to higher Orbes.

The Sun that light imparts to all, receives

From all his alimental recompence

In humid exhalations, and at Even

Sups with the Ocean: though in Heav'n the Trees

Of life ambrosial frutage bear, and vines

Yeild Nectar, though from off the boughs each Morn

We brush mellifluous Dewes, and find the ground

Cover'd with pearly grain: yet God hath here   430

Varied his bounty so with new delights,

As may compare with Heaven; and to taste

Think not I shall be nice. So down they sat,

And to thir viands fell, nor seemingly

The Angel, nor in mist, the common gloss

Of Theologians, but with keen dispatch

Of real hunger, and concoctive heate

To transubstantiate; what redounds, transpires

Through Spirits with ease; nor wonder; if by fire

Of sooty coal the Empiric Alchimist   440

Can turn, or holds it possible to turn

Metals of drossiest Ore to perfet Gold

As from the Mine. Mean while at Table *Eve*

Ministerd naked, and thir flowing cups

With pleasant liquors crown'd: O innocence

Deserving Paradise! if ever, then,

Then had the Sons of God excuse to have bin

Enamour'd at that sight; but in those hearts

Love unlibidinous reign'd, nor jealousie

Was understood, the injur'd Lovers Hell.   450

   Thus when with meats & drinks they had suffic'd,

Not burd'nd Nature, sudden mind arose

In *Adam*, not to let th' occasion pass

Given him by this great Conference to know

Of things above his World, and of thir being

Who dwell in Heav'n, whose excellence he saw

Transcend his own so farr, whose radiant forms
Divine effulgence, whose high Power so far
Exceeded human, and his wary speech
Thus to th' Empyreal Minister he fram'd.   460
    Inhabitant with God, now know I well
Thy favour, in this honour done to man,
Under whose lowly roof thou hast voutsaf't
To enter, and these earthly fruits to taste,
Food not of Angels, yet accepted so,
As that more willingly thou couldst not seem
At Heav'ns high feasts to have fed: yet what compare?
    To whom the winged Hierarch repli'd.
O *Adam*, one Almightie is, from whom
All things proceed, and up to him return,   470
If not deprav'd from good, created all
Such to perfection, one first matter all,
Indu'd with various forms, various degrees
Of substance, and in things that live, of life;
But more refin'd, more spiritous, and pure,
As neerer to him plac't or neerer tending
Each in thir several active Sphears assignd,
Till body up to spirit work, in bounds
Proportiond to each kind. So from the root
Springs lighter the green stalk, from thence the leaves   480
More aerie, last the bright consummate floure
Spirits odorous breathes: flours and thir fruit
Mans nourishment, by gradual scale sublim'd
To vital Spirits aspire, to animal,
To intellectual, give both life and sense,

Fansie and understanding, whence the soule

Reason receives, and reason is her being,

Discursive, or Intuitive; discourse

Is oftest yours, the latter most is ours,

Differing but in degree, of kind the same.   490

Wonder not then, what God for you saw good

If I refuse not, but convert, as you,

To proper substance; time may come when men

With Angels may participate, and find

No inconvenient Diet, nor too light Fare:

And from these corporal nutriments perhaps

Your bodies may at last turn all to Spirit,

Improv'd by tract of time, and wingd ascend

Ethereal, as wee, or may at choice

Here or in Heav'nly Paradises dwell;   500

If ye be found obedient, and retain

Unalterably firm his love entire

Whose progenie you are. Mean while enjoy

Your fill what happiness this happie state

Can comprehend, incapable of more.

    To whom the Patriarch of mankind repli'd.

O favourable spirit, propitious guest,

Well hast thou taught the way that might direct

Our knowledge, and the scale of Nature set

From center to circumference, whereon   510

In contemplation of created things

By steps we may ascend to God. But say,

What meant that caution joind, *if ye be found*

Obedient? can wee want obedience then

To him, or possibly his love desert
Who formd us from the dust, and plac'd us here
Full to the utmost measure of what bliss
Human desires can seek or apprehend?
    To whom the Angel. Son of Heav'n and Earth,
Attend: That thou art happie, owe to God,   520
That thou continu'st such, owe to thy self,
That is, to thy obedience; therein stand.
This was that caution giv'n thee; be advis'd.
God made thee perfet, not immutable;
And good he made thee, but to persevere
He left it in thy power, ordaind thy will
By nature free, not over-rul'd by Fate
Inextricable, or strict necessity;
Our voluntarie service he requires,
Not our necessitated, such with him   530
Findes no acceptance, nor can find, for how
Can hearts, not free, be tri'd whether they serve
Willing or no, who will but what they must
By Destinie, and can no other choose?
My self and all th' Angelic Host that stand
In sight of God enthron'd, our happie state
Hold, as you yours, while our obedience holds;
On other surety none; freely we serve.
Because wee freely love, as in our will
To love or not; in this we stand or fall: 540
And som are fall'n, to disobedience fall'n,
And so from Heav'n to deepest Hell; O fall
From what high state of bliss into what woe!

To whom our great Progenitor. Thy words
Attentive, and with more delighted eare
Divine instructer, I have heard, then when
Cherubic songs by night from neighbouring Hills
Aereal Music send: nor knew I not
To be both will and deed created free;
Yet that we never shall forget to love 550
Our maker, and obey him whose command
Single, is yet so just, my constant thoughts
Assur'd me and still assure: though what thou tellst
Hath past in Heav'n, som doubt within me move,
But more desire to hear, if thou consent,
The full relation, which must needs be strange,
Worthy of Sacred silence to be heard;
And we have yet large day, for scarce the Sun
Hath finisht half his journey, and scarce begins
His other half in the great Zone of Heav'n. 560
    Thus *Adam* made request, and *Raphael*
After short pause assenting, thus began.
    High matter thou injoinst me, O prime of men,
Sad task and hard, for how shall I relate
To human sense th' invisible exploits
Of warring Spirits; how without remorse
The ruin of so many glorious once
And perfet while they stood; how last unfould
The secrets of another world, perhaps
Not lawful to reveal? yet for thy good 570
This is dispenc't, and what surmounts the reach
Of human sense, I shall delineate so,

By lik'ning spiritual to corporal forms,
As may express them best, though what if Earth
Be but the shaddow of Heav'n, and things therein
Each to other like, more then on earth is thought?
    As yet this world was not, and *Chaos* wilde
Reignd where these Heav'ns now rowl, where Earth now rests
Upon her Center pois'd, when on a day
(For Time, though in Eternitie, appli'd   580
To motion, measures all things durable
By present, past, and future) on such day
As Heav'ns great Year brings forth, th' Empyreal Host
Of Angels by Imperial summons call'd,
Innumerable before th' Almighties Throne
Forthwith from all the ends of Heav'n appeerd
Under thir Hierarchs in orders bright
Ten thousand thousand Ensignes high advanc'd,
Standards, and Gonfalons twixt Van and Reare
Streame in the Aire, and for distinction serve   590
Of Hierarchies, of Orders, and Degrees;
Or in thir glittering Tissues bear imblaz'd
Holy Memorials, acts of Zeale and Love
Recorded eminent. Thus when in Orbes
Of circuit inexpressible they stood,
Orb within Orb, the Father infinite,
By whom in bliss imbosom'd sat the Son,
A midst as from a flaming Mount, whose top
Brightness had made invisible, thus spake.
    Hear all ye Angels, Progenie of Light,   600
Thrones, Dominations, Princedoms, Vertues, Powers,

Hear my Decree, which unrevok't shall stand.

This day I have begot whom I declare

My onely Son, and on this holy Hill

Him have anointed, whom ye now behold

At my right hand; your Head I him appoint;

And by my Self have sworn to him shall bow

All knees in Heav'n, and shall confess him Lord:

Under his great Vice-gerent Reign abide

United as one individual Soule   610

For ever happie: him who disobeyes

Mee disobeyes, breaks union, and that day

Cast out from God and blessed vision, falls

Into utter darkness, deep ingulft, his place

Ordaind without redemption, without end.

   So spake th' Omnipotent, and with his words

All seemd well pleas'd, all seem'd, but were not all.

That day, as other solem dayes, they spent

In song and dance about the sacred Hill,

Mystical dance, which yonder starrie Spheare   620

Of Planets and of fixt in all her Wheeles

Resembles nearest, mazes intricate,

Eccentric, intervolv'd, yet regular

Then most, when most irregular they seem:

And in thir motions harmonie Divine

So smooths her charming tones, that Gods own ear

Listens delighted. Eevning now approachd

(For we have also our Eevning and our Morn,

We ours for change delectable, not need)

Forthwith from dance to sweet repast they turn   630

Desirous, all in Circles as they stood,

Tables are set, and on a sudden pil'd

With Angels Food, and rubied Nectar flows:

In Pearl, in Diamond, and massie Gold,

Fruit of delicious Vines, the growth of Heav'n.

They eat, they drink, and with refection sweet

Are fill'd, before th' all-bounteous King, who showrd

With copious hand, rejoycing in thir joy.

Now when ambrosial Night with Clouds exhal'd

From that high mount of God, whence light & shade   640

Spring both, the face of brightest Heav'n had changd

To grateful Twilight (for Night comes not there

In darker veile) and roseat Dews dispos'd

All but the unsleeping eyes of God to rest,

Wide over all the Plain, and wider farr

Then all this globous Earth in Plain outspred,

(Such are the Courts of God) Th' Angelic throng

Disperst in Bands and Files thir Camp extend

By living Streams among the Trees of Life,

Pavilions numberless, and sudden reard,   650

Celestial Tabernacles, where they slept

Fannd with coole Winds, save those who in thir course

Melodious Hymns about the sovran Throne

Alternate all night long: but not so wak'd

Satan, so call him now, his former name

Is heard no more in Heav'n; he of the first,

If not the first Arch-Angel, great in Power,

In favour and præeminence, yet fraught

With envie against the Son of God, that day

Honourd by his great Father, and proclaimd   660

Messiah King anointed, could not beare

Through pride that sight, and thought himself impaird.

Deep malice thence conceiving & disdain,

Soon as midnight brought on the duskie houre

Friendliest to sleep and silence, he resolv'd

With all his Legions to dislodge, and leave

Unworshipt, unobey'd the Throne supream

Contemptuous, and his next subordinate

Awak'ning, thus to him in secret spake.

    Sleepst thou Companion dear, what sleep can close   670

Thy eye-lids? and remembrest what Decree

Of yesterday, so late hath past the lips

Of Heav'ns Almightie. Thou to me thy thoughts

Wast wont, I mine to thee was wont to impart;

Both waking we were one; how then can now

Thy sleep dissent? new Laws thou seest impos'd;

New Laws from him who reigns, new minds may raise

In us who serve, new Counsels, to debate

What doubtful may ensue, more in this place

To utter is not safe. Assemble thou   680

Of all those Myriads which we lead the chief;

Tell them that by command, ere yet dim Night

Her shadowie Cloud withdraws, I am to haste,

And all who under me thir Banners wave,

Homeward with flying march where we possess

The Quarters of the North, there to prepare

Fit entertainment to receive our King

The great *Messiah*, and his new commands,

Who speedily through all the Hierarchies
Intends to pass triumphant, and give Laws.   690
    So spake the false Arch-Angel, and infus'd
Bad influence into th' unwarie brest
Of his Associate; hee together calls,
Or several one by one, the Regent Powers,
Under him Regent, tells, as he was taught,
That the most High commanding, now ere Night,
Now ere dim Night had disincumberd Heav'n,
The great Hierarchal Standard was to move;
Tells the suggested cause, and casts between
Ambiguous words and jealousies, to sound   700
Or taint integritie; but all obey'd
The wonted signal, and superior voice
Of thir great Potentate; for great indeed
His name, and high was his degree in Heav'n;
His count'nance, as the Morning Starr that guides
The starrie flock, allur'd them, and with lyes
Drew after him thc third part of Heav'ns Host:
Mean while th' Eternal eye, whose sight discernes
Abstrusest thoughts, from forth his holy Mount
And from within the golden Lamps that burne   710
Nightly before him, saw without thir light
Rebellion rising, saw in whom, how spred
Among the sons of Morn, what multitudes
Were banded to oppose his high Decree;
And smiling to his onely Son thus said.
    Son, thou in whom my glory I behold
In full resplendence, Heir of all my might,

Neerly it now concernes us to be sure
Of our Omnipotence, and with what Arms
We mean to hold what anciently we claim   720
Of Deitie or Empire, such a foe
Is rising, who intends to erect his Throne
Equal to ours, throughout the spacious North;
Nor so content, hath in his thought to trie
In battel, what our Power is, or our right.
Let us advise, and to this hazard draw
With speed what force is left, and all imploy
In our defence, lest unawares we lose
This our high place, our Sanctuarie, our Hill.
   To whom the Son with calm aspect and cleer   730
Light'ning Divine, ineffable, serene,
Made answer. Mightie Father, thou thy foes
Justly hast in derision, and secure
Laugh'st at thir vain designes and tumults vain,
Matter to mee of Glory, whom thir hate
Illustrates, when they see all Regal Power
Giv'n me to quell thir pride, and in event
Know whether I be dextrous to subdue
Thy Rebels, or be found the worst in Heav'n.
   So spake the Son, but *Satan* with his Powers   740
Farr was advanc't on winged sped, an Host
Innumerable as the Starrs of Night,
Or Starrs of Morning, Dew-drops, which the Sun
Impearls on every leaf and every flouer.
Regions they pass'd, the mightie Regencies
Of Seraphim and Potentates and Thrones

In thir triple Degrees, Regions to which
All thy Dominion, *Adam*, is no more
Then what this Garden is to all the Earth,
And all the Sea, from one entire globose   750
Stretcht into Longitude; which having pass'd
At length into the limits of the North
They came, and *Satan* to his Royal seat
High on a Hill, far blazing, as a Mount
Rais'd on a Mount, with Pyramids and Towrs
From Diamond Quarries hew'n, & Rocks of Gold,
The Palace of great *Lucifer*, (so call
That Structure in the Dialect of men
Interpreted) which not long after, hee
Affecting all equality with God,   760
In imitation of that Mount whereon
Messiah was declar'd in sight of Heav'n,
The Mountain of the Congregation call'd;
For thither he assembl'd all his Train,
Pretending so commanded to consult
About the great reception of thir King,
Thither to come, and with calumnious Art
Of counterfeted truth thus held thir ears.

    Thrones, Dominations, Princedomes, Vertues, Powers,
If these magnific Titles yet remain   770
Not meerly titular, since by Decree
Another now hath to himself ingross't
All Power, and us eclipst under the name
Of King anointed, for whom all this haste
Of midnight march, and hurried meeting here,

This onely to consult how we may best
With what may be devis'd of honours new
Receive him coming to receive from us
Knee-tribute yet unpaid, prostration vile,
Too much to one, but double how endur'd,   780
To one and to his image now proclaim'd?
But what if better counsels might erect
Our minds and teach us to cast off this Yoke?
Will ye submit your necks, and chuse to bend
The supple knee? ye will not, if I trust
To know ye right, or if ye know your selves
Natives and Sons of Heav'n possest before
By none, and if not equal all, yet free,
Equally free; for Orders and Degrees
Jarr not with liberty, but well consist.   790
Who can in reason then or right assume
Monarchie over such as live by right
His equals, if in power and splendor less,
In freedome equal? or can introduce
Law and Edict on us, who without law
Erre not, much less for this to be our Lord,
And look for adoration to th' abuse
Of those Imperial Titles which assert
Our being ordain'd to govern, not to serve?
    Thus farr his bold discourse without controule   800
Had audience, when among the Seraphim
Abdiel, then whom none with more zeale ador'd
The Deitie, and divine commands obei'd,
Stood up, and in a flame of zeale severe

The current of his fury thus oppos'd.

   O argument blasphemous, false and proud!

Words which no eare ever to hear in Heav'n

Expected, least of all from thee, ingrate

In place thy self so high above thy Peeres.

Canst thou with impious obloquie condemne   810

The just Decree of God, pronounc't and sworn,

That to his only Son by right endu'd

With Regal Scepter, every Soule in Heav'n

Shall bend the knee, and in that honour due

Confess him rightful King? unjust thou saist

Flatly unjust, to binde with Laws the free,

And equal over equals to let Reigne,

One over all with unsucceeded power.

Shalt thou give Law to God, shalt thou dispute

With him the points of libertie, who made   820

Thee what thou art, & formd the Pow'rs of Heav'n

Such as he pleasd, and circumscrib'd thir being?

Yet by exprience taught we know how good,

And of our good, and of our dignitie

How provident he is, how farr from thought

To make us less, bent rather to exalt

Our happie state under one Head more neer

United. But to grant it thee unjust,

That equal over equals Monarch Reigne:

Thy self though great & glorious dost thou count,   830

Or all Angelic Nature joind in one,

Equal to him begotten Son, by whom

As by his Word the mighty Father made

All things, ev'n thee, and all the Spirits of Heav'n

By him created in thir bright degrees,

Crownd them with Glory, & to thir Glory nam'd

Thrones, Dominations, Princedoms, Vertues, Powers

Essential Powers, nor by his Reign obscur'd,

But more illustrious made, since he the Head

One of our number thus reduc't becomes,   840

His Laws our Laws, all honour to him done

Returns our own. Cease then this impious rage,

And tempt not these; but hast'n to appease

Th' incensed Father, and th' incensed Son,

While Pardon may be found in time besought.

   So spake the fervent Angel, but his zeale

None seconded, as out of season judg'd,

Or singular and rash, whereat rejoic'd

Th' Apostat, and more haughty thus repli'd.

That we were formd then saist thou? & the work   850

Of secondarie hands, by task transferd

From Father to his Son? strange point and new!

Doctrin which we would know whence learnt: who saw

When this creation was? rememberst thou

Thy making, while the Maker gave thee being?

We know no time when we were not as now;

Know none before us, self-begot, self-rais'd

By our own quick'ning power, when fatal course

Had circl'd his full Orbe, the birth mature

Of this our native Heav'n, Ethereal Sons.   860

Our puissance is our own, our own right hand

Shall teach us highest deeds, by proof to try

Who is our equal: then thou shalt behold
Whether by supplication we intend
Address, and to begirt th' Almighty Throne
Beseeching or besieging. This report,
These tidings carrie to th' anointed King;
And fly, ere evil intercept thy flight.

He said, and as the sound of waters deep
Hoarce murmur echo'd to his words applause   870
Through the infinite Host, nor less for that
Thc flaming Seraph fearless, though alone
Encompass'd round with foes, thus answerd bold.

O alienate from God, O spirit accurst,
Forsak'n of all good; I see thy fall
Determind, and thy hapless crew involv'd
In this perfidious fraud, contagion spred
Both of thy crime and punishment: henceforth
No more be troubl'd how to quit the yoke
Of Gods *Messiah*; those indulgent Laws   880
Will not be now voutsaf't, other Decrees
Against thee are gon forth without recall;
That Golden Scepter which thou didst reject
Is now an Iron Rod to bruise and breake
Thy disobedience. Well thou didst advise,
Yet not for thy advise or threats I fly
These wicked Tents devoted, least the wrauth
Impendent, raging into sudden flame
Distinguish not: for soon expect to feel
His Thunder on thy head, devouring fire.   890
Then who created thee lamenting learne,

When who can uncreate thee thou shalt know.
    So spake the Seraph *Abdiel* faithful found,
Among the faithless, faithful only hee;
Among innumerable false, unmov'd,
Unshak'n, unseduc'd, unterrifi'd
His Loyaltie he kept, his Love, his Zeale;
Nor number, nor example with him wrought
To swerve from truth, or change his constant mind
Though single. From amidst them forth he passd,   900
Long way through hostile scorn, which he susteind
Superior, nor of violence fear'd aught;
And with retorted scorn his back he turn'd
On those proud Towrs to swift destruction doom'd.

PARADISE
LOST

BOOK VI

ALL night the dreadless Angel unpursu'd
Through Heav'ns wide Champain held his way, till Morn,
Wak't by the circling Hours, with rosie hand
Unbarr'd the gates of Light. There is a Cave
Within the Mount of God, fast by his Throne,
Where light and darkness in perpetual round
Lodge and dislodge by turns, which makes through Heav'n
Grateful vicissitude, like Day and Night;
Light issues forth, and at the other dore
Obsequious darkness enters, till her houre   10
To veile the Heav'n, though darkness there might well
Seem twilight here; and now went forth the Morn
Such as in highest Heav'n, arrayd in Gold
Empyreal, from before her vanisht Night,
Shot through with orient Beams: when all the Plain
Coverd with thick embatteld Squadrons bright,
Chariots and flaming Armes, and fierie Steeds
Reflecting blaze on blaze, first met his view:
Warr he perceav'd, warr in procinct, and found
Already known what he for news had thought   20
To have reported: gladly then he mixt

Among those friendly Powers who him receav'd
With joy and acclamations loud, that one
That of so many Myriads fall'n, yet one
Returnd not lost: On to the sacred hill
They led him high applauded, and present
Before the seat supream; from whence a voice
From midst a Golden Cloud thus milde was heard.
    Servant of God, well done, well hast thou fought
The better fight, who single hast maintaind   30
Against revolted multitudes the Cause
Of Truth, in word mightier then they in Armes;
And for the testimonie of Truth hast born
Universal reproach, far worse to beare
Then violence: for this was all thy care
To stand approv'd in sight of God, though Worlds
Judg'd thee perverse: the easier conquest now
Remains thee, aided by this host of friends,
Back on thy foes more glorious to return
Then scornd thou didst depart, and to subdue   40
By force, who reason for thir Law refuse,
Right reason for thir Law, and for thir King
Messiah, who by right of merit Reigns.
Goe *Michael* of Celestial Armies Prince,
And thou in Military prowess next
Gabriel, lead forth to Battel these my Sons
Invincible, lead forth my armed Saints
By Thousands and by Millions rang'd for fight;
Equal in number to that Godless crew
Rebellious, them with Fire and hostile Arms   50

Fearless assault, and to the brow of Heav'n

Pursuing drive them out from God and bliss,

Into thir place of punishment, the Gulf

Of *Tartarus*, which ready opens wide

His fiery *Chaos* to receave thir fall.

   So spake the Sovran voice, and Clouds began

To darken all the Hill, and smoak to rowl

In duskie wreathes, reluctant flames, the signe

Of wrauth awak't: nor with less dread the loud

Ethereal Trumpet from on high gan blow: 60

At which command the Powers Militant,

That stood for Heav'n, in mighty Quadrate joyn'd

Of Union irresistible, mov'd on

In silence thir bright Legions, to the sound

Of instrumental Harmonie that breath'd

Heroic Ardor to advent'rous deeds

Under thir God-like Leaders, in the Cause

Of God and his *Messiah*. On they move

Indissolubly firm; nor obvious Hill,

Nor streit'ning Vale, nor Wood, nor Stream divides   70

Thir perfet ranks; for high above the ground

Thir march was, and the passive Air upbore

Thir nimble tread; as when the total kind

Of Birds in orderly array on wing

Came summond over *Eden* to receive

Thir names of thee; so over many a tract

Of Heav'n they march'd, and many a Province wide

Tenfold the length of this terrene: at last

Farr in th' Horizon to the North appeer'd

From skirt to skirt a fierie Region, stretcht   80
In battailous aspect, and neerer view
Bristl'd with upright beams innumerable
Of rigid Spears, and Helmets throng'd, and Shields
Various, with boastful Argument portraid,
The banded Powers of *Satan* hasting on
With furious expedition; for they weend
That self same day by fight, or by surprize
To win the Mount of God, and on his Throne
To set the envier of his State, the proud
Aspirer, but thir thoughts prov'd fond and vain   90
In the mid way: thought strange to us it seemd
At first, that Angel should with Angel warr,
And in fierce hosting meet, who wont to meet
So oft in Festivals of joy and love
Unanimous, as sons of one great Sire
Hymning th' Eternal Father: but the shout
Of Battel now began, and rushing sound
Of onset ended soon each milder thought.
High in the midst exalted as a God
Th' Apostat in his Sun-bright Chariot sate   100
Idol of Majestie Divine, enclos'd
With Flaming Cherubim, and golden Shields;
Then lighted from his gorgeous Throne, for now
'Twixt Host and Host but narrow space was left,
A dreadful interval, and Front to Front
Presented stood in terrible array
Of hideous length: before the cloudie Van,
On the rough edge of battel ere it joyn'd,

Satan with vast and haughtie strides advanc't,
Came towring, armd in Adamant and Gold;   110
Abdiel that sight endur'd not, where he stood
Among the mightiest, bent on highest deeds,
And thus his own undaunted heart explores.

    O Heav'n! that such resemblance of the Highest
Should yet remain, where faith and fealtie
Remain not; wherfore should not strength & might
There fail where Vertue fails, or weakest prove
Where boldest; though to sight unconquerable?
His puissance, trusting in th' Almightie's aide,
I mean to try, whose Reason I have tri'd   120
Unsound and false; nor is it aught but just,
That he who in debate of Truth hath won,
Should win in Arms, in both disputes alike
Victor; though brutish that contest and foule,
When Reason hath to deal with force, yet so
Most reason is that Reason overcome.

    So pondering, and from his armed Pccrs
Forth stepping opposite, half way he met
His daring foe, at this prevention more
Incens't, and thus securely him defi'd.   130
    Proud, art thou met? thy hope was to have reacht
The highth of thy aspiring unoppos'd,
The Throne of God unguarded, and his side
Abandond at the terror of thy Power
Or potent tongue; fool, not to think how vain
Against th' Omnipotent to rise in Arms;
Who out of smallest things could without end

Have rais'd incessant Armies to defeat
Thy folly; or with solitarie hand
Reaching beyond all limit, at one blow   140
Unaided could have finisht thee, and whelmd
Thy Legions under darkness; but thou seest
All are not of thy Train; there be who Faith
Prefer, and Pietie to God, though then
To thee not visible, when I alone
Seemd in thy World erroneous to dissent
From all: my Sect thou seest, now learn too late
How few somtimes may know, when thousands err.
    Whom the grand foe with scornful eye askance
Thus answerd. Ill for thee, but in wisht houre   150
Of my revenge, first sought for thou returnst
From flight, seditious Angel, to receave
Thy merited reward, the first assay
Of this right hand provok't, since first that tongue
Inspir'd with contradiction durst oppose
A third part of the Gods, in Synod met
Thir Deities to assert, who while they feel
Vigour Divine within them, can allow
Omnipotence to none. But well thou comst
Before thy fellows, ambitious to win   160
From me som Plume, that thy success may show
Destruction to the rest: this pause between
(Unanswerd least thou boast) to let thee know;
At first I thought that Libertie and Heav'n
To heav'nly Soules had bin all one; but now
I see that most through sloth had rather serve,

Ministring Spirits, traind up in Feast and Song;
Such hast thou arm'd, the Minstrelsie of Heav'n,
Servilitie with freedom to contend,
As both thir deeds compar'd this day shall prove.   170
　　To whom in brief thus *Abdiel* stern repli'd.
Apostat, still thou errst, nor end wilt find
Of erring, from the path of truth remote:
Unjustly thou deprav'st it with the name
Of *Servitude* to serve whom God ordains,
Or Nature; God and Nature bid the same,
When he who rules is worthiest, and excells
Them whom he governs. This is servitude,
To serve th' unwise, or him who hath rebelld
Against his worthier, as thine now serve thee,   180
Thy self not free, but to thy self enthrall'd;
Yet leudly dar'st our ministring upbraid.
Reign thou in Hell thy Kingdom, let mee serve
In Heav'n God ever blest, and his Divine
Behests obey, worthiest to be obey'd,
Yet Chains in Hell, not Realms expect: mean while
From mee returnd, as erst thou saidst, from flight,
This greeting on thy impious Crest receive.
　　So saying, a noble stroke he lifted high,
Which hung not, but so swift with tempest fell   190
On the proud Crest of *Satan*, that no sight,
Nor motion of swift thought, less could his Shield
Such ruin intercept: ten paces huge
He back recoild; the tenth on bended knee
His massie Spear upstaid; as if on Earth

Winds under ground or waters forcing way
Sidelong, had push't a Mountain from his seat
Half sunk with all his Pines. Amazement seis'd
The Rebel Thrones, but greater rage to see
Thus foil'd thir mightiest, ours joy filld, and shout, 200
Presage of Victorie and fierce desire
Of Battel: whereat *Michael* bid sound
Th' Arch-angel trumpet; through the vast of Heav'n
It sounded, and the faithful Armies rung
Hosanna to the Highest: nor stood at gaze
The adverse Legions, nor less hideous joyn'd
The horrid shock: now storming furie rose,
And clamour such as heard in Heav'n till now
Was never, Arms on Armour clashing bray'd
Horrible discord, and the madding Wheeles 210
Of brazen Chariots rag'd; dire was the noise
Of conflict; over head the dismal hiss
Of fiery Darts in flaming volies flew,
And flying vaulted either Host with fire.
So under fierie Cope together rush'd
Both Battels maine, with ruinous assault
And inextinguishable rage; all Heav'n
Resounded, and had Earth bin then, all Earth
Had to her Center shook. What wonder? when
Millions of fierce encountring Angels fought 220
On either side, the least of whom could weild
These Elements, and arm him with the force
Of all thir Regions: how much more of Power
Armie against Armie numberless to raise

Dreadful combustion warring, and disturb,
Though not destroy, thir happie Native seat;
Had not th' Eternal King Omnipotent
From his strong hold of Heav'n high over-rul'd
And limited thir might; though numberd such   230
As each divided Legion might have seemd
A numerous Host, in strength each armed hand
A Legion; led in fight, yet Leader seemd
Each Warriour single as in Chief, expert
When to advance, or stand, or turn the sway
Of Battel, open when, and when to close
The ridge of grim Warr; no thought of flight,
None of retreat, no unbecoming deed
That argu'd fear; each on himself reli'd,
As onely in his arm the moment lay
Of victorie; deeds of eternal fame   240
Were don, but infinite: for wide was spred
That Warr and various; somtimes on firm ground
A standing fight, then soaring on main wing
Tormented all the Air; all Air seemd then
Conflicting Fire: long time in eeven scale
The Battel hung; till *Satan*, who that day
Prodigious power had shewn, and met in Armes
No equal, raunging through the dire attack
Of fighting Seraphim confus'd, at length
Saw where the Sword of *Michael* smote, and fell'd   250
Squadrons at once, with huge two-handed sway
Brandisht aloft the horrid edge came down
Wide wasting; such destruction to withstand

He hasted, and oppos'd the rockie Orb
Of tenfold Adamant, his ample Shield
A vast circumference: At his approach
The great Arch-Angel from his warlike toile
Surceas'd, and glad as hoping here to end
Intestine War in Heav'n, the arch foe subdu'd
Or Captive drag'd in Chains, with hostile frown   260
And visage all enflam'd first thus began.

   Author of evil, unknown till thy revolt,
Unnam'd in Heav'n, now plenteous, as thou seest
These Acts of hateful strife, hateful to all,
Though heaviest by just measure on thy self
And thy adherents: how hast thou disturb'd
Heav'ns blessed peace, and into Nature brought
Miserie, uncreated till the crime
Of thy Rebellion? how hast thou instill'd
Thy malice into thousands, once upright   270
And faithful, now prov'd false. But think not here
To trouble Holy Rest; Heav'n casts thee out
From all her Confines. Heav'n the seat of bliss
Brooks not the works of violence and Warr.
Hence then, and evil go with thee along
Thy ofspring, to the place of evil, Hell,
Thou and thy wicked crew; there mingle broiles,
Ere this avenging Sword begin thy doome,
Or som more sudden vengeance wing'd from God
Precipitate thee with augmented paine.   280

   So spake the prince of Angels; to whom thus
The Adversarie. Nor think thou with wind

Of airie threats to aw whom yet with deeds
Thou canst not. Hast thou turnd the least of these
To flight, or if to fall, but that they rise
Unvanquisht, easier to transact with mee
That thou shouldst hope, imperious, & with threats
To chase me hence? erre not that so shall end
The strife which thou call's evil, but wee style
The strife of Glorie: which we mean to win,   290
Or turn this Heav'n it self into the Hell
Thou fablest, here however to dwell free,
If not to reign: mean while thy utmost force,
And join him nam'd *Almightie* to thy aid,
I flie not, but have sought thee farr and nigh.
   They ended parle, and both addrest for fight
Unspeakable; for who, though with the tongue
Of Angels, can relate, or to what things
Liken on Earth conspicuous, that may lift
Human imagination to such highth   300
Of Godlike Power: for likest Gods they seemd,
Stood they or mov'd, in stature, motion, arms
Fit to decide the Empire of great Heav'n.
Now wav'd thir fierie Swords, and in the Aire
Made horrid Circles; two broad Suns thir Shields
Blaz'd opposite, while expectation stood
In horror; from each hand with speed retir'd
Where erst was thickest fight, th' Angelic throng,
And left large field, unsafe within the wind
Of such commotion, such as to set forth   310
Great things by small, If Natures concord broke,

Among the Constellations warr were sprung,

Two Planets rushing from aspect maligne

Of fiercest opposition in mid Skie,

Should combat, and thir jarring Shears confound.

Together both with next to Almightie Arme,

Uplifted imminent one stroke they aim'd

That might determine, and not need repeate,

As not of power, at once; not odds appeerd

In might or swift prevention; but the sword   320

Of *Michael* from the Armorie of God

Was giv'n him temperd so, that neither keen

Nor solid might resist that edge: it met

The sword of *Satan* with steep force to smite

Descending, and in half cut sheere, nor staid,

But with swift wheele reverse, deep entring shar'd

All his right side; then *Satan* first knew pain,

And writh'd him to and fro convolv'd; so sore

The griding sword with discontinuous wound

Pass'd through him, but th' Ethereal substance clos'd   330

Not long divisible, and from the gash

A stream of Nectarous humor issuing flow'd

Sanguin, such as Celestial Spirits may bleed,

And all his Armour staind ere while so bright.

Forthwith on all sides to his aide was run

By Angels many and strong, who interpos'd

Defence, while others bore him on thir Shields

Back to his Chariot; where it stood retir'd

From off the files of warr; there they him laid

Gnashing for anguish and despite and shame   340

To find himself not matchless, and his pride
Humbl'd by such rebuke, so farr beneath
His confidence to equal God in power.
Yet soon he heal'd; for Spirits that live throughout
Vital in every part, not as frail man
In Entrailes, Heart or Head, Liver or Reines,
Cannot but by annihilating die;
Nor in thir liquid texture mortal wound
Receive, no more then can the fluid Aire:
All Heart they live, all Head, all Eye, all Eare,   350
All Intellect, all Sense, and as they please,
They limn themselves, and colour, shape or size
Assume, as likes them best, condense or rare.
   Mean while in other parts like deeds deservd
Memorial, where the might of *Gabriel* fought,
And with fierce Ensignes pierc'd the deep array
Of *Moloc* furious King, who him defi'd,
And at his Chariot wheeles to drag him bound
Threatn'd, nor from the Holie One of Heav'n
Refrein'd his tongue blasphemous; but anon   360
Down clov'n to the waste, with shatterd Armes
And uncouth paine fled bellowing. On each wing
Uriel and *Raphael* his vaunting foe,
Though huge, and in a Rock of Diamond Armd,
Vanquish'd *Adramelec*, and *Asmadai*,
Two potent Thrones, that to be less then Gods
Disdain'd, but meaner thoughts learnd in thir flight,
Mangl'd with gastly wounds through Plate and Maile.
Nor stood unmindful *Abdiel* to annoy

The Atheist crew, but with redoubl'd blow 370
Ariel and *Arioc,* and the violence
Of *Ramiel* scorcht and blasted overthrew.
I might relate of thousands, and thir names
Eternize here on Earth; but those elect
Angels contented with thir fame in Heav'n
Seek not the praise of men: the other sort
In might though wondrous and in Acts of Warr,
Nor of Renown less eager, yet by doome
Canceld from Heav'n and sacred memorie,
Nameless in dark oblivion let them dwell. 380
For strength from Truth divided and from Just,
Illaudable, naught merits but dispraise
And ignominie, yet to glorie aspires
Vain glorious, and through infamie seeks fame:
Therfore Eternal silence be thir doome.
   And now thir mightiest quelld, the battel swerv'd,
With many an inrode gor'd; deformed rout
Enter'd, and foul disorder; all the ground
With shiverd armour strow'n, and on a heap
Chariot and Charioter lay overturnd 390
And fierie foaming Steeds; what stood, recoyld
Orewearied, through the faint Satanic Host
Defensive scarse, or with pale fear surpris'd,
Then first with fear surpris'd and sense of paine
Fled ignominious, to such evil brought
By sinne of disobedience, till that hour
Not liable to fear or flight or paine.
Far otherwise th' inviolable Saints

In Cubic Phalanx firm advanc't entire,

Invulnerable, impenitrably arm'd: 400

Such high advantages thir innocence

Gave them above thir foes, not to have sinnd,

Not to have disobei'd; in fight they stood

Unwearied, unobnoxious to be pain'd

By wound, though from thir place by violence mov'd.

   Now Night her course began, and over Heav'n

Inducing darkness, grateful truce impos'd,

And silence on the odious dinn of Warr:

Under her Cloudie covert both retir'd,

Victor and Vanquisht: on the foughten field   410

Michael and his Angels prevalent

Encamping, plac'd in Guard thir Watches round,

Chrerubic waving fires: on th' other part

Satan with his rebellious disappeerd,

Far in the dark dislodg'd, and void of rest,

His Potentates to Councel call'd by night;

And in the midst thus undismai'd began.

   O now in danger tri'd, now known in Armes

Not to be overpowerd, Companions deare,

Found worthy not of Libertie alone,   420

Too mean pretense, but what we more affect,

Honour, Dominion, Glorie, and renowne,

Who have sustaind one day in doubtful fight,

(And if one day, why not Eternal dayes?)

What Heavens Lord had powerfullest to send

Against us from about his Throne, and judg'd

Sufficient to subdue us to his will,

But proves not so: then fallible, it seems,
Of future we may deem him, though till now
Omniscient thought. True is, less firmly arm'd,   430
Some disadvantage we endur'd and paine,
Till now not known, but known as soon contemnd,
Since now we find this our Empyreal forme
Incapable of mortal injurie
Imperishable, and though peirc'd with wound,
Soon closing, and by native vigour heal'd.
Of evil then so small as easie think
The remedie; perhaps more valid Armes,
Weapons more violent, when next we meet,
May serve to better us, and worse our foes,   440
Or equal what between us made the odds,
In Nature none: if other hidden cause
Left them Superiour, while we can preserve
Unhurt our mindes, and understanding sound,
Due search and consultation will disclose.

   He sat; and in th' assembly next upstood
Nisroc, of Principalities the prime;
As one he stood escap't from cruel fight,
Sore toild, his riv'n Armes to havoc hewn,
And cloudie in aspect thus answering spake.   450
Deliverer from new Lords, leader to free
Enjoyment of our right as Gods; yet hard
For Gods, and too unequal work we find
Against unequal armes to fight in paine,
Against unpaind, impassive; from which evil
Ruin must needs ensue; for what availes

Valour or strength, though matchless, quelld with pain
Which all subdues, and makes remiss the hands
Of Mightiest. Sense of pleasure we may well
Spare out of life perhaps, and not repine,   460
But live content, which is the calmest life:
But pain is perfet miserie, the worst
Of evils, and excessive, overturnes
All patience. He who therefore can invent
With what more forcible we may offend
Our yet unwounded Enemies, or arme
Our selves with like defence, to mee deserves
No less then for deliverance what we owe.
    Whereto with look compos'd *Satan* repli'd.
Not uninvented that, which thou aright   470
Beleivst so main to our success, I bring;
Which of us who beholds the bright surface
Of this Ethereous mould whereon we stand,
This continent of spacious Heav'n, adornd
With Plant, Fruit, Flour Ambrosial, Gemms & Gold,
Whose Eye so superficially surveyes
These things, as not to mind from whence they grow
Deep under ground, materials dark and crude,
Of spiritous and fierie spume, till toucht
With Heav'ns ray, and temperd they shoot forth   480
So beauteous, op'ning to the ambient light.
These in thir dark Nativitie the Deep
Shall yeild us, pregnant with infernal flame,
Which into hallow Engins long and round
Thick-rammd, at th' other bore with touch of fire

Dilated and infuriate shall send forth

From far with thundring noise among our foes

Such implements of mischief as shall dash

To pieces, and orewhelm whatever stands

Adverse, that they shall fear we have disarmd   490

The Thunderer of his only dreaded bolt.

Nor long shall be our labour, yet ere dawne,

Effect shall end our wish. Mean while revive;

Abandon fear; to strength and counsel joind

Think nothing hard, much less to be despaird.

He ended, and his words thir drooping chere

Enlightn'd, and thir languisht hope reviv'd.

Th' invention all admir'd, and each, how hee

To be th' inventer miss'd, so easie it seemd

Once found, which yet unfound most would have thought   500

Impossible: yet haply of thy Race

In future dayes, if Malice should abound,

Some one intent on mischief, or inspir'd

With dev'lish machination might devise

Like instrument to plague the Sons of men

For sin, on warr and mutual slaughter bent.

Forthwith from Councel to the work they flew,

None arguing stood, innumerable hands

Were ready, in a moment up they turnd

Wide the Celestial soile, and saw beneath   510

Th' originals of Nature in thir crude

Conception; Sulphurous and Nitrous Foame

They found, they mingl'd, and with suttle Art,

Concocted and adusted they reduc'd

To blackest grain, and into store conveyd:
Part hidd'n veins diggd up (nor hath this Earth
Entrails unlike) of Mineral and Stone,
Whereof to found thir Engins and thir Balls
Of missive ruin; part incentive reed
Provide, pernicious with one touch to fire.   520
So all ere day-spring, under conscious Night
Secret they finish'd, and in order set,
With silent circumspection unespi'd.
Now when fair Morn Orient in Heav'n appeerd
Up rose the Victor Angels, and to Arms
The matin Trumpet Sung: in Arms they stood
Of Golden Panoplie, refulgent Host,
Soon banded; others from the dawning Hills
Lookd round, and Scouts each Coast light-armed scoure,
Each quarter, to descrie the distant foe,   530
Where lodg'd, or whither fled, or if for fight,
In motion or in alt: him soon they met
Under spred Ensignes moving nigh, in slow
But firm Battalion; back with speediest Sail
Zophiel, of Cherubim the swiftest wing,
Came flying, and in mid Aire aloud thus cri'd.
    Arme, Warriours, Arme for fight, the foe at hand,
Whom fled we thought, will save us long pursuit
This day, fear not his flight; so thick a Cloud
He comes, and settl'd in his face I see   540
Sad resolution and secure: let each
His Adamantine coat gird well, and each
Fit well his Helme, gripe fast his orbed Shield,

Born eevn or high, for this day will pour down,
If I conjecture aught, no drizling showr,
But ratling storm of Arrows barbd with fire.
So warnd he them aware themselves, and soon
In order, quit of all impediment;
Instant without disturb they took Allarm,
And onward move Embattelld; when behold   550
Not distant far with heavie pace the Foe
Approaching gross and huge; in hollow Cube
Training his devilish Enginrie, impal'd
On every side with shaddowing Squadrons Deep,
To hide the fraud. At interview both stood
A while, but suddenly at head appeerd
Satan: And thus was heard Commanding loud.
    Vangard, to Right and Left the Front unfould;
That all may see who hate us, how we seek
Peace and composure, and with open brest   560
Stand readie to receive them, if they like
Our overture, and turn not back perverse;
But that I doubt, however witness Heaven,
Heav'n witness thou anon, while we discharge
Freely our part: yee who appointed stand
Do as you have in charge, and briefly touch
What we propound, and loud that all may hear.
    So scoffing in ambiguous words, he scarce
Had ended; when to Right and Left the Front
Divided, and to either Flank retir'd.   570
Which to our eyes discoverd new and strange,
A triple-mounted row of Pillars laid

On Wheels (for like to Pillars most they seem'd
Or hollow'd bodies made of Oak or Firr
With branches lopt, in Wood or Mountain fell'd)
Brass, Iron, Stonie mould, had not thir mouthes
With hideous orifice gap't on us wide,
Portending hollow truce; at each behind
A Seraph stood, and in his hand a Reed
Stood waving tipt with fire; while we suspense,   580
Collected stood within our thoughts amus'd,
Not long, for sudden all at once thir Reeds
Put forth, and to a narrow vent appli'd
With nicest touch. Immediate in a flame,
But soon obscur'd with smoak, all Heav'n appeerd,
From those deep-throated Engins belcht, whose roar
Emboweld with outragious noise the Air,
And all her entrails tore, disgorging foule
Thir devillish glut, chaind Thunderbolts, and Hail
Of Iron Globes, which on the Victor Host   590
Level'd, with such impetuous furie smote,
That whom they hit, none on thir feet might stand,
Though standing else as Rocks, but down they fell
By thousands, Angel on Arch-Angel rowl'd;
The sooner for thir Arms, unarm'd they might
Have easily as Spirits evaded swift
By quick contraction or remove; but now
Foule dissipation follow'd and forc't rout;
Nor serv'd it to relax thir serried files,
What should they do? if on they rusht, repulse   600
Repeated, and indecent overthrow

Doubl'd, would render them yet more despis'd,

And to thir foes a laughter; for in view

Stood rankt of Seraphim another row

In posture to displode thir second tire

Of Thunder: back defeated to return

They worse abhorr'd. *Satan* beheld thir plight,

And to his Mates thus in derision call'd.

  O Friends, why come not on these Victors proud?

Ere while they fierce were coming, and when wee,   610

To entertain them fair with open Front

And Brest, (what could we more?) propounded terms

Of composition, strait they chang'd thir minds,

Flew off, and into strange vagaries fell,

As they would dance, yet for a dance they seemd

Somwhat extravagant and wilde, perhaps

For joy of offerd peace: but I suppose

If our proposals once again were heard

We should compel them to a quick result.

  To whom thus *Belial* in like gamesom mood.   620

Leader, the terms we sent were terms of weight,

Of hard contents, and full of force urg'd home,

Such as we might perceive amus'd them all,

And stumbl'd many, who receives them right,

Had need from head to foot well understand;

Not understood, this gift they have besides,

They shew us when our foes walk not upright.

  So they among themselves in pleasant veine

Stood scoffing, highthn'd in thir thoughts beyond

All doubt of Victorie, eternal might   630

To match with thir inventions they presum'd
So easie, and of his Thunder made a scorn,
And all his Host derided, while they stood
A while in trouble; but they stood not long,
Rage prompted them at length, & found them arms
Against such hellish mischief fit to oppose.
Forthwith (behold the excellence, the power
Which God hath in his mighty Angels plac'd)
Thir Arms away they threw, and to the Hills
(For Earth hath this variety from Heav'n   640
Of pleasure situate in Hill and Dale)
Light as the Lightning glimps they ran, they flew,
From thir foundations loosning to an fro
They pluckt the seated Hills with all thir load,
Rocks, Waters, Woods, and by the shaggie tops
Up lifting bore them in thir hands: Amaze,
Be sure, and terrour seis'd the rebel Host,
When coming towards them so dread they saw
The bottom of the Mountains upward turn'd,
Till on those cursed Engins triple-row   650
They saw them whelmd, and all thir confidence
Under the weight of Mountains buried deep,
Themselves invaded next, and on thir heads
Main Promontories flung, which in the Air
Came shadowing, and opprest whole Legions arm'd,
Thir armor help'd thir harm, crush't in and brus'd
Into thir substance pent, which wrought them pain
Implacable, and many a dolorous groan,
Long strugling underneath, ere they could wind

Out of such prison, though Spirits of purest light,   660

Purest at first, now gross by sinning grown.

The rest in imitation to like Armes

Betook them, and the neighbouring Hills uptore;

So Hills amid the Air encounterd Hills

Hurl'd to and fro with jaculation dire,

That under ground they fought in dismal shade;

Infernal noise; Warr seem'd a civil Game

To this uproar; horrid confusion heapt

Upon confusion rose: and now all Heav'n

Had gone to wrack, with ruin overspred,   670

Had not th' Almightie Father where he sits

Shrin'd in his Sanctuarie of Heav'n secure,

Consulting on the sum of things, foreseen

This tumult, and permitted all, advis'd:

That his great purpose he might so fulfill,

To honour his Anointed Son aveng'd

Upon his enemies, and to declare

All power on him transferr'd: whence to his Son

Th' Assessor of his Throne he thus began.

   Effulgence of my Glorie, Son belov'd,   680

Son in whose face invisible is beheld

Visibly, what by Deitie I am,

And in whose hand what by Decree I doe,

Second Omnipotence, two dayes are past,

Two dayes, as we compute the dayes of Heav'n,

Since *Michael* and his Powers went forth to tame

These disobedient; sore hath been thir fight,

As likeliest was, when two such Foes met arm'd;

For to themselves I left them, and thou knowst,
Equal in their Creation they were form'd, 690
Save what sin hath impaird, which yet hath wrought
Insensibly, for I suspend thir doom;
Whence in perpetual fight they needs must last
Endless, and no solution will be found:
Warr wearied hath perform'd what Warr can do,
And to disorder'd rage let loose the reines,
With Mountains as with Weapons arm'd, which makes
Wild work in Heav'n, and dangerous to the maine.
Two dayes are therefore past, the third is thine;
For thee I have ordain'd it, and thus farr 700
Have sufferd, that the Gloirie may be thine
Of ending this great Warr, since none but Thou
Can end it. Into thee such Vertue and Grace
Immense I have transfus'd, that all may know
In Heav'n and Hell thy Power above compare,
And this perverse Commotion governd thus,
To manifest thee worthiest to be Heir
Of all things, to be Heir and to be King
By Sacred Unction, thy deserved right.
Go then thou Mightiest in thy Fathers might, 710
Ascend my Chariot, guide the rapid Wheeles
That shake Heav'ns basis, bring forth all my Warr,
My Bow and Thunder, my Almightie Arms
Gird on, and Sword upon thy puissant Thigh;
Pursue these sons of Darkness, drive them out
From all Heav'ns bounds into the utter Deep:
There let them learn, as likes them, to despise

God and *Messiah* his anointed King.

    He said, and on his Son with Rayes direct

Shon full, he all his Father full exprest   720

Ineffably into his face receiv'd,

And thus the filial Godhead answerng spake.

    O Father, O Supream of heav'nly Thrones,

First, Highest, Holiest, Best, thou alwayes seekst

To glorifie thy Son, I alwayes thee,

As is most just; this I my Glorie account,

My exaltation, and my whole delight,

That thou in me well pleas'd, declarst thy will

Fulfill'd, which to fulfil is all my bliss.

Scepter and Power, thy giving, I assume,   730

And gladlier shall resign, when in the end

Thou shalt be All in All, and I in thee

For ever, and in mee all whom thou lov'st:

But whom thou hat'st, I hate, and can put on

Thy terrors, as I put thy mildness on,

Image of thee in all things; and shall soon,

Armd with thy might, rid heav'n of these rebell'd,

To thir prepar'd ill Mansion driven down

To chains of Darkness, and th' undying Worm,

That from thy just obedience could revolt,   740

Whom to obey is happiness entire.

Then shall thy Saints unmixt, and from th' impure

Farr separate, circling thy holy Mount

Unfained *Halleluiahs* to thee sing,

Hymns of high praise, and I among them chief.

So said, he o're his Scepter bowing, rose

From the right hand of Glorie where he sate,
And the third sacred Morn began to shine
Dawning through Heav'n: forth rush'd with whirlwind sound
The Chariot of Paternal Deitie,   750
Flashing thick flames, Wheele within Wheele undrawn,
It self instinct with Spirit, but convoyd
By four Cherubic shapes, four Faces each
Had wondrous, as with Starrs thir bodies all
And Wings were set with Eyes, with Eyes the Wheels
Of Beril, and careering Fires between;
Over thir heads a chrystal Firmament,
Whereon a Saphir Throne, inlaid with pure
Amber, and colours of the showrie Arch.
Hee in Celestial Panoplie all armd   760
Of radiant *Urim*, work divinely wrought,
Ascended, at this right hand Victorie
Sate Eagle-wing'd, beside him hung his Bow
And Quiver with three-bolted Thunder stor'd,
And from about him fierce Effusion rowld
Of smoak and bickering flame, and sparkles dire;
Attended with ten thousand thousand Saints,
He onward came, farr off his coming shon,
And twentie thousand (I thir number heard)
Chariots of God, half on each hand were seen: 770
Hee on the wings of Cherub rode sublime
On the Crystallin Skie, in Saphir Thron'd.
Illustrious farr and wide, but by his own
First seen, them unexpected joy surpriz'd,
When the great Ensign of *Messiah* blaz'd

Aloft by Angels born, his Sign in Heav'n:
Under whose Conduct *Michael* soon reduc'd
His Armie, circumfus'd on either Wing,
Under thir Head imbodied all in one.
Before him Power Divine his way prepar'd;   780
At his command the uprooted Hills retir'd
Each to his place, they heard his voice and went
Obsequious, Heav'n his wonted face renewd,
And with fresh Flourets Hill and Valley smil'd.
This saw his hapless Foes, but stood obdur'd,
And to rebellious fight rallied thir Powers
Insensate, hope conceiving from despair.
In heav'nly Spirits could such perverseness dwell?
But to convince the proud what Signs availe,
Or Wonders move th' obdurate to relent?   790
They hard'nd more by what might most reclame,
Grieving to see his Glorie, at the sight
Took envie, and aspiring to his highth,
Stood reimbattell'd fierce, by force or fraud
Weening to prosper, and at length prevaile
Against God and *Messiah*, or to fall
In universal ruin last, and now
To final Battel drew, disdaining flight,
Or faint retreat; when the great Son of God
To all his Host on either hand thus spake.   800
    Stand still in bright array ye Saints, here stand
Ye Angels arm'd, this day from Battel rest;
Faithful hath been your Warfare, and of God
Accepted, fearless in his righteous Cause,

And as ye have receivd, so have ye don
Invincibly; but of this cursed crew
The punishment to other hand belongs,
Vengeance is his, or whose he sole appoints;
Number to this dayes work is not ordain'd
Nor multitude, stand onely and behold   810
Gods indignation on these Godless pourd
By mee; not you but mee they have despis'd,
Yet envied; against mee is all thir rage,
Because the Father, t' whom in Heav'n supream
Kingdom and Power and Glorie appertains,
Hath honourd me according to his will.
Therefore to mee thir doom he hath assign'd;
That they may have thir wish, to trie with mee
In Battel which the stronger proves, they all,
Or I alone against them, since by strength   820
They measure all, of other excellence
Not emulous, nor care who them excells;
Nor other strife with thcm do I voutsafe.
    So spake the Son, and into terrour chang'd
His count'nance too severe to be beheld
And full of wrauth bent on his Enemies.
At once the Four spred out thir Starrie wings
With dreadful shade contiguous, and the Orbes
Of his fierce Chariot rowld, as with the sound
Of torrent Floods, or of a numerous Host.   830
Hee on his impious Foes right onward drove,
Gloomie as Night; under his burning Wheeles
The stedfast Empyrean shook throughout,

All but the Throne it self of God. Full soon
Among them he arriv'd; in his right hand
Grasping ten thousand Thunders, which he sent
Before him, such as in thir Soules infix'd
Plagues; they astonisht all resistance lost,
All courage; down thir idle weapons drop'd;
O're Shields and Helmes, and helmed heads he rode   840
Of Thrones and mighty Seraphim prostrate,
That wish'd the Mountains now might be again
Thrown on them as a shelter from his ire.
Nor less on either side tempestuous fell
His arrows, from the fourfold-visag'd Foure,
Distinct with eyes, and from the living Wheels,
Distinct alike with multitude of eyes,
One Spirit in them rul'd, and every eye
Glar'd lightning, and shot forth pernicious fire
Among th' accurst, that witherd all thir strength,   850
And of thir wonted vigour lef them draind,
Exhausted, spiritless, afflicted, fall'n.
Yet half his strength he put not forth, but check'd
His Thunder in mid Volie, for he meant
Not to destroy, but root them out of Heav'n:
The overthrown he rais'd, and as a Heard
Of Goats or timerous flock together throngd
Drove them before him Thunder-struck, pursu'd
With terrors and with furies to the bounds
And Chrystall wall of Heav'n, which op'ning wide,   860
Rowld inward, and a spacious Gap disclos'd
Into the wastful Deep; the monstrous sight

Strook them with horrow backward, but far worse
Urg'd them behind; headlong themselvs they threw
Down from the verge of Heav'n, Eternal wrauth
Burnt after them to the bottomless pit.
　　Hell heard th' unsufferable noise, Hell saw
Heav'n ruining from Heav'n and would have fled
Affrighted; but strict Fate had cast too deep
Her dark foundations, and too fast had bound.   870
Nine dayes they fell; confounded *Chaos* roard,
And felt tenfold confusion in thir fall
Through his wilde Anarchie, so huge a rout
Incumberd him with ruin: Hell at last
Yawning receavd them whole, and on them clos'd,
Hell thir fit habitation fraught with fire
Unquenchable, the house of woe and paine.
Disburd'nd Heav'n rejoic'd, and soon repaird
Her mural breach, returning whence it rowld.
Sole Victor from th' expulsion of his Foes   880
Messiah his triumphal Chariot turnd:
To meet him all his Saints, who silent stood
Eye witnesses of his Almightie Acts,
With Jubilie advanc'd; and as they went,
Shaded with branching Palme, each order bright,
Sung Triumph, and him sung Victorious King,
Son, Heire, and Lord, to him Dominion giv'n,
Worthiest to Reign: he celebrated rode
Triumphant through mid Heav'n, into the Courts
And Temple of his mightie Father Thron'd   890
On high; who into Glorie him receav'd,

Where now he sits at the right hand of bliss.

   Thus measuring things in Heav'n by things on Earth

At thy request, and that thou maist beware

By what is past, to thee I have reveal'd

What might have else to human Race bin hid;

The discord which befel, and Warr in Heav'n

Among th' Angelic Powers, and the deep fall

Of those too high aspiring, who rebelld

With *Satan*, hee who envies now thy state,   900

Who now is plotting how he may seduce

Thee also from obedience, that with him

Bereavd of happiness thou maist partake

His punishment, Eternal miserie;

Which would be all his solace and revenge,

As a despite don against the most High,

Thee once to gaine Companion of his woe.

But list'n not to his Temptations, warne

Thy weaker; let it profit thee to have heard

By terrible Example the reward   910

Of disobedience; firm they might have stood,

Yet fell; remember, and fear to transgress.

       The End of the Sixth Book.

PARADISE
LOST

BOOK VII.

DEscend from Heav'n *Urania*, by that name
If rightly thou art call'd, whose Voice divine
Following, above th' *Olympian* Hill I soare,
Above the flight of *Pegasean* wing.
The meaning, not the Name I call: for thou
Nor of the Muses nine, nor on the top
Of old *Olympus* dwell'st, but Heav'nlie borne,
Before the Hills appeerd, or Fountain flow'd,
Thou with Eternal wisdom didst converse,
Wisdom thy Sister, and with her didst play   10
In presence of th' Almightie Father, pleas'd
With thy Celestial Song. Up led by thee
Into the Heav'n of Heav'ns I have presum'd,
An Earthlie Guest, and drawn Empryeal Aire,
Thy tempring; with like safetie guided down
Return me to my Native Element:
Least from this flying Steed unrein'd, (as once
Bellerophon, though from a lower Clime)
Dismounted, on th' *Aleian* Field I fall
Erroneous, there to wander and forlorne.   20
Half yet remaines unsung, but narrower bound

Within the visible Diurnal Spheare;
Standing on Earth, not rapt above the Pole,
More safe I Sing with mortal voice, unchang'd
To hoarce or mute, though fall'n on evil dayes,
On evil dayes though fall'n, and evil tongues;
In darkness, and with dangers compast round,
And solitude; yet not alone, while thou
Visit'st my slumbers Nightly, or when Morn
Purples the East: still govern thou my Song,   30
Urania, and fit audience find, though few.
But drive farr off the barbarous dissonance
Of *Bacchus* and his Revellers, the Race
Of that wilde Rout that tore the *Thracian* Bard
In *Rhodope*, where Woods and Rocks and Eares
To rapture, till the savage clamor dround
Both Harp and Voice; nor could the Muse defend
Her Son. So fail not thou, who thee implores:
For thou art Heav'nlie, shee an empty dreame.
    Say Goddess, what ensu'd when *Raphael*,   40
The affable Arch-angel, had forewarn'd
Adam by dire example to beware
Apostasie, by what befell in Heaven
To those Apostates, least the like befall
In Paradise to *Adam* or his Race,
Charg'd not to touch the interdicted Tree,
If they transgress, and slight that sole command,
So easily obeyd amid the choice
Of all tasts else to please thir appetite,
Though wandring. He with his consorted *Eve*   50

The storie heard attentive, and was fill'd
With admiration, and deep Muse to heare
Of things so high and strange, things to thir thought
So unimaginable as hate in Heav'n,
And Warr so neer the Peace of God in bliss
With such confusion: but the evil soon
Driv'n back redounded as a flood on those
From whom it sprung, impossible to mix
With Blessedness. Whence *Adam* soon repeal'd
The doubts that in his heart arose: and now   60
Led on, yet sinless, with desire to know
What neerer might concern him, how this World
Of Heav'n and Earth conspicuous first began,
When, and whereof created, for what cause,
What within *Eden* or without was done
Before his memorie, as one whose drouth
Yet scarce allay'd still eyes the current streame,
Whose liquid murmur heard new thirst excites,
Proceeded thus to ask his Heav'nly Guest.

Great things, and full of wonder in our eares,   70
Farr differing from this World, thou hast reveal'd
Divine Interpreter, by favour sent
Down from the Empyrean to forewarne
Us timely of what might else have bin our loss,
Unknown, which human knowledg could not reach:
For which to the infinitly Good we owe
Immortal thanks, and his admonishment
Receave with solemne purpose to observe
Immutably his sovran will, the end

Of what we are. But since thou hast voutsaf't   80
Gently for our instruction to impart
Things above Earthly thought, which yet concernd
Our knowing, as to highest wisdom seemd,
Deign to descend now lower, and relate
What may no less perhaps availe us known,
How first began this Heav'n which we behold
Distant so high, with moving Fires adornd
Innumerable, and this which yeelds or fills
All space, the ambient Aire wide interfus'd
Imbracing round this florid Earth, what cause   90
Mov'd the Creator in his holy Rest
Through all Eternitie so late to build
In *Chaos*, and the work begun, how soon
Absolv'd, if unforbid thou maist unfould
What wee, not to explore the secrets aske
Of his Eternal Empire, but the more
To magnifie his works, the more we know.
And the great Light of Day yet wants to run
Much of his Race though steep, suspens in Heav'n
Held by thy voice, thy potent voice he heares,   100
And longer will delay to heare thee tell
His Generation, and the rising Birth
Of Nature from the unapparent Deep:
Or if the Starr of Eevning and the Moon
Haste to thy audience, Night with her will bring
Silence, and Sleep listning to thee will watch,
Or we can bid his absence, till thy Song
End, and dismiss thee ere the Morning shine.

Thus *Adam* his illustrous Guest besought:

And thus the Godlike Angel answerd milde.   110

This also thy request with caution askt

Obtaine: though to recount Almightie works

What words or tongue of Seraph can suffice,

Or heart of man suffice to comprehend?

Yet what thou canst attain, which best may serve

To glorifie the Maker, and inferr

Thee also happier, shall not be withheld

Thy hearing, such Commission from above

I have receav'd, to answer thy desire

Of knowledge within bounds; beyond abstain   120

To ask, nor let thine own inventions hope

Things not reveal'd, which th 'invisible King,

Onely Omniscient, hath supprest in Night,

To none communicable in Earth or Heaven:

Anough is left besides to search and know.

But Knowledge is as food, and needs no less

Her Temperance over Appetite, to know

In measure what the mind may well contain,

Oppresses else with Surfet, and soon turns

Wisdom to Folly, as Nourishment to Winde.   130

Know then, that after *Lucifer* from Heav'n

(So call him, brighter once amidst the Host

Of Angels, then that Starr the Starrs among)

Fell with his flaming Legions through the Deep

Into his place, and the great Son returnd

Victorious with his Saints, th' Omnipotent

Eternal Father from his Throne beheld

Thir multitude, and to his Son thus spake.

   At least our envious Foe hath fail'd, who thought

All like himself rebellious, by whose aid   140

This inaccessible high strength, the seat

Of Deitie supream, us dispossest,

He trusted to have seis'd, and into fraud

Drew many, whom thir place knows here no more;

Yet farr the greater part have kept, I see,

Thir station, Heav'n yet populous retaines

Number sufficient to possess her Realmes

Though wide, and this high Temple to frequent

With Ministeries due and solemn Rites:

But least his heart exalt him in the harme   150

Already done, to have dispeopl'd Heav'n,

My damage fondly deem'd, I can repaire

That detriment, if such it be to lose

Self-lost, and in a moment will create

Another World, out of one man a Race

Of men innumerable, there to dwell,

Not here, till by degrees of merit rais'd

They open to themselves at length the way

Up hither, under long obedience tri'd,

And Earth tbe chang'd to Heavn, & Heav'n to Earth,   160

One Kingdom, Joy and Union without end.

Mean while inhabit laxe, ye Powers of Heav'n,

And thou my Word, begotten Son, by thee

This I perform, speak thou, and be it don:

My overshadowing Spirit and might with thee

I send along, ride forth, and bid the Deep

Within appointed bounds be Heav'n and Earth,

Boundless the Deep, because I am who fill

Infinitude, nor vacuous the space.

Though I uncircumscrib'd my self retire,   170

And put not forth my goodness, which is free

To act or not, Necessitie and Chance

Approach not mee, and what I will is Fate.

　So spake th' Almightie, and to what he spake

His Word, the Filial Godhead, gave effect.

Immediate are the Acts of God, more swift

Then time or motion, but to human ears

Cannot without process of speech be told,

So told as earthly notion can receave.

Great triumph and rejoycing was in Heav'n   180

When such was heard declar'd the Almightie's will;

Glorie they sung to the most High, good will

To future men, and in thir dwellings peace:

Glorie to him whose just avenging ire

Had driven out th' ungodly from his sight

And th' habitations of the just; to him

Glorie and praise, whose wisdom had ordain'd

Good out of evil to create, in stead

Of Spirits maligne a better Race to bring

Into thir vacant room, and thence diffuse   190

His good to Worlds and Ages infinite.

So sang the Hierarchies: Mean while the Son

On his great Expedition now appeer'd,

Girt with Omnipotence, with Radiance crown'd

Of Majestie Divine, Sapience and Love

Immense, and all his Father in him shon.

About his Chariot numberless were pour'd

Cherub and Seraph, Potentates and Thrones,

And Vertues, winged Spirits, and Chariots wing'd,

From the Armoury of God, where stand of old   200

Myriads between two brazen Mountains lodg'd

Against a solemn day, harnest at hand,

Celestial Equipage; and now came forth

Spontaneous, for within them Spirit livd,

Attendant on thir Lord: Heav'n op'nd wide

Her ever during Gates, Harmonious sound

On golden Hinges moving, to let forth

The King of Glorie in his powerful Word

And Spirit coming to create new Worlds.

On heav'nly ground they stood, and from the shore   210

They view'd the vast immeasurable Abyss

Outrageous as a Sea, dark, wasteful, wilde,

Up from the bottom turn'd by furious windes

And surging waves, as Mountains to assault

Heav'ns highth, and with the Center mix the Pole.

 Silence, ye troubl'd waves, and thou Deep, peace,

Said then th' Omnific Word, your discord end:

 Nor staid, but on the Wings of Cherubim

Uplifted, in Paternal Glorie rode

Farr into *Chaos,* and the World unborn;   220

For *Chaos* heard his voice: him all his Traine

Follow'd in bright procession to behold

Creation, and the wonders of his might.

Then staid the fervid Wheeles, and in his hand

He took the golden Compasses, prepar'd
In God Eternal store, to circumscribe
This Universe, and all created things:
One foot he center'd, and the other turn'd
Round through the vast profunditie obscure,
And said, thus farr extend, thus farr thy bounds,   230
This be thy just Circumference, O World.
Thus God the Heav'n created, thus the Earth,
Matter unform'd and void: Darkness profound
Cover'd th' Abyss: but on the watrie calme
His brooding wings the Spirit of God outspred,
And vital vertue infus'd, and vital warmth
Throughout the fluid Mass, but downward purg'd
The black tartareous cold infernal dregs
Adverse to life: then founded, then conglob'd
Like things to like, the rest to several place   240
Disparted, and between spun out the Air,
And Earth self-ballanc't on her Center hung.
    Let ther be Light, said God, and forthwith Light
Ethereal, first of things, quintessence pure
Sprung from the Deep, and from her Native East
To journie through the airie gloom began,
Sphear'd in a radiant Cloud, for yet the Sun
Was not; shee in a cloudie Tabernacle
Sojourn'd the while. God saw the Light was good;
And light from darkness by the Hemisphere   250
Divided: Light the Day, and Darkness Night
He nam'd. Thus was the first Day Eev'n and Morn:
Nor past uncelebrated, nor unsung

By the Celestial Quires, when Orient Light
Exhaling first from Darkness they beheld;
Birth-day of Heav'n and Earth; with joy and shout
The hollow Universal Orb they fill'd,
And touch't thir Golden Harps, & hymning prais'd
God and his works, Creatour him they sung,
Both when first Eevning was, and when first Morn.   260
    Again, God said, let ther be Firmament
Amid the Waters, and let it divide
The Waters from the Waters: and God made
The Firmament, expanse of liquid, pure,
Transparent, Elemental Air, diffus'd
In circuit to the uttermost convex
Of this great Round: partition firm and sure,
The Waters underneath from those above
Dividing: for as Earth, so hee the World
Built on circumfluous Waters calme, in wide   270
Crystallin Ocean, and the loud misrule
Of *Chaos* farr remov'd, least fierce extreames
Contiguous might distemper the whole frame:
And Heav'n he nam'd the Firmament: So Eev'n
And Morning *Chorus* sung the second Day.
    The Earth was form'd, but in the Womb as yet
Of Waters, Embryon immature involv'd,
Appeer'd not: over all the face of Earth
Main Ocean flow'd, not idle, but with warme
Prolific humour soft'ning all her Globe,   280
Fermented the great Mother to conceave,
Satiate with genial moisture, when God said

Be gather'd now ye Waters under Heav'n
Into one place, and let dry Land appeer.
Immediately the Mountains huge appeer
Emergent, and thir broad bare backs upheave
Into the Clouds, thir tops ascend the Skie:
So high as heav'd the tumid Hills, so low
Down sunk a hollow bottom broad and deep,
Capacious bed of Waters: thither they   290
Hasted with glad precipitance, uprowld
As drops on dust conglobing from the drie;
Part rise in crystal Wall, or ridge direct,
For haste; such flight the great command impress'd
On the swift flouds: as Armies at the call
Of Trumpet (for of Armies thou hast heard)
Troop to thir Standard, so the watrie throng,
Wave rowling after Wave, where way they found,
If steep, with torrent rapture, if through Plaine,
Soft-ebbing; nor withstood them Rock or Hill,   300
But they, or under ground, or circuit wide
With Serpent errour wandring, found thir way,
And on the washie Oose deep Channels wore;
Easie, e're God had bid the ground be drie,
All but within those banks, where Rivers now
Stream, and perpetual draw thir humid traine.
The dry Land, Earth, and the great receptacle
Of congregated Waters he call'd Seas:
And saw that it was good, and said, Let th' Earth
Put forth the verdant Grass, Herb yeilding Seed,   310
And Fruit Tree yeilding Fruit after her kind;

Whose Seed is in her self upon the Earth.

He scarce had said, when the bare Earth, till then

Desert and bare, unsightly, unadorn'd,

Brought forth the tender Grass, whose verdure clad

Her Universal Face with pleasant green,

Then Herbs of every leaf, that sudden flour'd

Op'ning thir various colours, and made gay

Her bosom smelling sweet: and these scarce blown,

Forth flourish't thick the clustring Vine, forth crept   320

The swelling Gourd, up stood the cornie Reed

Embattell'd in her field: add the humble Shrub,

And Bush with frizl'd hair implicit: last

Rose as in Dance the stately Trees, and spred

Thir branches hung with copious Fruit; or gemm'd

Thir Blossoms: with high Woods the Hills were crown'd,

With tufts the vallies & each fountain side,

With borders long the Rivers. That Earth now

Seemd like to Heav'n, a seat where Gods might dwell,

Or wander with delight, and love to haunt   330

Her sacred shades : though God had yet not rain'd

Upon the Earth, and man to till the ground

None was, but from the Earth a dewie Mist

Went up and waterd all the ground, and each

Plant of the field, which e're it was in the Earth

God made, and every Herb, before it grew

On the green stemm; God saw that it was good:

So Eev'n and Morn recorded the Third Day.

    Again th' Almightie spake: Let there be Lights

High in th' expanse of Heaven to divide   340

The Day from Night; and let them be for Signes,

For Seasons, and for Dayes, and circling Years,

And let them be for Lights as I ordaine

Thir Office in the Firmament of Heav'n

To give Light on the Earth; and it was so.

And God made two great Lights, great for thir use

To Man, the greater to have rule by Day,

The less by Night alterne: and made the Starrs,

And set them in the Firmament of Heav'n

To illuminate the Earth, and rule the Day   350

In thir vicissitude, and rule the Night,

And Light from Darkness to divide. God saw,

Surveying his great Work, that it was good:

For of Celestial Bodies first the Sun

A mightie Spheare he fram'd, unlightsom first,

Though of Ethereal Mould: then form'd the Moon

Globose, and everie magnitude of Starrs,

And sowd with Starrs the Heav'n thick as a field:

Of Light by farr the greater part he took,

Transplanted from her cloudie Shrine, and plac'd   360

In the Suns orb, made porous to receive

And drink the liquid Light, firm to retaine

Her gather'd beams, great Palace now of Light.

Hither as to thir Fountain other Starrs

Repairing, in thir gold'n Urns draw Light,

And hence the Morning Planet guilds her horns;

By tincture or reflection they augment

Thir small peculiar, though from human sight

So farr remote, with diminution seen.

First in his East the glorious Lamp was seen,   370
Regent of Day, and all th' Horizon round
Invested with bright Rayes, jocond to run
His Longitude through Heav'ns high rode: the gray
Dawn, and the *Pleiades* before him danc'd
Shedding sweet influence: less bright the Moon,
But opposite in leveld West was set
His mirror, with full face borrowing her Light
From him, for other light she needed none
In that aspect, and still that distance keepes
Till night, then in the East her turn she shines,   380
Revolvd on Heav'ns great Axle, and her Reign
With thousand lesser Lights dividual holds,
With thousand thousand Starres, that then appeer'd
Spangling the Hemisphere: then first adornd
With thir bright Luminaries that Set and Rose,
Glad Eevning & glad Morn crownd the fourth day.
   And God said, let the Waters generate
Reptil with Spawn abundant, living Soule:
And let Fowle flie above the Earth, with wings
Displayd on the op'n Firmament of Heav'n.   390
And God created the great Whales, and each
Soul living, each that crept, which plenteously
The waters generated by thir kindes,
And every Bird of wing after his kinde;
And saw that it was good, and bless'd them, saying,
Be fruitful, multiply, and in the Seas
And Lakes and running Streams the waters fill;
And let the Fowle be multiply'd on the Earth.

Forthwith the Sounds and Seas, each Creek & Bay

With Frie innumerable swarme, and Shoales   400

Of Fish that with thir Finns and shining Scales

Glide under the green Wave, in Sculles that oft

Bank the mid Sea: part single or with mate

Graze the Sea weed thir pasture, & through Groves

Of Coral stray, or sporting with quick glance

Show to the Sun thir wav'd coats dropt with Gold,

Or in thir Pearlie shells at ease, attend

Moist nutriment, or under Rocks thir food

In jointed Armour watch: on smooth the Seale,

And bended Dolphins play: part huge of bulk   410

Wallowing unweildie, enormous in thir Gate

Tempest the Ocean: there Leviathan

Hugest of living Creatures, on the Deep

Stretcht like a Promontorie sleeps or swimmes,

And seems a moving Land, and at his Gilles

Draws in, and at his Trunck spouts out a Sea.

Mean while the tepid Caves, and Fens and shoares

Thir Brood as numerous hatch, from the Egg that soon

Bursting with kindly rupture forth disclos'd

Thir callow young, but featherd soon and fledge   420

They summ'd thir Penns, and soaring th' air sublime

With clang despis'd the ground, under a cloud

In prospect; there the Eagle and the Stork

On Cliffs and Cedar tops thir Eyries build:

Part loosly wing the Region, part more wise

In common, rang'd in figure wedge thir way,

Intelligent of seasons, and set forth

Thir Aierie Caravan high over Sea's

Flying, and over Lands with mutual wing

Easing thir flight; so stears the prudent Crane   430

Her annual Voiage, born on Windes; the Aire

Floats, as they pass, fann'd with unnumber'd plumes:

From Branch to Branch the smaller Birds with song

Solac'd the Woods, and spred thir painted wings

Till Ev'n, nor then the solemn Nightingal

Ceas'd warbling, but all night tun'd her soft layes:

Others on Silver Lakes and Rivers Bath'd

Thir downie Brest; the Swan with Arched neck

Between her white wings mantling proudly, Rowes

Her state with Oarie feet: yet oft they quit   440

The Dank, and rising on stiff Pennons, towre

The mid Aereal Skie: Others on ground

Walk'd firm; the crested Cock whose clarion sounds

The silent hours, and th' other whose gay Traine

Adorns him, colour'd with the Florid hue

Of Rainbows and Starrie Eyes. The Waters thus

With Fish replenisht, and the Aire with Fowle,

Ev'ning and Morn solemniz'd the Fift day.

   The Sixt, and of Creation last arose

With Eevning Harps and Mattin, when God said,   450

Let th' Earth bring forth Soul living in her kinde,

Cattell and Creeping things, and Beast of the Earth,

Each in their kinde. The Earth obey'd, and strait

Op'ning her fertil Woomb teem'd at a Birth

Innumerous living Creatures, perfet formes,

Limb'd and full grown: out of the ground up rose

As from his Laire the wilde Beast where he wonns
In Forrest wilde, in Thicket, Brake, or Den;
Among the Trees in Pairs they rose, they walk'd:
The Cattel in the Fields and Meddowes green: 460
Those rare and solitarie, these in flocks
Pasturing at once, and in broad Herds upsprung.
The grassie Clods now Calv'd, now half appeer'd
The Tawnie Lion, pawing to get free
His hinder parts, then springs as broke from Bonds,
And Rampant shakes his Brinded main; the Ounce,
The Libbard, and the Tyger, as the Moale
Rising, the crumbl'd Earth above them threw
In Hillocks; the swift Stag from under ground
Bore up his branching head: scarse from his mould   470
Behemoth biggest born of Earth upheav'd
His vastness: Fleec't the Flocks and bleating rose,
As Plants: ambiguous between Sea and Land
The River Horse and scalie Crocodile.
At once came forth whatever creeps the ground,
Insect or Worme; those wav'd thir limber fans
For wings, and smallest Lineaments exact
In all the Liveries dect of Summers pride
With spots of Gold and Purple, azure and green:
These as a line thir long dimension drew,   480
Streaking the ground with sinuous trace; not all
Minims of Nature; some of Serpent kinde
Wondrous in length and corpulence involv'd
Thir Snakie foulds, and added wings. First crept
The Parsimonious Emmet, provident

Of future, in small room large heart enclos'd,

Pattern of just equalitie perhaps

Hereafter, join'd in her popular Tribes

Of Commonalitie: swarming next appeer'd

The Femal Bee that feeds her Husband Drone   490

Deliciously, and builds her waxen Cells

With Honey stor'd: the rest are numberless,

And thou thir Natures know'st, and gav'st them Names,

Needless to thee repeated; nor unknown

The Serpent suttl'st Beast of all the field,

Of huge extent somtimes, with brazen Eyes

And hairie Main terrific, though to thee

Not noxious, but obedient at thy call.

Now Heav'n in all her Glorie shon, and rowld

Her motions, as the great first-Movers hand   500

First wheeld thir course; Earth in her rich attire

Consummate lovly smil'd; Aire, Water, Earth,

By Fowl, Fish, Beast, was flown, was swum, was walkt

Frequent; and of the Sixt day yet remain'd;

There wanted yet the Master work, the end

Of all yet don; a Creature who not prone

And Brute as other Creatures, but endu'd

With Sanctitie of Reason, might erect

His Stature, and upright with Front serene

Govern the rest, self-knowing, and from thence   510

Magnanimous to correspond with Heav'n,

But grateful to acknowledge whence his good

Descends, thither with heart and voice and eyes

Directed in Devotion, to adore

And worship God Supream, who made him chief
Of all his works: therefore the Omnipotent
Eternal Father (For where is not hee
Present) thus to his Son audibly spake.

    Let us make now Man in our image, Man
In our similitude, and let them rule   520
Over the Fish and Fowle of Sea and Aire,
Beast of the Field, and over all the Earth,
And every creeping thing that creeps the ground.
This said, he formd thee, *Adam*, thee O Man
Dust of the ground, and in thy nostrils breath'd
The breath of Life; in his own Image hee
Created thee, in the Image of God
Express, and thou becam'st a living Soul.
Male he created thee, but thy consort
Femal for Race; then bless'd Mankinde, and said,   530
Be fruitful, multiplie, and fill the Earth,
Subdue it, and throughout Dominion hold
Over Fish of the Sea, and Fowle of the Aire,
And every living thing that moves on the Earth.
Wherever thus created, for no place
Is yet distinct by name, thence, as thou know'st
He brought thee into this delicious Grove,
This Garden, planted with the Trees of God,
Delectable both to behold and taste;
And freely all thir pleasant fruit for food   540
Gave thee, all sorts are here that all th' Earth yeelds,
Varietie without end; but of the Tree
Which tasted works knowledge of Good and Evil,

Thou mai'st not; in the day thou eat'st, thou di'st;
Death is the penaltie impos'd, beware,
And govern well thy appetite, least sin
Surprise thee, and her black attendant Death.
Here finish'd hee, and all that he had made
View'd, and behold all was entirely good;
So Ev'n and Morn accomplish'd the Sixt day:　　　　550
Yet not till the Creator from his work
Desisting, though unwearied, up returnd
Up to the Heav'n of Heav'ns his high abode,
Thence to behold this new created World
Th' addition of his Empire, how it shew'd
In prospect from his Throne, how good, how faire,
Answering his great Idea. Up he rode
Followd with acclamation and the sound
Symphonious of ten thousand Harpes that tun'd
Angelic harmonies: the Earth, the Aire　　　　560
Resounded, (thou remember'st, for thou heardst)
The Heav'ns and all the Constellations rung,
The Planets in thir stations list'ning stood,
While the bright Pomp ascended jubilant.
Open, ye everlasting Gates, they sung,
Open, ye Heav'ns, your living dores; let in
The great Creator from his work returnd
Magnificent, his Six days work, a World;
Open, and henceforth oft; for God will deigne
To visit oft the dwellings of just Men　　　　570
Delighted, and with frequent intercourse
Thither will send his winged Messengers

On errands of supernal Grace. So sung
The glorious Train ascending: He through Heav'n,
That open'd wide her blazing Portals, led
To Gods Eternal house direct the way,
A broad and ample rode, whose dust is Gold
And pavement Starrs, as Starrs to thee appeer,
Seen in the Galaxie, that Milkie way
Which nightly as a circling Zone thou seest   580
Pouderd with Starrs. And now on Earth the Seaventh
Ecv'ning arose in *Eden*, for the Sun
Was set, and twilight from the East came on,
Forerunning Night; when at the holy mount
Of Heav'ns high-seated top, th' Impereal Throne
Of Godhead, fixt for ever firm and sure,
The Filial Power arriv'd, and sate him down
With his great Father, for he also went
Invisible, yet staid (such priviledge
Hath Omnipresence) and the work ordain'd,   590
Author and end of all things, and from work
Now resting, bless'd and hallowd the Seav'nth day,
As resting on that day from all his work,
But not in silence holy kept; the Harp
Had work and rested not, the solemn Pipe,
And Dulcimer, all Organs of sweet stop,
All sounds on Fret by String or Golden Wire
Temper'd soft Tunings, intermixt with Voice
Choral or Unison: of incense Clouds
Fuming from Golden Censers hid the Mount.   600
Creation and the Six dayes acts they sung,

Great are thy works, *Jehovah*, infinite

Thy power; what thought can measure thee or tongue

Relate thee; greater now in thy return

Then from the Giant Angels; thee that day

Thy Thunders magnifi'd; but to create

Is greater then created to destroy.

Who can impair thee, mighty King, or bound

Thy Empire? easily the proud attempt

Of Spirits apostat and thir Counsels vaine   610

Thou hast repeld, while impiously they thought

Thee to diminish, and from thee withdraw

The number of thy worshippers. Who seekes

To lessen thee, against his purpose serves

To manifest the more thy might: his evil

Thou usest, and from thence creat'st more good.

Witness this new-made World, another Heav'n

From Heaven Gate not farr, founded in view

On the cleer *Hyaline*, the Glassie Sea;

Of amplitude almost immense, with Starr's   620

Numerous, and every Starr perhaps a World

Of destind habitation; but thou know'st

Thir seasons: among these the seat of men,

Earth with her nether Ocean circumfus'd,

Thir pleasant dwelling place. Thrice happie men,

And sons of men, whom God hath thus advanc't,

Created in his Image, there to dwell

And worship him, and in reward to rule

Over his Works, on Earth, in Sea, or Air,

And multiply a Race of Worshippers   630

Holy and just: thrice happie if they know
Thir happiness, and persevere upright.
　　So sung they, and the Empyrean rung,
With *Halleluiahs:* Thus was Sabbath kept.
And thy request think now fulfill'd, that ask'd
How first this World and face of things began,
And what before thy memorie was don
From the beginning, that posteritie
Informd by thee might know; if else thou seekst
Aught, not surpassing human measure, say.　　　　640
　　To whom thus *Adam* gratefully repli'd.
What thanks sufficient, or what recompence
Equal have I to render thee, Divine
Hystorian, who thus largely hast allayd
The thirst I had of knowledge, and voutsaf't
This friendly condescention to relate
Things else by me unsearchable, now heard
VVith wonder, but delight, and, as is due,
With glorie attributed to the high
Creator; some thing yet of doubt remaines,　　　　650
VVhich onely thy solution can resolve.
VVhen I behold this goodly Frame, this VVorld
Of Heav'n and Earth consisting, and compute,
Thir magnitudes, this Earth a spot, a graine,
An Atom, with the Firmament compar'd
And all her numberd Starrs, that seem to rowle
Spaces incomprehensible (for such
Thir distance argues and thir swift return
Diurnal) meerly to officiate light

Round this opacous Earth, this punctual spot,   660
One day and night; in all thir vast survey
Useless besides, reasoning I oft admire,
How Nature wise and frugal could commit
Such disproportions, with superfluous hand
So many nobler Bodies to create,
Greater so manifold to this one use,
For aught appeers, and on thir Orbs impose
Such restless revolution day by day
Repeated, while the sedentarie Earth,
That better might with farr less compass move,   670
Serv'd by more noble then her self, attaines
Her end without least motion, and receaves,
As Tribute such a sumless journey brought
Of incorporeal speed, her warmth and light;
Speed, to describe whose swiftness Number failes.
 So spake our Sire, and by his count'nance seemd
Entring on studious thoughts abstruse, which *Eve*
Perceaving where she sat retir'd in sight,
With lowliness Majestic from her seat,
And Grace that won who saw to wish her stay,   680
Rose, and went forth among her Fruits and Flours,
To visit how they prosper'd, bud and bloom,
Her Nurserie; they at her coming sprung
And toucht by her fair tendance gladlier grew.
Yet went she not, as not with such discourse
Delighted, or not capable her eare
Of what was high: such pleasure she reserv'd,
Adam relating, she sole Auditress;

Her Husband the Relater she preferr'd
Before the Angel, and of him to ask   690
Chose rather; hee, she knew would intermix
Grateful digressions, and solve high dispute
With conjugal Caresses, from his Lip
Not Words alone pleas'd her. O when meet now
Such pairs, in Love and mutual Honour joyn'd?
With Goddess-like demeanour forth she went;
Not unattended, for on her as Queen
A pomp of winning Graces waited still,
And from about her shot Darts of desire
Into all Eyes to wish her still in sight.   700
And *Raphael* now to *Adam*'s doubt propos'd
Benevolent and facil thus repli'd.
   To ask or search I blame thee not, for Heav'n
Is as the Book of God before thee set,
Wherein to read his wondrous Works, and learne
His Season, Hours, or Days, or Months, or Yeares:
This to attain, whether Heav'n move or Earth,
Imports not, if thou reck'n right, the rest
From Man or Angel the great Architect
Did wisely to conceal, and not divulge   710
His secrets to be scann'd by them who ought
Rather admire; or if they list to try
Conjecture, he his Fabric of the Heav'ns
Hath left to thir disputes, perhaps to move
His laughter at thir quaint Opinions wide
Hereafter, when they come to model Heav'n
And calculate the Starrs, how they will weild

The mightie frame, how build, unbuild, contrive

To save appeerances, how gird the Sphear

With Centric and Eccentric scribl'd o're,   720

Cycle and Epicycle, Orb in Orb:

Alreadie by thy reasoning this I guess,

Who art to lead thy ofspring, and supposest

That Bodies bright and greater should not serve

The less not bright, nor Heav'n such journies run,

Earth sitting still, when she alone receaves

The benefit: consider first, that Great

Or Bright inferrs not Excellence: the Earth

Though, in comparison of Heav'n, so small,

Nor glistering, may of solid good containe   730

More plenty then the Sun that barren shines,

Whose vertue on it self workes no effect,

But in the fruitful Earth; there first receavd

His beams, unactive else, thir vigor find.

Yet not to Earth are those bright Luminaries

Officious, but to thee Earths habitant.

And for the Heav'ns wide Circuit, let it speak

The Makers high magnificence, who built

So spacious, and his Line stretcht out so farr;

That Man may know he dwells not in his own;   740

An Edifice too large for him to fill,

Lodg'd in a small partition, and the rest

Ordain'd for uses to his Lord best known.

The swiftness of those Circles attribute,

Though numberless, to his Omnipotence,

That to corporeal substances could adde

Speed almost Spiritual; mee thou thinkst not slow,

Who since the Morning hour set out from Heav'n

Where God resides, and ere mid-day arriv'd

In *Eden,* distance inexpressible   750

By Numbers that have name. But this I urge,

Admitting Motion in the Heav'ns, to shew

Invalid that which thee to doubt it mov'd;

Not that I so affirm, though so it seem

To thee who hast thy dwelling here on Earth.

God to remove his wayes from human sense,

Plac'd Heav'n from Earth so farr, that earthly sight,

If it presume, might erre in things too high,

And no advantage gaine. What if the Sun

Be Center to the World, and other Starrs   760

By his attractive vertue and thir own

Incited, dance about him various rounds?

Thir wandring course now high, now low, then hid,

Progressive, retrograde, or standing still,

In six thou seest, and what if sev'nth to these

The Planet Earth, so stedfast though she seem,

Insensibly three different Motions move?

Which else to several Sphears thou must ascribe

Mov'd contrarie with thwart obliquities,

Or save the Sun his labour, and that swift   770

Nocturnal and Diurnal rhomb suppos'd,

Invisible else above all Starrs, the Wheele

Of Day and Night; which needs not thy beleefe,

If Earth industrious of her self fetch Day

Travelling East, and with her part averse

From the Suns beam meet Night, her other part
Still luminous by his ray. What if that light
Sent from her through the wide transpicuous aire,
To the terrestrial Moon be as a Starr
Enlightning her by Day, as she by Night   780
This Earth? reciprocal, if Land be there,
Feilds and Inhabitants: Her spots thou seest
As Clouds, and Clouds may rain, and Rain produce
Fruits in her soft'nd Soile, for some to eate
Allotted there; and other Suns perhaps
With thir attendant Moons thou wilt descrie
Communicating Male and Femal Light,
Which two great Sexes animate the World,
Stor'd in each Orb perhaps with some that live.
For such vast room in Nature unpossest   790
By living Soule, desert and desolate,
Onely to shine, yet scarce to contribute
Each Orb a glimps of Light, conveyd so farr
Down to this habitable, which returnes
Light back to them, is obvious to dispute.
But whether thus these things, or whether not,
Whether the Sun predominant in Heav'n
Rise on the Earth, or Earth rise on the Sun,
Hee from the East his flaming rode begin,
Or Shee from West her silent course advance   800
With inoffensive pace that spinning sleeps
On her soft Axle, while she paces Eev'n,
And bears thee soft with the smooth Air along,
Sollicit not thy thoughts with matters hid,

Leave them to God above, him serve and feare;
Of other Creatures, as him pleases best,
Wherever plac't, let him dispose: joy thou
In what he gives to thee, this Paradise
And thy faire *Eve*; Heav'n is for thee too high
To know what passes there; be lowlie wise: 810
Think onely what concernes thee and thy being;
Dream not of other Worlds, what Creatures there
Live, in what state, condition or degree,
Contented that thus farr hath been reveal'd
Not of Earth onely but of highest Heav'n.
   To whom thus *Adam* cleerd of doubt, repli'd.
How fully hast thou satisfi'd mee, pure
Intelligence of Heav'n, Angel serene,
And freed from intricacies, taught to live,
The easiest way, nor with perplexing thoughts   820
To interrupt the sweet of Life, from which
God hath bid dwell farr off all anxious cares,
And not molest us, unless we our selves
Seek them with wandring thoughts, and notions vaine.
But apt the Mind or Fancie is to roave
Uncheckt, and of her roaving is no end;
Till warn'd, or by experience taught, she learne,
That not to know at large of things remote
From use, obscure and suttle, but to know
That which before us lies in daily life,   830
Is the prime Wisdom, what is more, is fume,
Or emptiness, or fond impertinence,
And renders us in things that most concerne

Unpractis'd, unprepar'd, and still to seek.

Therefore from this high pitch let us descend

A lower flight, and speak of things at hand

Useful, whence haply mention may arise

Of somthing not unseasonable to ask

By sufferance, and thy wonted favour deign'd.

Thee I have heard relating what was don   840

Ere my remembrance: now hear mee relate

My Storie, which perhaps thou hast not heard;

And Day is yet not spent; till then thou seest

How suttly to detaine thee I devise,

Inviting thee to hear while I relate,

Fond, were it not in hope of thy reply:

For while I sit with thee, I seem in Heav'n,

And sweeter thy discourse is to my eare

Then Fruits of Palm-tree pleasantest to thirst

And hunger both, from labour, at the houre   850

Of sweet repast; they satiate, and soon fill,

Though pleasant, but thy words with Grace Divine

Imbu'd, bring to thir sweetness no satietie.

    To whom thus *Raphael* answer'd heav'nly meek.

Nor are thy lips ungraceful, Sire of men,

Nor tongue ineloquent; for God on thee

Abundantly his gifts hath also pour'd

Inward and outward both, his image faire:

Speaking or mute all comliness and grace

Attends thee, and each word, each motion formes.   860

Nor less think wee in Heav'n of thee on Earth

Then of our fellow servant, and inquire

Gladly into the wayes of God with Man:

For God we see hath honour'd thee, and set

On Man his equal Love: say therefore on;

For I that Day was absent, as befell,

Bound on a voyage uncouth and obscure,

Farr on excursion toward the Gates of Hell;

Squar'd in full Legion (such command we had)

To see that none thence issu'd forth a spie,   870

Or enemie, while God was in his work,

Least hee incenst at such eruption bold,

Destruction with Creation might have mixt.

Not that they durst without his leave attempt,

But us he sends upon his high behests

For state, as Sovran King, and to enure

Our prompt obedience. Fast we found, fast shut

The dismal Gates, and barricado'd strong;

But long ere our approaching heard within

Noise, other then the sound of Dance or Song,   880

Torment, and lowd lament, and furious rage.

Glad we return'd up to the coasts of Light

Ere Sabbath Eev'ning: so we had in charge.

But thy relation now; for I attend,

Pleas'd with thy words no less then thou with mine.

So spake the Godlike Power, and thus our Sire.

For Man to tell how human Life began

Is hard; for who himself beginning knew?

Desire with thee still longer to converse

Induc'd me. As new wak't from soundest sleep   890

Soft on the flourie herb I found me laid

In Balmie Sweat, which with his Beames the Sun
Soon dri'd, and on the reaking moisture fed.
Strait toward Heav'n my wondring Eyes I turnd,
And gaz'd a while the ample skie, till rais'd
By quick instinctive motion up I sprung,
As thitherward endevoring, and upright
Stood on my feet; about me round I saw
Hill, Dale, and shadie Woods, and sunnie Plaines,
And liquid Lapse of murmuring Sreams; by these,   900
Creatures that livd, and movd, and walk'd, or flew,
Birds on the branches warbling; all things smil'd,
With fragrance and with joy my heart oreflow'd.
My self I then perus'd, and Limb by Limb
Survey'd, and sometimes went, and sometimes ran
With supple joints, and lively vigour led:
But who I was, or where, or from what cause,
Knew not; to speak I tri'd, and forthwith spake,
My Tongue obey'd and readily could name
What e're I saw. Thou Sun, said I, faire Light,   910
And thou enlight'nd Earth, so fresh and gay,
Ye Hills and Dales, ye Rivers, Woods, and Plaines,
And ye that live and move, fair Creatures, tell,
Tell, if ye saw, how came I thus, how here?
Not of my self; by some great Maker then,
In goodness and in power præeminent;
Tell me, how may I know him, how adore,
From whom I have that thus I move and live,
And feel that I am happier then I know.
While thus I call'd, and stray'd I knew not whither,   920

From where I first drew Aire, and first beheld
This happie Light, when answer none return'd,
On a green shadie Bank profuse of Flours
Pensive I sate me down; there gentle sleep
First found me, and with soft oppression seis'd
My droused sense, untroubl'd, though I thought
I then was passing to my former state
Insensible, and forthwith to dissolve:
When suddenly stood at my Head a dream,
Whose inward apparition gently mov'd   930
My Fancy to believe I yet had being,
And livd: One came, methought, of shape Divine,
And said, thy Mansion wants thee, *Adam*, rise,
First Man, of Men innumerable ordain'd
First Father, call'd by thee I come thy Guide
To the Garden of bliss, thy seat prepar'd.
So saying, by the hand he took me rais'd,
And over Fields and Waters, as in Aire
Smooth sliding without step, last led me up
A woodie Mountain; whose high top was plaine,   940
A Circuit wide, enclos'd, with goodliest Trees
Planted, with Walks, and Bowers, that what I saw
Of Earth before scarse pleasant seemd. Each Tree
Load'n with fairest Fruit, that hung to the Eye
Tempting, stirr'd in me sudden appetite
To pluck and eate; whereat I wak'd, and found
Before mine Eyes all real, as the dream
Had lively shadowd: Here had new begun
My wandring, had not hee who was my Guide

Up hither, from among the Trees appeer'd,   950
Presence Divine. Rejoycing, but with aw
In adoration at his feet I fell
Submiss: he rear'd me, & Whom thou soughtst I am,
Said mildely, Author of all this thou seest
Above, or round about thee or beneath.
This Paradise I give thee, count it thine
To Till and keep, and of the Fruit to eate:
Of every Tree that in the Garden growes
Eate freely with glad heart; fear here no dearth:
But of the Tree whose operation brings   960
Knowledg of good and ill, which I have set
The Pledge of thy Obedience and thy Faith,
Amid the Garden by the Tree of Life,
Remember what I warne thee, shun to taste,
And shun the bitter consequence: for know,
The day thou eat'st thereof, my sole command
Transgrest, inevitably thou shalt dye;
From that day mortal, and this happie State
Shalt loose, expell'd from hence into a World
Of woe and sorrow. Sternly he pronounc'd   970
The rigid interdiction, which resounds
Yet dreadful in mine eare, though in my choice
Not to incur; but soon his cleer aspect
Return'd and gratious purpose thus renew'd.
Not onely these fair bounds, but all the Earth
To thee and to thy Race I give; as Lords
Possess it, and all things that therein live,
Or live in Sea, or Aire, Beast, Fish, and Fowle.

In signe whereof each Bird and Beast behold
After thir kindes; I bring them to receave   980
From thee thir Names, and pay thee fealtie
With low subjection; understand the same
Of Fish within thir watry residence,
Not hither summond, since they cannot change
Thir Element to draw the thinner Aire.
As thus he spake, each Bird and Beast behold
Approaching two and two, These cowring low
With blandishment, each Bird stoop'd on his wing.
I nam'd them, as thy pass'd, and understood
Thir Nature, with such knowledg God endu'd   990
My sudden apprehension: but in these
I found not what me thought I wanted still;
And to the Heav'nly vision thus presum'd.
    O by what Name, for thou above all these,
Above mankinde, or aught then mankinde higher,
Surpassest farr my naming, how may I
Adore thee, Author of this Universe,
And all this good to man, for whose well being
So amply, and with hands so liberal
Thou hast provided all things: but with mee   1000
I see not who partakes. In solitude
What happiness, who can enjoy alone,
Or all enjoying, what contentment find?
Thus I presumptuous; and the vision bright,
As with a smile more bright'nd, thus repli'd.
    What call'st thou solitude, is not the Earth
With various living creatures, and the Aire

Replenisht, and all these at thy command
To come and play before thee, know'st thou not
Thir language and thir wayes, they also know,   1010
And reason not contemptibly; with these
Find pastime, and beare rule; thy Realm is large.
So spake the Universal Lord, and seem'd
So ordering. I with leave of speech implor'd,
And humble deprecation thus repli'd.

    Let not my words offend thee, Heav'nly Power,
My Maker, be propitious while I speak.
Hast thou not made me here thy substitute,
And these inferiour farr beneath me set?
Among unequals what societie   1020
Can sort, what harmonie or true delight?
Which must be mutual, in proportion due
Giv'n and receiv'd; but in disparitie
The one intense, the other still remiss
Cannot well suite with either, but soon prove
Tedious alike: Of fellowship I speak
Such as I seek, fit to participate
All rational delight, wherein the brute
Cannot be human consort; they rejoyce
Each with thir kinde, Lion with Lioness;   1030
So fitly them in pairs thou hast combin'd;
Much less can Bird with Beast, or Fish with Fowle
So well converse, nor with the Ox the Ape;
Wors then can Man with Beast, and least of all.

    Whereto th' Almighty answer'd, not displeas'd.
A nice and suttle happiness I see

Thou to thy self proposest, in the choice

Of thy Associates, *Adam*, and wilt taste

No pleasure, though in pleasure, solitarie.

What thinkst thou then of mee, and this my State,   1040

Seem I to thee sufficiently possest

Of happiness, or not? who am alone

From all Eternitie, for none I know

Second to mee or like, equal much less.

How have I then with whom to hold converse

Save with the Creatures which I made, and those

To me inferiour, infinite descents

Beneath what other Creatures are to thee?

   He ceas'd, I lowly answer'd. To attaine

The highth and depth of thy Eternal wayes   1050

All human thoughts come short, Supream of things;

Thou in thy self art perfet, and in thee

Is no deficience found; not so is Man,

But in degree, the cause of his desire

By conversation with his like to help,

Or solace his defects. No need that thou

Shouldst propagat, already infinite;

And through all numbers absolute, though One;

But Man by number is to manifest

His single imperfection, and beget   1060

Like of his like, his Image multipli'd,

In unitie defective, which requires

Collateral love, and deerest amitie.

Thou in thy secresie although alone,

Best with thy self accompanied, seek'st not

Social communication, yet so pleas'd,

Canst raise thy Creature to what highth thou wilt

Of Union or Communion, deifi'd;

I by conversing cannot these erect

From prone, nor in thir wayes complacence find.   1070

Thus I embold'nd spake, and freedom us'd

Permissive, and acceptance found, which gain'd

This answer from the gracious voice Divine.

   Thus farr to try thee, *Adam*, I was pleas'd,

And finde thee knowing not of Beasts alone,

Which thou hast rightly nam'd, but of thy self,

Expressing well the spirit within thee free,

My Image, not imparted to the Brute,

Whose fellowship therefore unmeet for thee

Good reason was thou freely shouldst dislike,   1080

And be so minded still; I, ere thou spak'st,

Knew it not good for Man to be alone,

And no such companie as then thou saw'st

Intended thee, for trial onely brought,

To see how thou could'st judge of fit and meet:

What next I bring shall please thee, be assur'd,

Thy likeness, thy fit help, thy other self,

Thy wish, exactly to thy hearts desire.

   Hee ended, or I heard no more, for now

My earthly by his Heav'nly overpowerd,   1090

Which it had long stood under, streind to the highth

In that celestial Colloquie sublime,

As with a object that excels the sense,

Dazl'd and spent, sunk down, and sought repair

Of sleep, which instantly fell on me, call'd

By Nature as in aide, and clos'd mine eyes.

Mine eyes he clos'd, but op'n left the Cell

Of Fancie my internal sight, by which

Abstract as in a transe methought I saw,

Though sleeping, where I lay, and saw the shape   1100

Still glorious before whom awake I stood;

Who stooping op'nd my left side, and took

From thence a Rib, with cordial spirits warme,

And Life-blood streaming fresh; wide was the wound,

But suddenly with flesh fill'd up & heal'd:

The Rib he formd and fashond with his hands;

Under his forming hands a Creature grew,

Manlike, but different sex, so lovly faire,

That what seemd fair in all the World, seemd now

Mean, or in her summd up, in her containd   1110

And in her looks, which from that time infus'd

Sweetness into my heart, unfelt before,

And into all things from her Aire inspir'd

The spirit of love and amorous delight.

She disappeerd, and left me dark, I wak'd

To find her, or for ever to deplore

Her loss, and other pleasures all abjure:

When out of hope, behold her, not farr off,

Such as I saw her in my dream, adornd

With what all Earth or Heaven could bestow   1120

To make her amiable: On she came,

Led by her Heav'nly Maker, though unseen,

And guided by his voice, nor uninformd

Of nuptial Sanctitie and marriage Rites:
Grace was in all her steps, Heav'n in her Eye,
In every gesture dignitie and love.
I overjoyd could not forbear aloud.

    This turn hath made amends; thou hast fulfill'd
Thy words, Creator bounteous and benigne,
Giver of all things faire, but fairest this   1130
Of all thy gifts, nor enviest. I now see
Bone of my Bone, Flesh of my Flesh, my Self
Before me; Woman is her Name, of Man
Extracted; for this cause he shall forgoe
Father and Mother, and to his Wife adhere;
And they shall be one Flesh, one Heart, one Soule.

    She heard me thus, and though divinely brought,
Yet Innocence and Virgin Modestie,
Her vertue and the conscience of her worth,
That would be woo'd, and not unsought be won,   1140
Not obvious, not obtrusive, but retir'd,
The more desirable, or to say all,
Nature her self, though pure of sinful thought,
Wrought in her so, that seeing me, she turn'd;
I follow'd her, she what was Honour knew,
And with obsequious Majestie approv'd
My pleaded reason. To the Nuptial Bowre
I led her blushing like the Morn: all Heav'n,
And happie Constellations on that houre
Shed thir selectest influence; the Earth   1150
Gave sign of gratulation, and each Hill;
Joyous the Birds; fresh Gales and gentle Aires

Whisper'd it to the Woods, and from thir wings
Flung Rose, flung Odours from the spicie Shrub,
Disporting, till the amorous Bird of Night
Sung Spousal, and bid haste the Eevning Starr
On his Hill top, to light the bridal Lamp.
Thus I have told thee all my State, and brought
My Storie to the sum of earthly bliss
Which I enjoy, and must confess to find   1160
In all things else delight indeed, but such
As us'd or not, works in the mind no change,
Nor vehement desire, these delicacies
I mean of Taste, Sight, Smell, Herbs, Fruits, & Flours,
Walks, and the melodie of Birds; but here
Farr otherwise, transported I behold,
Transported touch; here passion first I felt,
Commotion strange, in all enjoyments else
Superiour and unmov'd, here onely weake
Against the charm of Beauties powerful glance.   1170
Or Nature faild in mee, and left some part
Not proof enough such Object to sustain,
Or from my side subducting, took perhaps
More then enough; at least on her bestow'd
Too much of Ornament, in outward shew
Elaborate, of inward less exact.
For well I understand in the prime end
Of Nature her th' inferiour, in the mind
And inward Faculties, which most excell,
In outward also her resembling less   1180
His Image who made both, and less expressing

The character of that Dominion giv'n
O're other Creatures; yet when I approach
Her loveliness, so absolute she seems
And in her self compleat, so well to know
Her own, that what she wills to do or say,
Seems wisest, vertuousest, discreetest, best;
All higher knowledge in her presence falls
Degraded, Wisdom in discourse with her
Looses discount'nanc't, and like folly shewes;   1190
Authoritie and Reason on her waite,
As one intended first, not after made
Occasionally; and to consummate all,
Greatness of mind and nobleness thir seat
Build in her loveliest, and create an awe
About her, as a guard Angelic plac't.
To whom the Angel with contracted brow.
   Accuse not Nature, she hath don her part;
Do thou but thine, and be not diffident
Of Wisdom, she deserts thee not, if thou   1200
Dismiss not her, when most thou needst her nigh,
By attributing overmuch to things
Less excellent, as thou thy self perceav'st,
For what admir'st thou, what transports thee so,
An outside? fair no doubt, and worthy well
Thy cherishing, thy honouring, and thy love,
Not thy subjection: weigh with her thy self;
Then value: Oft times nothing profits more
Then self-esteem, grounded on just and right
Well manag'd; of that skill the more thou know'st,   1210

The more she will acknowledge thee her Head,
And to realities yeild all her shows;
Made so adorn for thy delight the more,
So awful, that with honour thou maist love
Thy mate, who sees when thou art seen least wise.
But if the sense of touch whereby mankind
Is propagated seem such dear delight
Beyond all other, think the same voutsaf't
To Cattel and each Beast; which would not be
To them made common & divulg'd, if aught   122(
Therein enjoy'd were worthy to subdue
The Soule of Man, or passion in him move.
What higher in her societie thou findst
Attractive, human, rational, love still;
In loving thou dost well, in passion not,
Wherein true Love consists not; love refines
The thoughts, and heart enlarges, hath his seat
In Reason, and is judicious, is the scale
By which to heav'nly Love thou maist ascend,
Not sunk in carnal pleasure, for which cause   123(
Among the Beasts no Mate for thee was found.
    To whom thus half abash't *Adam* repli'd.
Neither her out-side formd so fair, nor aught
In procreation common to all kindes
(Though higher of the genial Bed by far,
And with mysterious reverence I deem)
So much delights me, as those graceful acts,
Those thousand decencies that daily flow
From all her words and actions, mixt with Love

And sweet compliance, which declare unfeign'd   1240
Union of Mind, or in us both one Soule;
Harmonie to behold in wedded pair
More grateful then harmonious sound to the eare.
Yet these subject not; I to thee disclose
What inward thence I feel, not therefore foild,
Who meet with various objects, from the sense
Variously representing; yet still free
Approve the best, and follow what I approve.
To love thou blam'st me not, for love thou saist
Leads up to Heav'n, is both the way and guide;   1250
Bear with me then, if lawful what I ask;
Love not the heav'nly Spirits, and how thir Love
Express they, by looks onely, or do they mix
Irradiance, virtual or immediate touch?
    To whom the Angel with a smile that glow'd
Celestial rosie red, Loves proper hue,
Answer'd. Let it suffice thee that thou know'st
Us happie, and without Love no happiness.
Whatever pure thou in the body enjoy'st
(And pure thou wert created) we enjoy   1260
In eminence, and obstacle find none
Of membrane, joynt, or limb, exclusive barrs:
Easier then Air with Air, if Spirits embrace,
Total they mix, Union of Pure with Pure
Desiring; nor restrain'd conveyance need
As Flesh to mix with Flesh, or Soul with Soul.
But I can now no more; the parting Sun
Beyond the Earths green Cape and verdant Isles

Hesperean sets, my Signal to depart.

Be strong, live happie, and love, but first of all   1270

Him whom to love is to obey, and keep

His great command; take heed least Passion sway

Thy Judgement to do aught, which else free Will

Would not admit; thine and of all thy Sons

The weal or woe in thee is plac't; beware.

I in thy persevering shall rejoyce,

And all the Blest: stand fast; to stand or fall

Free in thine own Arbitrement it lies,

Perfet within, no outward aid require;

And all temptation to transgress repel.   1280

So saying, he arose; whom *Adam* thus

Follow'd with benediction. Since to part,

Go heavenly Guest, Ethereal Messenger,

Sent from whose sovran goodness I adore.

Gentle to me and affable hath been

Thy condescension, and shall be honour'd ever

With grateful Memorie: thou to mankind

Be good and friendly still, and oft return.

So parted they, the Angel up to Heav'n

From the thick shade, and *Adam* to his Bowre.   1290

PARADISE
LOST

BOOK VIII.

NO more of talk where God or Angel Guest
With Man, as with his Friend, familiar us'd
To sit indulgent, and with him partake
Rural repast, permitting him the while
Venial discourse unblam'd: I now must change
Those Notes to Tragic; foul distrust, and breach
Disloyal on the part of Man, revolt,
And disobedience: On the part of Heav'n
Now alienated, distance and distaste,
Anger and just rebuke, and judgement giv'n,   10
That brought into this World a world of woe,
Sinne and her shadow Death, and Miserie
Deaths Harbinger: Sad task, yet argument
Not less but more Heroic then the wrauth
Of stern *Achilles* on his Foe pursu'd
Thrice Fugitive about *Troy* Wall; or rage
Of *Turnus* for *Lavinia* disespous'd,
Or *Neptun*'s ire or *Juno*'s, that so long
Perplex'd the *Greek* and *Cytherea*'s Son;
If answerable style I can obtaine   20
Of my Celestial Patroness, who deignes
Her nightly visitation unimplor'd,

And dictates to me slumbring, or inspires

Easie my unpremeditated Verse

Since first this Subject for Heroic Song

Pleas'd me long choosing, and beginning late;

Not sedulous by Nature to indite

Warrs, hitherto the onely Argument

Heroic deem'd, chief maistrie to dissect

With long and tedious havoc fabl'd Knights   30

In Battels feign'd; the better fortitude

Of Patience and Heroic Martyrdom

Unsung; or to describe Races and Games,

Or tilting Furniture, emblazon'd Shields,

Impreses quaint, Caparisons and Steeds;

Bases and tinsel Trappings, gorgious Knights

At Joust and Torneament; then marshal'd Feast

Serv'd up in Hall with Sewers, and Seneshals;

The skill of Artifice or Office mean,

Not that which justly gives Heroic name   40

To Person or to Poem. Mee of these

Nor skilld nor studious, higher Argument

Remaines, sufficient of it self to raise

That name, unless an age too late, or cold

Climat, or Years damp my intended wing

Deprest, and much they may, if all be mine,

Not Hers who brings it nightly to my Ear.

     The Sun was sunk, and after him the Starr

Of *Hesperus,* whose Office is to bring

Twilight upon the Earth, short Arbiter   50

Twixt Day and Night, and now from end to end

Nights Hemisphere had veild the Horizon round:

When *Satan* who late fled before the threats

Of *Gabriel* out of *Eden*, now improv'd

In meditated fraud and malice, bent

On mans destruction, maugre what might hap

Of heavier on himself, fearless return'd.

By Night he fled, and at Midnight return'd

From compassing the Earth, cautious of day,

Since *Uriel* Regent of the Sun descri'd   60

His entrance, and forewarnd the Cherubim

That kept thir watch; thence full of anguish driv'n,

The space of seven continu'd Nights he rode

With darkness, thrice the Equinoctial Line

He circl'd, four times cross'd the Carr of Night

From Pole to Pole, traversing each Colure;

On the eighth return'd, and on the Coast averse

From entrance or Cherubic Watch, by stealth

Found unsuspected way. There was a place,

Now not, though Sin, not Time, first wraught the change,   70

Where *Tigris* at the foot of Paradise

Into a Gulf shot under ground, till part

Rose up a Fountain by the Tree of Life;

In with the River sunk, and with it rose

Satan involv'd in rising Mist, then sought

Where to lie hid; Sea he had searcht and Land

From *Eden* over *Pontus*, and the Poole

Mæotis, up beyond the River *Ob*;

Downward as farr Antartic; and in length

West from *Orontes* to the Ocean barr'd   80

At *Darien*, thence to the Land where flowes
Ganges and *Indus:* thus the Orb he roam'd
With narrow search; and with inspection deep
Consider'd every Creature, which of all
Most opportune might serve his Wiles, and found
The Serpent suttlest Beast of all the Field.
Him after long debate, irresolute
Of thoughts revolv'd, his final sentence chose
Fit Vessel, fittest Imp of fraud, in whom
To enter, and his dark suggestions hide   90
From sharpest sight: for in the wilie Snake,
Whatever sleights none would suspicious mark,
As from his wit and native suttletie
Proceeding, which in other Beasts observ'd
Doubt might beget of Diabolic pow'r
Active within beyond the sense of brute.
Thus he resolv'd, but first from inward griefe
His bursting passion into plaints thus pour'd:
    O Earth, how like to Heav'n, if not preferr'd
More justly, Seat worthier of Gods, as built   100
With second thoughts, reforming what was old!
For what God after better worse would build?
Terrestrial Heav'n, danc't round by other Heav'ns
That shine, yet bear thir bright officious Lamps,
Light above Light, for thee alone, as seems,
In thee concentring all thir precious beams
Of sacred influence: As God in Heav'n
Is Center, yet extends to all, so thou
Centring receav'st from all those Orbs; in thee
Not in themselves, all thir known vertue appeers   110

Productive in Herb, Plant, and nobler birth

Of Creatures animate with gradual life

Of Growth, Sense, Reason, all summ'd up in Man.

With what delight could I have walkt thee round

If I could joy in aught, sweet interchange

Of Hill and Vallie, Rivers, Woods and Plaines,

Now Land, now Sea, & Shores with Forrest crownd,

Rocks, Dens, and Caves; but I in none of these

Find Place or refuge; and the more I see

Pleasures about me, so much more I feel   120

Torment within me, as from the hateful siege

Of contraries; all good to me becomes

Bane, and in Heav'n much worse would be my state.

But neither here seek I, no nor in Heav'n

To dwell, unless by maistring Heav'ns Supreame;

Nor hope to be my self less miserable

By what I seek, but others to make such

As I, though thereby worse to me redound:

For onely in destroying I finde ease

To my relentless thoughts; and him destroyd,   130

Or won to what may work his utter loss,

For whom all this was made, all this will soon

Follow, as to him linkt in weal or woe,

In wo then; that destruction wide may range:

To mee shall be the glorie sole among

The infernal Powers, in one day to have marr'd

What he *Almightie* styl'd, six Nights and Days

Continu'd making, and who knows how long

Before had bin contriving, though perhaps

Not longer then since I in one Night freed   140

From servitude inglorious welnigh half
Th' Angelic Name, and thinner left the throng
Of his adorers: hee to be aveng'd,
And to repaire his numbers thus impair'd,
Whether such vertue spent of old now faild
More Angels to Create, if they at least
Are his Created or to spite us more,
Determin'd to advance into our room
A Creature form'd of Earth, and him endow,
Exalted from so base original,   150
With Heav'nly spoils, our spoils: What he decreed
He effected; Man he made, and for him built
Magnificent this World, and Earth his seat,
Him Lord pronounc'd, and, O indignitie!
Subjected to his service Angel wings,
And flaming Ministers to watch and tend
Thir earthie Charge: Of these the vigilance
I dread, and to elude, thus wrapt in mist
Of midnight vapor glide obscure, and prie
In every Bush and Brake, where hap may finde   160
The Serpent sleeping, in whose mazie foulds
To hide me, and the dark intent I bring.
O foul descent! that I who erst contended
With Gods to sit the highest, am now constraind
Into a Beast, and mixt with bestial slime,
This essence to incarnate and imbrute,
That to the hight of Deitie aspir'd;
But what will not Ambition and Revenge

Descend to? who aspires must down as low

As high he soard, obnoxious first or last   170

To basest things. Revenge, at first though sweet,

Bitter ere long back on it self recoiles;

Let it; I reck not, so it light well aim'd,

Since higher I fall short, on him who next

Provokes my envie, this new Favorite

Of Heav'n, this Man of Clay, Son of despite,

Whom us the more to spite his Maker rais'd

From dust: spite then with spite is best repaid.

   So saying, through each Thicket Danck or Drie,

Like a black mist low creeping, he held on   180

His midnight search, where soonest he might finde

The Serpent: him fast sleeping soon he found

In Labyrinth of many a round self-rowld,

His head the midst, well stor'd with suttle wiles:

Not yet in horrid Shade or dismal Den,

Nor nocent yet, but on the grassie Herbe

Fearless unfeard he slept: in at his Mouth

The Devil enterd, and his brutal sense,

In heart or head, possessing soon inspir'd

With act intelligential; but his sleep   190

Disturbd not, waiting close th' approach of Morn.

Now whenas sacred Light began to dawne

In *Eden* on the humid Flours, that breathd

Thir morning Incense, when all things that breath,

From th' Earths great Altar send up silent praise

To the Creator, and his Nostrils fill

With gratefull Smell, forth came the human pair
And joynd thir vocal Worship to the Quire
Of Creatures wanting voice, that done, partake
The season, prime for sweetest Sents and Aires: 200
Then commune how that day they best may ply
Thir growing work: for much thir work outgrew
The hands dispatch of two Gardning so wide.
And *Eve* first to her Husband thus began.
    Adam, well may we labour still to dress
This Garden, still to tend Plant, Herb and Flour,
Our pleasant task enjoyn'd, but till more hands
Aid us, the work under our labour grows,
Luxurious by restraint; what we by day
Lop overgrown, or prune, or prop, or bind,   210
One night or two with wanton growth derides
Tending to wilde. Thou therefore now advise
Or hear what to my mind first thoughts present,
Let us divide our labours, thou where choice
Leads thee, or where most needs, whether to wind
The Woodbine round this Arbour, or direct
The clasping Ivie where to climb, while I
In yonder Spring or Roses intermixt
With Myrtle, find what to redress till Noon:
For while so near each other thus all day   220
Our task we choose, what wonder if so near
Looks intervene and smiles, or object new
Casual discourse draw on, which intermits
Our dayes work brought to little, though begun
Early, and th' hour of Supper comes unearn'd.

    To whom mild answer *Adam* thus return'd.

Sole *Eve,* Associate sole, to me beyond

Compare above all living Creatures deare,

Well hast thou motion'd, wel thy thoughts imployd

How we might best fulfill the work which here   230

God hath assign'd us, nor of me shalt pass

Unprais'd: for nothing lovelier can be found

In woman, then to studie houshold good,

And good workes in her Husband to promote.

Yet not so strictly hath our Lord impos'd

Labour, as to debarr us when we need

Refreshment, whether food, or talk between,

Food of the mind, or this sweet intercourse

Of looks and smiles, for smiles from Reason flow,

To brute deni'd, and are of Love the food,   240

Love not the lowest end of human life.

For not to irksom toile, but to delight

He made us, and delight to Reason joyn'd.

These paths and Bowers doubt not but our joynt hands

Will keep from Wilderness with ease, as wide

As we need walk, till younger hands ere long

Assist us: But if much converse perhaps

Thee satiate, to short absence I could yeild.

For solitude somtimes is best societie,

And short retirement urges sweet returne.   250

But other doubt possesses me, least harm

Befall thee sever'd from me; for thou knowst

What hath bin warn'd us, what malicious Foe

Envying our happiness, and of his own

Despairing, seeks to work us woe and shame

By sly assault; and somwhere nigh at hand

Watches, no doubt, with greedy hope to find

His wish and best advantage, us asunder,

Hopeless to circumvent us joynd, where each

To other speedie aide might lend at need;   260

Whether his first design be to withdraw

Our fealtie from God, or to disturb

Conjugal Love, then which perhaps no bliss

Enjoy'd by us excites his envie more;

Or this, or worse, leave not the faithful side

That gave thee being, stil shades thee and protects.

The Wife, where danger or dishonour lurks,

Safest and seemliest by her Husband staies,

Who guards her, or with her the worst endures.

     To whom the Virgin Majestie of *Eve*,   270

As one who loves, and some unkindess meets,

With sweet austeer composure thus reply'd.

     Ofspring of Heav'n and Earth, and all Earths Lord,

That such an Enemie we have, who seeks

Our ruin, both by thee informd I learne,

And from the parting Angel over-heard

As in a shadie nook I stood behind,

Just then returnd at shut of Evening Flours.

But that thou shouldst my firmness therfore doubt

To God or thee, because we have a foe   280

May tempt it, I expected not to hear.

His violence thou fearst not, being such,

As wee, not capable of death or paine,

Can either not receave, or can repell.

His fraud is then thy fear, which plain inferrs

Thy equal fear that my firm Faith and Love

Can by his fraud be shak'n or seduc't;

Thoughts, which how found they harbour in thy brest,

Adam, missthought of her to thee so dear?

To whom with healing words *Adam* reply'd.   290

Daughter of God and Man, immortal *Eve*,

For such thou art, from sin and blame entire:

Not diffident of thee do I dissuade

Thy absence from my sight, but to avoid

Th' attempt it self, intended by our Foe.

For hee who tempts, though in vain, at least asperses

The tempted with dishonour foul, suppos'd

Not incorruptible of Faith, not prooff

Against temptation: thou thy self with scorne

And anger wouldst resent the offer'd wrong,   300

Though ineffectual found: misdeem not then,

If such affront I labour to avert

From thee alone, which on us both at once

The Enemie, though bold, will hardly dare,

Or daring, first on mee th' assault shall light.

Nor thou his malice and false guile contemn;

Suttle he needs must be, who could seduce

Angels, nor think superfluous others aid.

I from the influence of thy looks receave

Access in every Vertue, in thy sight   310

More wise, more watchful, stronger, if need were

Of outward strength; while shame, thou looking on,

Shame to be overcome or over-reacht
Would utmost vigor raise, and rais'd unite.
Why shouldst not thou like sense within thee feel
When I am present, and thy trial choose
With me, best witness of thy Vertue tri'd.

   So spake domestick *Adam* in his care
And Matrimonial Love, but *Eve,* who thought
Less attributed to her Faith sincere,   320
Thus her reply with accent sweet renewd.

   If this be our condition, thus to dwell
In narrow circuit strait'nd by a Foe,
Suttle or violent, we not endu'd
Single with like defence wherever met,
How are we happie, still in fear of harm?
But harm precedes not sin: onely our Foe
Tempting affronts us with his foul esteem
Of our integritie: his foul esteeme
Sticks no dishonor on our Front, but turns   330
Foul on himself; then wherfore shund or feard
By us? who rather double honour gaine
From his surmise prov'd false, finde peace within,
Favour from Heav'n, our witness from th' event.
And what is Faith, Love, Vertue unassaid
Alone, without exterior help sustaind?
Let us not then suspect our happie State
Left so imperfet by the Maker wise,
As not secure to single or combin'd.
Fraile is our happiness, if this be so,   340

And *Eden* were no *Eden* thus expos'd.

　　To whom thus *Adam* fervently repli'd.

O Woman, best are all things as the will

Of God ordaind them, his creating hand

Nothing imperfet or deficient left

Of all that he Created, much less Man,

Or ought that might his happie State secure,

Secure from outward force; within himself

The danger lies, yet lies within his power:

Against his will he can receave no harme.　　　　　　　350

But God left free the Will, for what obeyes

Reason, is free, and Reason he made right,

But bid her well beware, and still erect,

Least by some faire appeering good surpris'd

She dictate false, and missinforme the Will

To do what God expresly hath forbid.

Not then mistrust, but tender love enjoynes,

That I should mind thee oft, and mind thou me.

Firm we subsist, yet possible to swerve,

Since Reason not impossibly may meet　　　　　　　360

Some specious object by the Foe subornd,

And fall into deception unaware,

Not keeping strictest watch, as she was warnd.

Seek not temptation then; which to avoide

Were better, and most likelie if from mee

Thou sever not: Trial will come unsought.

Wouldst thou approve thy constancie, approve

First thy obedience; th' other who can know,

Not seeing thee attempted, who attest?

But if thou think, trial unsought may finde   370

Us both securer then thus warnd thou seemst,

Go; for thy stay, not free, absents thee more;

Go in thy native innocence, relie

On what thou hast of vertue, summon all,

For God towards thee hath done his part, do thine.

   So spake the Patriarch of Mankinde, but *Eve*

Persisted, yet submiss, though last, repli'd.

With thy permission then, and thus forewarnd

Chiefly by what thy own last reasoning words

Touched onely, that our trial, when least sought,   380

May finde us both perhaps farr less prepar'd,

The willinger I goe, nor much expect

A Foe so proud will first the weaker seek;

So bent, the more shall shame him his repulse.

Thus saying, from her Husbands hand her hand

Soft she withdrew, and like a Wood-Nymph light

Oread or *Dryad*, or of *Delia*'s Traine,

Betook her to the Groves, but *Delia*'s self

In gate surpass'd and Goddess-like deport,

Though not as shee with Bow and Quiver armd,   390

But with such Gardning Tools as Art yet rude,

Guiltless of fire had formd, or Angels brought.

To *Pales*, or *Pomona*, thus adornd,

Likest she seemd, *Pomona* when she fled

Vertumnus, or to *Ceres* in her Prime,

Yet Virgin of *Proserpina* from *Jove*.

Her long with ardent look his Eye pursu'd

Delighted, but desiring more her stay.

Oft he to her his charge of quick returne

Repeated, shee to him as oft engag'd   400

To be returnd by Noon amid the Bowre,

And all things in best order to invite

Noontide repast, or Afternoons repose.

O much deceav'd, much failing, hapless *Eve*,

Of thy presum'd return! event perverse!

Thou never from that houre in Paradise

Foundst either sweet repast, or sound repose;

Such ambush hid among sweet Flours and Shades

Waited with hellish rancor imminent

To intercept thy way, or send thee back   410

Despoild of Innocence, of Faith, of Bliss.

For now, and since first break of dawne the Fiend,

Meer Serpent in appearance, forth was come,

And on his Quest, where likeliest he might finde

The onely two of Mankinde, but in them

The whole included Race, his purposd prey.

In Bowre and Field he sought, where any tuft

Of Grove or Garden-Plot more pleasant lay,

Thir tendance or Plantation for delight,

By Fountain or by shadie Rivulet   420

He sought them both, but wish'd his hap might find

Eve separate, he wish'd, but not with hope

Of what so seldom chanc'd, when to his wish,

Beyond his hope, *Eve* separate he spies,

Veild in a Cloud of Fragrance, where she stood,

Half spi'd, so thick the Roses bushing round

About her glowd, oft stooping to support
Each Flour of slender stalk, whose head though gay
Carnation, Purple, Azure, or spect with Gold,
Hung drooping unsustaind, them she upstaies   430
Gently with Mirtle band, mindless the while,
Her self, though fairest unsupported Flour,
From her best prop so farr, and storm so nigh.
Neerer he drew, and many a walk travers'd
Of stateliest Covert, Cedar, Pine, or Palme,
Then voluble and bold, now hid, now seen
Among thick-wov'n Arborets and Flours
Imborderd on each Bank, the hand of *Eve*:
Spot more delicious then those Gardens feign'd
Or of reviv'd *Adonis*, or renownd   440
Alcinous, host of old *Laertes* Son,
Or that, not Mystic, where the Sapient King
Held dalliance with his faire *Egyptian* Spouse.
Much hee the Place admir'd, the Person more.
As onc who long in populous City pent,
Where Houses thick and Sewers annoy the Aire,
Forth issuing on a Summers Morn to breathe
Among the pleasant Villages and Farmes
Adjoynd, from each thing met conceaves delight,
The smell of Grain, or tedded Grass, or Kine,   450
Or Dairie, each rural sight, each rural sound;
If chance with Nymphlike step fair Virgin pass,
What pleasing seemd, for her now pleases more,
She most, and in her look summs all Delight.
Such Pleasure took the Serpent to behold

This Flourie Plat, the sweet recess of *Eve*

Thus earlie, thus alone; her Heav'nly forme

Angelic, but more soft, and Feminine,

Her graceful Innocence, her every Aire

Of gesture or lest action overawd   460

His Malice, and with rapine sweet bereav'd

His fierceness of the fierce intent it brought:

That space the Evil one abstracted stood

From his own evil, and for the time remaind

Stupidly good, of enmitie disarm'd,

Of guile, of hate, of envie, of revenge;

But the hot Hell that alwayes in him burnes,

Though in mid Heav'n, soon ended his delight,

And tortures him now more, the more he sees

Of pleasure not for him ordain'd: then soon   470

Fierce hate he recollects, and all his thoughts

Of mischief, gratulating, thus excites.

Thoughts, whither have ye led me, with what sweet

Compulsion thus transported to forget

What hither brought us, hate, not love, nor hope

Of Paradise for Hell, hope here to taste

Of pleasure, but all pleasure to destroy,

Save what is in destroying, other joy

To me is lost. Then let me not let pass

Occasion which now smiles, behold alone   480

The Woman, opportune to all attempts,

Her Husband, for I view far round, not nigh,

Whose higher intellectual more I shun,

And strength, of courage hautie, and of limb

Heroic built, though of terrestrial mould,
Foe not informidable, exempt from wound,
I not; so much hath Hell debas'd, and paine
Infeebl'd me, to what I was in Heav'n.
Shee fair, divinely fair, fit Love for Gods,
Not terrible, though terrour be in Love   490
And beautie, not approacht by stronger hate,
Hate stronger, under shew of Love well feign'd,
The way which to her ruin now I tend.
So spake the Enemie of Mankind, enclos'd
In Serpent, Inmate bad, and toward *Eve*
Address'd his way, not with indented wave,
Prone on the ground, as since, but on his reare,
Circular base of rising foulds, that tour'd
Fould above fould a surging Maze, his Head
Crested aloft, and Carbuncle his Eyes;   500
With burnisht Neck of verdant Gold, erect
Amidst his circling Spires, that on the grass
Floted redundant: pleasing was his shape,
And lovely, never since of Serpent kind
Lovelier, not those that in *Illyria* chang'd
Hermione and *Cadmus*, or the God
In *Epidaurus*; nor to which transformd
Ammonian Jove, or *Capitoline* was seen,
Hee with *Olympias*, this with her who bore
Scipio the highth of *Rome*. With tract oblique   510
At first, as one who sought access, but feard
To interrupt, side-long he works his way.
As when a Ship by skilful Stearsman wrought

Nigh Rivers mouth or Foreland, where the Wind
Veres oft, as oft so steers, and shifts her Saile;
So varied hee, and of his tortuous Traine
Curld many a wanton wreath in sight of *Eve*,
To lure her Eye; shee busied heard the sound
Of rusling Leaves, but minded not, as us'd
To such disport before her through the Field,   520
From every Beast, more duteous at her call,
Then at *Circean* call the Herd disguis'd.
Hee boulder now, uncall'd before her stood;
But in a gaze admiring: Oft he bowd
His turret Crest, and sleek enamel'd Neck,
Fawning, and lick'd the ground whereon she trod.
His gentle dumb expression turnd at length
The Eye of *Eve* to mark his play; he glad
Of her attention gaind, with Serpent Tongue
Organic, or impulse of vocal Air,   530
His fraudulent temptation thus began.
     Wonder not, sovran Mistress, if perhaps
Thou canst, who art sole Wonder, much less arm
Thy looks, the Heav'n of mildness, with disdain,
Displeas'd that I approach thee thus, and gaze
Insatiate, I thus single, nor have feard
Thy awful brow, more awful thus retir'd.
Fairest resemblance of thy Maker faire,
Thee all things living gaze on, all things thine
By gift, and thy Celestial Beautie adore   540
With ravishment beheld, there best beheld
Where universally admir'd; but here

In this enclosure wild, these Beasts among,
Beholders rude, and shallow to discerne
Half what in thee is fair, one man except,
Who sees thee? (and what is one?) who shouldst be seen
A Goddess among Gods, ador'd and serv'd
By Angels numberless, thy daily Train.
    So gloz'd the Tempter, and his Proem tun'd;
Into the Heart of *Eve* his words made way,   550
Though at the voice much marveling; at length
Not unamaz'd she thus in answer spake.
What may this mean? Language of Man pronounc't
By Tongue of Brute, and human sense exprest?
The first at lest of these I thought deni'd
To Beasts, whom God on thir Creation-Day
Created mute to all articulat sound;
The latter I demurre, for in thir looks
Much reason, and in thir actions oft appeers.
Thee, Serpent, suttlest beast of all the field   560
I knew, but not with human voice endu'd;
Redouble then this miracle, and say,
How cam'st thou speakable of mute, and how
To me so friendly grown above the rest
Of brutal kind, that daily are in sight?
Say, for such wonder claims attention due.
    To whom the guileful Tempter thus reply'd.
Empress of this fair World, resplendent *Eve*,
Easie to mee it is to tell thee all
What thou commandst, and right thou shouldst be obeyd: 570

I was at first as other Beasts that graze
The trodden Herb, of abject thoughts and low,
As was my food, nor aught but food discern'd
Or Sex, and apprehended nothing high:
Till on a day roaving the field, I chanc'd
A goodly Tree farr distant to behold
Loaden with fruit of fairest colours mixt,
Ruddie and Gold: I nearer drew to gaze;
When from the boughes a savorie odour blow'n,
Grateful to appetite, more pleas'd my sense   580
Then smell of sweetest Fenel, or the Teats
Of Ewe or Goat dropping with Milk at Eevn,
Unsuckt of Lamb or Kid, that tend thir play.
To satisfie the sharp desire I had
Of tasting those fair Apples, I resolv'd
Not to deferr; hunger and thirst at once,
Powerful perswaders, quick'nd at the scent
Of that alluring fruit, urg'd me so keene.
About the Mossie Trunk I wound me soon,
For high from ground the branches would require   590
Thy utmost reach or *Adams:* Round the Tree
All other Beasts that saw, with like desire
Longing and envying stood, but could not reach.
Amid the Tree now got, where plentie hung
Tempting so nigh, to pluck and eat my fill
I spar'd not, for such pleasure till that hour
At Feed or Fountain never had I found.
Sated at length, ere long I might perceave

Strange alteration in me, to degree

Of Reason in my inward Powers, and Speech   600

Wanted not long, though to this shape retaind.

Thenceforth to Speculations high or deep

I turnd my thoughts, and with capacious mind

Considerd all things visible in Heav'n,

Or Earth, or Middle, all things fair and good;

But all that fair and good in thy Divine

Semblance, and in thy Beauties heav'nly Ray

United I beheld; no Fair to thine

Equivalent or second, which compel'd

Mee thus, though importune perhaps, to come   610

And gaze, and worship thee of right declar'd

Sovran of Creatures, universal Dame.

    So talk'd the spirited sly Snake; and *Eve*

Yet more amaz'd unwarie thus reply'd.

    Serpent, thy overpraising leaves in doubt

The vertue of that Fruit, in thee first prov'd:

But say, where grows the Tree, from hence how far?

For many are the Trees of God that grow

In Paradise, and various, yet unknown

To us, in such abundance lies our choice,   620

As leaves a greater store of Fruit untoucht,

Still hanging incorruptible, till men

Grow up to thir provision, and more hands

Help to disburden Nature of her Bearth.

    To whom the wilie Adder, blithe and glad.

Empress, the way is readie, and not long,

Beyond a row of Myrtles, on a Flat,

Fast by a Fountain, one small Thicket past
Of blowing Myrrh and Balme; if thou accept
My conduct, I can bring thee thither soon.   630
    Lead then, said *Eve.* Hee leading swiftly rowld
In tangles, and made intricate seem strait,
To mischief swift. Hope elevates, and joy
Bright'ns his Crest, as when a wandring Fire
Compact of unctuous vapor, which the Night
Condenses, and the cold invirons round,
Kindl'd through agitation to a Flame,
Which oft, they say, some evil Spirit attends,
Hovering and blazing with delusive Light,
Misleads th' amaz'd Night-wanderer from his way   640
To Boggs and Mires, & oft through Pond or Poole,
There swallow'd up and lost, from succour farr.
So glister'd the dire Snake, and into fraud
Led *Eve* our credulous Mother, to the Tree
Of prohibition, root of all our woe;
Which when she saw, thus to her guide she spake.
    Serpent, we might have spar'd our coming hither,
Fruitless to me, though Fruit be here to excess,
The credit of whose vertue rest with thee,
Wondrous indeed, if cause of such effects.   650
But of this Tree we may not taste nor touch;
God so commanded, and left that Command
Sole Daughter of his voice; the rest, we live
Law to our selves, our Reason is our Law.
    To whom the Tempter guilefully repli'd.
Indeed? hath God then said that of the Fruit

Of all these Garden Trees ye shall not eate,
Yet Lords declar'd of all in Earth or Aire?

   To whom thus *Eve* yet sinless. Of the Fruit
Of each Tree in the Garden we may eate,   660
But of the Fruit of this fair Tree amidst
The Garden, God hath said, Ye shall not eate
Thereof, nor shall ye touch it, least ye die.

   She scarse had said, though brief, when now more bold
The Tempter, but with shew of Zeale and Love
To Man, and indignation at his wrong,
New part puts on, and as to passion mov'd,
Fluctuats disturbed, yet comely, and in act
Rais'd, as of som great matter to begin.
As when of old som Orator renound   670
In *Athens* or free *Rome*, where Eloquence
Flourishd, since mute, to som great cause addrest,
Stood in himself collected, while each part,
Motion, each act won audience ere the tongue,
Somtimes in highth began, as no delay
Of Preface brooking through his Zeal of Right.
So standing, moving, or to highth upgrown
The Tempter all impassiond thus began.

   O Sacred, Wise, and Wisdom-giving Plant,
Mother of Science, Now I feel thy Power   680
Within me cleere, not onely to discerne
Things in thir Causes, but to trace the wayes
Of highest Agents, deemd however wise.
Queen of this Universe, doe not believe
Those rigid threats of Death; ye shall not Die:

How should ye? by the Fruit? it gives you Life
To Knowledge? By the Threatner, look on mee,
Mee who have touch'd and tasted, yet both live,
And life more perfet have attaind then Fate
Meant mee, by ventring higher then my Lot.   690
Shall that be shut to Man, which to the Beast
Is open? or will God incense his ire
For such a petty Trespass, and not praise
Rather your dauntless vertue, whom the pain
Of Death denounc't, whatever thing Death be,
Deterrd not from atchieving what might leade
To happier life, knowledge of Good and Evil;
Of good, how just? of evil, if what is evil
Be real, why not known, since easier shunnd?
God therefore cannot hurt ye, and be just;   700
Not just, not God; not feard then, nor obeid:
Your feare it self of Death removes the feare.
Why then was this forbid? Why but to awe,
Why but to keep ye low and ignorant,
His worshippers; he knows that in the day
Ye Eate thereof, your Eyes that seem so cleere,
Yet are but dim, shall perfetly be then
Op'nd and cleerd, and ye shall be as Gods,
Knowing both Good and Evil as they know.
That ye should be as Gods, since I as Man,   710
Internal Man, is but proportion meet,
I of brute human, yee of human Gods.
So ye shall die perhaps, by putting off
Human, to put on Gods, death to be wisht,

Though threat'nd, which no worse then this can bring.
And what are Gods that Man may not become
As they, participating God-like food?
The Gods are first, and that advantage use
On our belief, that all from them proceeds;
I question it, for this fair Earth I see,   720
Warm'd by the Sun, producing every kind,
Them nothing: If they all things, who enclos'd
Knowledge of Good and Evil in this Tree,
That whoso eats thereeof, forthwith attains
Wisdom without their leave? and wherein lies
Th' offence, that Man should thus attain to know?
What can your knowledge hurt him, or this Tree
Impart against his will if all be his?
Or is it envie, and can envie dwell
In heav'nly brests? these, these and many more   730
Causes import your need of this fair Fruit.
Goddess humane, reach then, and freely taste.
    He ended, and his words replete with guile
Into her heart too easie entrance won:
Fixt on the Fruit she gaz'd, which to behold
Might tempt alone, and in her ears the sound
Yet rung of his perswasive words, impregn'd
With Reason, to her seeming, and with Truth;
Meanwhile the hour of Noon drew on, and wak'd
An eager appetite, rais'd by the smell   740
So savorie of that Fruit, which with desire,
Inclinable now grown to touch or taste,
Sollicited her longing eye; yet first

Pausing a while, thus to her self she mus'd.

   Great are thy Vertues, doubtless, best of Fruits,

Though kept from Man, & worthy to be admir'd,

Whose taste, too long forborn, at first assay

Gave elocution to the mute, and taught

The Tongue not made for Speech to speak thy praise:

Thy praise hee also who forbids thy use,   750

Conceales not from us, naming thee the Tree

Of Knowledge, knowledge both of good and evil;

Forbids us then to taste, but his forbidding

Commends thee more, while it inferrs the good

By thee communicated, and our want:

For good unknown, sure is not had, or had

And yet unknown, is as not had at all.

In plain then, what forbids he but to know,

Forbids us good, forbids us to be wise?

Such prohibitions binde not. But if Death   760

Bind us with after-bands, what profits then

Our inward freedom? In the day we eate

Of this fair Fruit, our doom is, we shall die.

How dies the Serpent? hee hath eat'n and lives,

And knows and speaks, and reasons, and discernes,

Irrational till then. For us alone

Was death invented? or to us deni'd

This intellectual food, for beasts reserv'd?

For Beasts it seems: yet that one Beast which first

Hath tasted, envies not, but brings with joy   770

The good befall'n him, Author unsuspect,

Friendly to man, farr from deceit or guile.

What fear I then, rather what know to feare
Under this ignorance of Good and Evil,
Of God or Death, of Law or Penaltie?
Here grows the Cure of all, this Fruit Divine,
Fair to the Eye, inviting to the Taste,
Of vertue to make wise: what hinders then
To reach, and feed at once both Bodie and Mind?
   So saying, her rash hand in evil hour   780
Forth reaching to the Fruit, she pluck'd, she eat:
Earth felt the wound, and Nature from her seat
Sighing through all her Works gave signs of woe,
That all was lost. Back to the Thicket slunk
The guiltie Serpent, and well might, for *Eve*
Intent now wholly on her taste, naught else
Regarded, such delight till then, as seemd,
In Fruit she never tasted, whether true
Or fansied so, through expectation high
Of knowledg, nor was God-head from her thought.   790
Greedily she ingorg'd without restraint,
And knew not eating Death: Satiate at length,
And hight'nd as with Wine, jocond and boon,
Thus to her self she pleasingly began.
   O Sovran, vertuous, precious of all Trees
In Paradise, of operation blest
To Sapience, hitherto obscur'd, infam'd,
And thy fair Fruit let hang, as to no end
Created; but henceforth my early care,
Not without Song, each Morning, and due praise   800
Shall tend thee, and the fertil burden ease

Of thy full branches offer'd free to all;
Till dieted by thee I grow mature
In knowledge, as the Gods who all things know;
Though others envie what they cannot give;
For had the gift bin theirs, it had not here
Thus grown. Experience, next to thee I owe,
Best guide; not following thee, I had remaind
In Ignorance, thou op'nst Wisdoms way,
And giv'st access, though secret she retire.   810
And I perhaps am secret; Heav'n is high,
High and remote to see from thence distinct
Each thing on Earth; and other care perhaps
May have diverted from continual watch
Our great Forbidder, safe with all his Spies
About him. But to *Adam* in what sort
Shall I appeer? shall I to him make known
As yet my change, and give him to partake
Full happiness with mee, or rather not,
But keep the odds of Knowledge in my power   820
Without Copartner? so to add what wants
in Femal Sex, the more to draw his Love,
And render me more equal, and perhaps,
A thing not undesireable, somtime
Superior; for inferior who is free?
This may be well: but what if God have seen,
And Death ensue? then I shall be no more,
And *Adam* wedded to another *Eve*,
Shall live with her enjoying, I extinct;
A death to think. Confirm'd then I resolve,   830

Adam shall share with me in bliss or woe:
So dear I love him, that with him all deaths
I could endure, without him live no life.

So saying, from the Tree her step she turnd,
But first low Reverence don, as to the power
That dwelt within, whose presence had infus'd
Into the plant sciential sap, deriv'd
From Nectar, drink of Gods. *Adam* the while
Waiting desirous her return, had wove
Of choicest Flours a Garland to adorne   840
Her Tresses, and her rural labours crown
As Reapers oft are wont thir Harvest Queen.
Great joy he promis'd to his thoughts, and new
Solace in her return, so long delay'd;
Yet oft his heart, divine of somthing ill,
Misgave him; hee the faultring measure felt;
And forth to meet her went, the way she took
That Morn when first they parted; by the Tree
Of Knowledge he must pass, there he her met,
Scarse from the Tree returning; in her hand   850
A bough of fairest fruit that downie smil'd,
New gatherd, and ambrosial smell diffus'd.
To him she hasted, in her face excuse
Came Prologue, and Apologie to prompt,
Which with bland wors at will she thus addrest.

Hast thou not wonderd, *Adam*, at my stay?
Thee I have misst, and thought it long, depriv'd
Thy presence, agonie of love till now
Not felt, nor shall be twice, for never more
Mean I to trie, what rash untri'd I sought,   860

The paine of absence from thy sight. But strange
Hath bin the cause, and wonderful to heare:
This Tree is not as we are told, a Tree
Of danger tasted, nor to evil unknown
Op'ning the way, but of Divine effect
To open Eyes, and make them Gods who taste;
And hath bin tasted such: the Serpent wise,
Or not restraind as wee, or not obeying,
Hath eat'n of the fruit, and is become,
Not dead, as we are threatn'd, but thence forth   870
Endu'd with human voice and human sense,
Reasoning to admiration, and with mee
Perswasively hath so prevaild, that I
Have also tasted, and have also found
Th' effects to correspond, opener mine Eyes,
Dimm erst, dilated Spirits, ampler Heart.
And growing up to Godhead; which for thee
Chiefly I sought, without thee can despise.
For bliss, as thou hast part, to me is bliss,
Tedious, unshar'd with thee, and odious soon.   880
Thou therfore also taste, that equal Lot
May joyne us, equal Joy, as equal Love;
Least thou not tasting, different degree
Disjoyne us, and I then too late renounce
Deitie for thee, when Fate will not permit.
    Thus *Eve* with Countnance blithe her storie told;
But in her Cheek distemper flushing glowd.
On th' other side, *Adam*, soon as he heard
The fatal Trespass don by *Eve*, amaz'd,
Astonied stood and Blank, while horror chill   890

Ran through his veins, and all his joynts relax'd;
From his slack hand the Garland wreath'd for *Eve*
Down drop'd, and all the faded Roses shed:
Speechless he stood and pale, till thus at length
First to himself he inward silence broke.

   O fairest of Creation, last and best
Of all Gods Works, Creature in whom excell'd
Whatever can to sight or thought be formd,
Holy, divine, good, amiable, or sweet!
How are thou lost, how on a suddcn lost,   900
Defac't, deflourd. and now to Death devote?
Rather how hast thou yeelded to transgress
The strict forbiddance, how to violate
The sacred Fruit forbidd'n! som cursed fraud
Of Enemie hath beguil'd thee, yet unknown,
And mee with thee hath ruind, for with thee
Certain my resolution is to Die;
How can I live without thee, how forgoe
Thy sweet Converse and Love so dearly joyn'd,
To live again in these wilde Woods forlorn?   910
Should God create another *Eve*, and I
Another Rib afford, yet loss of thee
Would never from my heart; no no, I feel
The Link of Nature draw me: Flesh of Flesh,
Bone of my Bone thou art, and from thy State
Mine never shall be parted, bliss or woe.

   So having said, as one from sad dismay
Recomforted, and after thoughts disturbd

Submitting to what seemd remediless,

Thus in calme mood his Words to *Eve* he turnd. 920

   Bold deed thou hast presum'd, adventrous *Eve,*

And peril great provok't, who thus hast dar'd

Had it bin onely coveting to Eye

That sacred Fruit, sacred to abstinence,

Much more to taste it under banne to touch.

But past who can recall, or don undoe?

Not God Omnipotent, nor Fate, yet so

Perhaps thou shalt not Die, perhaps the Fact

Is not so hainous now, foretasted Fruit,

Profan'd first by the Serpent, by him first 930

Made common and unhallowd ere our taste;

Nor yet on him found deadly, he yet lives,

Lives, as thou saidst, and gaines to live as Man

Higher degree of Life, inducement strong

To us, as likely tasting to attaine

Proportional ascent, which cannot be

But to be Gods, or Angels Demi-gods.

Nor can I think that God, Creator wise,

Though threatning, will in earnest so destroy

Us his prime Creatures, dignifi'd so high, 940

Set over all his Works, which in our Fall,

For us created, needs with us must faile,

Dependent made; so God shall uncreate,

Be frustrate, do, undo, and labour loose,

Not well conceav'd of God, who though his Power

Creation could repeate, yet would be loath

Us to abolish, least the Adversary
Triumph and say; Fickle their State whom God
Most Favors, who can please him long? Mee first
He ruind, now Mankind; whom will he next?   950
Matter of scorne, not to be given the Foe.
However I with thee have fixt my Lot,
Certain to undergoe like doom, if Death
Consort with thee, Death is to mee as Life;
So forcible within my heart I feel
Thc Bond of Nature draw me to my owne,
My own in thee, for what thou art is mine;
Our State cannot be severd, we are one,
One Flesh; to loose thee were to loose my self.
   So *Adam*, and thus *Eve* to him repli'd.   960
O glorious trial of exceeding Love,
Illustrious evidence, example high!
Ingaging me to emulate, but short
Of thy perfection, how shall I attaine,
Adam, from whose deare side I boast me sprung,
And gladly of our Union heare thee speak,
One Heart, one Soul in both; whereof good prooff
This day affords, declaring thee resolvd,
Rather then Death or aught then Death more dread
Shall separate us, linkt in Love so deare,   970
To undergoe with mee one Guilt, one Crime,
If any be, of tasting this fair Fruit,
Whose vertue, for of good still good proceeds,
Direct, or by occasion hath presented
This happie trial of thy Love, which else

So eminently never had bin known.
Were it I thought Death menac't would ensue
This my attempt, I would sustain alone
The worst, and not perswade thee, rather die
Deserted, then oblige thee with a fact   980
Pernicious to thy Peace, chiefly assur'd
Remarkably so late of thy so true,
So faithful Love unequald; but I feel
Farr otherwise th' event, not Death, but Life
Augmented, op'nd Eyes, new Hopes, new Joyes,
Taste so Divine, that what of sweet before
Hath toucht my sense, flat seems to this, and harsh.
On my experience, *Adam*, freely taste,
And fear of Death deliver to the Windes.
   So saying, she embrac'd him, and for joy   990
Tenderly wept, much won that he his Love
Had so enobl'd, as of choice to incurr
Divine displeasure for her sake, or Death.
In recompence (for such compliance bad
Such recompense best merits) from the bough
She gave him of that fair enticing Fruit
With liberal hand: he scrupl'd not to eat
Against his better knowledge, not deceav'd,
But fondly overcome with Femal charm.
Earth trembl'd from her entrails, as again   1000
In pangs, and Nature gave a second groan,
Skie lowr'd, and muttering Thunder, som sad drops
Wept at compleating of the mortal Sin
Original; while *Adam* took no thought,

Eating his fill, nor *Eve* to iterate
Her former trespass fear'd, the more to soothe
Him with her lov'd socieite, that now
As with new Wine intoxicated both
They swim in mirth, and fansie that they feel
Divinitie within them breeding wings   101(
Wherewith to scorn the Earth: but that false Fruit
Farr other operation first displaid,
Carnal desire enflaming, hee on *Eve*
Began to cast lascivious Eyes, she him
As wantonly repaid; in Lust they burne:
Till *Adam* thus 'gan *Eve* to dalliance move.
    Eve, now I see thou art exact of taste,
And elegant, of Sapience no small part,
Since to each meaning savour we apply,
And Palate call judicious; I the praise   102(
Yeild thee, so well this day thou hast purvey'd.
Much pleasure we have lost, while we abstain'd
From this delightful Fruit, nor known till now
True relish, tasting; if such pleasure be
In things to us forbidden, it might be wish'd,
For this one Tree had bin forbidden ten.
But come, so well refresh't, now let us play,
As meet is, after such delicious Fare;
For never did thy Beautie since the day
I saw thee first and wedded thee, adorn'd   103(
With all perfections, so enflame my sense
With ardor to enjoy thee, fairer now
Then ever, bountie of this vertuous Tree.

So said he, and forbore not glance or toy
Of amorous intent, well understood
Of *Eve*, whose Eye darted contagious Fire.
Her hand he seis'd, and to a shadie bank,
Thick overhead with verdant roof imbowr'd
He led her nothing loath; Flours were the Couch,
Pansies, and Violets, and Asphodel,   1040
And Hyacinth, Earths freshest softest lap.
There they thir fill of Love and Loves disport
Took largely, of thir mutual guilt the Seale,
The solace of thir sin, till dewie sleep
Oppress'd them, wearied with thir amorous play.
Soon as the force of that fallacious Fruit,
That with exhilerating vapour bland
About thir spirits had plaid, and inmost powers
Made erre, was now exhal'd, and grosser sleep
Bred of unkindly fumes, with conscious dreams   1050
Encumberd, now had left them, up they rose
As from unrest, and each the other viewing,
Soon found thir Eyes how op'nd, and thir minds
How dark'nd; innocence, that as a veile
Had shadow'd them from knowing ill, was gon,
Just confidence, and native righteousness,
And honour from about them, naked left
To guiltie shame hee cover'd, but his Robe
Uncover'd more. So rose the *Danite* strong
Herculean Samson from the Harlot-lap   1060
Of *Philistean Dalilah*, and wak'd
Shorn of his strength, They destitute and bare

Of all thir vertue: silent, and in face
Confounded long they sate, as struck'n mute,
Till *Adam*, though not less then *Eve* abasht,
At length gave utterance to these words constraind.
   O *Eve*, in evil hour thou didst give eare
To that false Worm, of whomsoever taught
To counterfet Mans voice, true in our Fall,
False in our promis'd Rising; since our Eyes   1070
Op'nd we find indeed, and find we know
Both Good and Evil, Good lost, and Evil got,
Bad Fruit of Knowledge, if this be to know,
Which leaves us naked thus, of Honour void,
Of Innocence, of Faith, of Puritie,
Our wonted Ornaments now soild and staind,
And in our Faces evident the signes
Of foul concupiscence; whence evil store;
Even shame, the last of evils; of the first
Be sure then. How shall I behold the face   1080
Henceforth of God or Angel, earst with joy
And rapture so oft beheld? those heav'nly shapes
Will dazle now this earthly, with thir blaze
Insufferably bright. O might I here
In solitude live savage, in some glade
Obscur'd, where highest Woods impenetrable
To Starr or Sun-light, spread thir umbrage broad,
And brown as Evening: Cover me ye Pines,
Ye Cedars, with innumerable boughs
Hide me, where I may never see them more.   1090

But let us now, as in bad plight devise
What best may for the present serve to hide
The Parts of each from other, that seem most
To shame obnoxious, and unseemliest seen,
Some Tree whose broad smooth Leaves together sowd,
And girded on our loyns, may cover round
Those middle parts, that this new commer, Shame,
There sit not, and reproach us as unclean.
    So counsel'd hee, and both together went
Into the thickest Wood, there soon they chose   1100
The Figtree, not that kind for Fruit renown'd,
But such as at this day to *Indians* known
In *Malabar* or *Decan* spreds her Armes
Braunching so broad and long, that in the ground
The bended Twigs take root, and Daughters grow
About the Mother Tree, a Pillard shade
High overarch't, and echoing Walks between;
There oft the *Indian* Herdsman shunning heate
Shelters in coole, and tends his pasturing Herds
As Loopholes cut through thickest shade: Those Leaves   1110
They gatherd, broad as *Amazonian* Targe,
And with what skill they had, together sowd,
To gird thir waste, vain Covering if to hide
Thir guilt and dreaded shame; O how unlike
To that first naked Glorie. Such of late
Columbus found th' *American* so girt
With featherd Cincture, naked else and wilde
Among the Trees on Iles and woodie Shores.

Thus fenc't, and as they thought, thir shame in part
Coverd, but not at rest or ease of Mind,   1120
They sate them down to weep, nor onely Teares
Raind at thir Eyes, but high Winds worse within
Began to rise, high Passions, Anger, Hate,
Mistrust, Suspicion, Discord, and shook sore
Thir inward State of Mind, calme Region once
And full of Peace, now tost and turbulent:
For Understanding rul'd not, and the Will
Heard not her lore, both in subjection now
To sensual Appetite, who from beneathe
Usurping over sovran Reason claimd   1130
Superior sway: From thus distemperd brest,
Adam, estrang'd in look and alterd stile,
Speech intermitted thus to *Eve* renewd.
    Would thou hadst heark'nd to my words, & stai'd
With me, as I besought thee, when that strange
Desire of wandring this unhappie Morn,
I know not whence possessd thee; we had then
Remaind still happie, not as now, despoild
Of all our good, sham'd, naked, miserable.
Let none henceforth seek needless cause to approve   1140
The Faith they owe; when earnestly they seek
Such proof, conclude, they then begin to faile.
    To whom soon mov'd with touch of blame thus *Eve*.
What words have past thy Lips, *Adam* severe,
Imput'st thou that to my default, or will
Of wandering, as thou call'st it, which who knows
But might as ill have happ'nd thou being by,

Or to thy self perhaps: hadst thou bin there,
Or here th' attempt, thou couldst not have discernd
Fraud in the Serpent, speaking as he spake;   1150
No ground of enmitie between us known,
Why hee should mean me ill, or seek to harme.
Was I to have never parted from thy side?
As good have grown there still a liveless Rib.
Being as I am, why didst not thou the Head
Command me absolutely not to go,
Going into such danger as thou saidst?
Too facil then thou didst not much gainsay,
Nay, didst permit, approve, and fair dismiss.
Hadst thou bin firm and fixt in thy dissent,   1160
Neither had I transgress'd, nor thou with mee.
　　To whom then first incenst *Adam* repli'd.
Is this the Love, is this the recompence
Of mine to thee, ingrateful *Eve*, exprest
Immutable when thou wert lost, not I,
Who might have liv'd and joyd immortal bliss,
Yet willingly chose rather Death with thee:
And am I now upbraided, as the cause
Of thy transgressing? not enough severe,
It seems, in thy restraint: what could I more?   1170
I warn'd thee, I admonish'd thee, foretold
The danger, and the lurking Enemie
That lay in wait; beyond this had bin force,
And force upon free Will hath here no place.
But confidence then bore thee on, secure
Either to meet no danger, or to finde

Matter of glorious trial; and perhaps

I also err'd in overmuch admiring

What seemd in thee so perfet, that I thought

No evil durst attempt thee, but I rue   1180

That errour now, which is become my crime,

And thou th' accuser. Thus it shall befall

Him who to worth in Woman overtrusting

Lets her Will rule; restraint she will not brook,

And left to her self, if evil thence ensue,

Shee first his weak indulgence will accuse.

    Thus they in mutual accusation spent

The fruitless hours, but neither self-condemning,

And of thir vain contest appeer'd no end.

The end of the Eighth Book.

PARADISE
LOST

BOOK IX.

MEanwhile the hainous and despightfull act
Of *Satan* done in Paradise, and how
Hee in the Serpent had perverted *Eve*,
Her Husband shee, to taste the fatall fruit,
Was known in Heav'n; for what can scape the Eye
Of God All-seeing, or deceave his Heart
Omniscient, who in all things wise and just,
Hinder'd not *Satan* to attempt the minde
Of Man, with strength entire, and free Will arm'd,
Complete to have discover'd and repulst   10
Whatever wiles of Foe or seeming Friend.
For still they knew, and ought to have still remember'd
The high Injunction not to taste that Fruit,
Whoever tempted; which they not obeying,
Incurr'd, what could they less, the penaltie,
And manifold in sin, deserv'd to fall.
Up into Heav'n from Paradise in hast
Th' Angelic Guards ascended, mute and sad
For Man, for of his state by this they knew,
Much wondring how the suttle Fiend had stoln   20
Entrance unseen. Soon as th' unwelcome news
From Earth arriv'd at Heaven Gate, displeas'd

All were who heard, dim sadness did not spare

That time Celestial visage, yet mixt

With pitie, violated not thir bliss.

About the new-arriv'd, in multitudes

Th' ethereal People ran, to hear and know

How all befell: they towards the Throne Supream

Accountable made haste to make appear

With righteous plea, thir utmost vigilance,   30

And easily approv'd; when the most High

Eternal Father from his secret Cloud,

Amidst in Thunder utter'd thus his voice

   Assembl'd Angels, and ye Powers return'd

From unsuccessful charge, be not dismaid,

Nor troubl'd at these tidings from the Earth,

Which your sincerest care could not prevent,

Foretold so lately what would come to pass,

When first this Tempter cross'd the Gulf from Hell.

I told ye then he should prevail and speed   40

On his bad Errand, Man should be seduc't

And flatter'd out of all, believing lies

Against his Maker; no Decree of mine

Concurring to necessitate his Fall,

Or touch with lightest moment of impulse

His free Will, to her own inclining left

In eeven scale. But fall'n he is, and now

What rests, but that the mortal Sentence pass

On his transgression, Death denounc't that day,

Which he presumes already vain and void,   50

Because not yet inflicted, as he fear'd,

By some immediate stroak; but soon shall find
Forbearance no acquittance ere day end.
Justice shall not return as bountie scorn'd.
But whom send I to judge them? whom but thee
Vicegerent Son, to thee I have transferr'd
All Judgement, whether in Heav'n, or Earth, or Hell.
Easie it may be seen that I intend
Mercie collegue with Justice, sending thee
Mans Friend, his Mediator, his design'd   60
Both Ransom and Redeemer voluntarie,
And destin'd Man himself to judge Man fall'n.
  So spake the Father, and unfoulding bright
Toward the right hand of Glorie, on the Son
Blaz'd forth unclouded Deitie; he full
Resplendent all his Father manifest
Express'd and thus divinely answer'd milde.
  Father Eternal, thine is to decree,
Mine both in Heav'n and Earth to do thy will
Supream, that thou in mee thy Son belov'd   70
Mayst ever rest well pleas'd. I go to judge
On Earth these thy transgressors, but thou knowst,
Whoever judg'd, the worst on mee must light,
When time shall be, for so I undertook
Before thee; and not repenting, this obtaine
Of right, that I may mitigate thir doom
On me deriv'd, yet I shall temper so
Justice with Mercie, as may illustrate most
Them fully satisfied, and thee appease.
Attendance none shall need, nor Train, where none   80

Are to behold the Judgement, but the judg'd,
Those two; the third best absent is condemn'd,
Convict by flight, and Rebel to all Law
Conviction to the Serpent none belongs.
    Thus saying, from his radiant Seat he rose
Of high collateral glorie: him Thrones and Powers,
Princedoms, and Dominations ministrant
Accompanied to Heaven Gate, from whence
Eden and all the Coast in prospect lay.
Down he descended strait; the speed of Gods   90
Time counts not, though with swiftest minutes wing'd.
Now was the Sun in Western cadence low
From Noon, and gentle Aires due at thir hour
To fan the Earth now wak'd, and usher in
The Eevning coole when he from wrauth more coole
Came the mild Judge and Intercessor both
To sentence Man: the voice of God they heard
Now walking in the Garden, by soft windes
Brought to thir Ears, while day declin'd, they heard,
And from his presence hid themselves among   100
The thickest Trees, both Man and Wife, till God
Approaching, thus to *Adam* call'd aloud.
    Where art thou *Adam*, wont with joy to meet
My coming seen far off? I miss thee here,
Not pleas'd, thus entertaind with solitude,
Where obvious dutie erewhile appear'd unsaught:
Or come I less conspicuous, or what change
Absents thee, or what chance detains? Come forth.
He came, and with him *Eve*, more loth, though first
To offend, discount'nanc't both, and discompos'd;   110

Love was not in thir looks, either to God

Or to each other, but apparent guilt,

And shame, and perturbation, and despaire,

Anger, and obstinancie, and hate, and guile.

Whence *Adam* faultring long, thus answer'd brief.

   I heard thee in the Garden, and of thy voice

Affraid, being naked, hid my self. To whom

The gracious Judge without revile repli'd.

   My voice thou oft hast heard, and hast not fear'd,

But still rejoyc't, how is it now become   120

So dreadful to thee? that thou are naked, who

Hath told thee? hast thou eaten of the Tree

Whereof I gave thee charge thou shouldst not eat?

   To whom thus *Adam* sore beset repli'd.

O Heav'n! in evil strait this day I stand

Before my Judge, either to undergoe

My self the total Crime, or to accuse

My other self, the partner of my life;

Whose failing, while her Faith to me remaines,

I should conceal, and not expose to blame   130

By my complaint; but strict necessitie

Subdues me, and calamitous constraint,

Least on my head both sin and punishment,

However insupportable, be all

Devolv'd; though should I hold my peace, yet thou

Wouldst easily detect what I conceale.

This Woman whom thou mad'st to be my help,

And gav'st me as thy perfet gift, so good,

So fit, so acceptable, so Divine,

That from her hand I could suspect no ill,   140

And what she did, whatever in it self,
Her doing seem'd to justifie the deed;
Shee gave me of the Tree, and I did eate.
    To whom the sovran Presence thus repli'd.
Was shee thy God, that her thou didst obey
Before his voice, or was shee made thy guide,
Superior, or but equal, that to her
Thou did'st resigne thy Manhood, and the Place
Wherein God set thee above her made of thee,
And for thee, whose perfection farr excell'd   150
Hers in all real dignitie: Adornd
She was indeed, and lovely to attract
Thy Love, not thy Subjection, and her Gifts
Were such as under Government well seem'd,
Unseemly to beare rule, which was thy part
And person, had'st thou known thy self aright.
    So having said, he thus to *Eve* in few:
Say Woman, what is this which thou hast done?
    To whom sad *Eve* with shame nigh overwhelm'd,
Confessing soon, yet not before her Judge   160
Bold or loquacious, thus abasht repli'd.
    The Serpent me beguil'd and I did eate.
    Which when the Lord God heard, without delay
To Judgement he proceeded on th' accus'd
Serpent though brute, unable to transferre
The Guilt on him who made him instrument
Of mischief, and polluted from the end
Of his Creation; justly then accurst,

As vitiated in Nature: more to know
Concern'd not Man (since he no further knew)   170
Nor alter'd his offence; yet God at last
To Satan first in sin his doom apply'd,
Though in mysterious terms, judg'd as then best:
And on the Serpent thus his curse let fall.
   Because thou hast done this, thou art accurst
Above all Cattel, each Beast of the Field;
Upon thy Belly groveling thou shalt goe,
And dust shalt eat all the days of thy Life.
Between Thee and the Woman I will put
Enmitie, and between thine and her Seed;   180
Her Seed shall bruise thy head, thou bruise his heel.
   So spake this Oracle, then verifi'd
When *Jesus* son of *Mary* second *Eve*,
Saw Satan fall like Lightning down from Heav'n,
Prince of the Aire; then rising from his Grave
Spoild Principalities and Powers, triumpht
In open shew, and with ascension bright
Captivity led captive through the Aire,
The Realme it self of Satan long usurpt,
Whom he shall tread at last under our feet;   190
Eevn hee who now foretold his fatal bruise,
And to the Woman thus his Sentence turn'd.
   Thy sorrow I will greatly multiplie
By thy Conception; Childern thou shalt bring
In sorrow forth, and to thy Husbands will
Thine shall submit, hee over thee shall rule.

On *Adam* last thus judgement he pronounc'd.
Because thou hast heark'nd to the voice of thy Wife,
And eaten of the Tree concerning which
I charg'd thee, saying: Thou shalt not eate thereof,   200
Curs'd is the ground for thy sake, thou in sorrow
Shalt eate thereof all the days of thy Life;
Thornes also and Thistles it shall bring thee forth
Unbid, and thou shalt eate th' Herb of th' Field,
In the sweat of thy Face shalt thou eate Bread,
Till thou return unto the ground, for thou
Out of the ground wast taken, know thy Birth,
For dust thou art, and shalt to dust returne.
    So judg'd he Man, both Judge and Saviour sent,
And th' instant stroke of Death denounc't that day   210
Remov'd farr off; then pittying how they stood
Before him naked to the aire, that now
Must suffer change, disdain'd not to begin
Thenceforth the forme of servant to assume,
As when he wash'd his servants feet, so now
As Father of his Familie he clad
Thir nakedness with Skins of Beasts, or slain,
Or as the Snake with youthful Coate repaid;
And thought not much to cloath his Enemies:
Nor hee thir outward onely with the Skins   220
Of Beasts, but inward nakedness, much more
Opprobrious, with his Robe of righteousness,
Araying cover'd from his Fathers sight.
To him with swift ascent he up returnd,
Into his blissful bosom reassum'd

In glory as of old, to him appeas'd
All, though all-knowing, what had past with Man
Recounted, mixing intercession sweet.
Meanwhile ere thus was sin'd and judg'd on Earth,
Within the Gates of Hell sate Sin and Death,   230
In counterview within the Gates, that now
Stood open wide, belching outrageous flame
Farr into *Chaos*, since the Fiend pass'd through,
Sin opening, who thus now to Death began.

   O Son, why sit we here each other viewing
Idlely, while Satan our great Author thrives
In other Worlds, and happier Seat provides
For us his ofspring deare? It cannot be
But that success attends him; if mishap,
Ere this he had return'd, with fury driv'n   240
By his Avengers, since no place like this
Can fit his punichment, or their revenge.
Methinks I feel new strength within me rise,
Wings growing, and Dominion giv'n me large
Beyond this Deep; whatever drawes me on,
Or sympathie, or som connatural force
Powerful at greatest distance to unite
With secret amity things of like kinde
By secretest conveyance. Thou my Shade
Inseparable must with mee along: 250
For Death from Sin no power can separate.
But least the difficultie of passing back
Stay his returne perhaps over this Gulfe
Impassable, impervious, let us try

Adventrous work, yet to thy power and mine

Not unagreeable, to found a path

Over this Maine from Hell to that new World

Where Satan now prevailes, a Monument

Of merit high to all th' infernal Host,

Easing thir passage hence, for intercourse,   260

Or transmigration, as thir lot shall lead.

Nor can I miss the way, so strongly drawn

By this new felt attraction and instinct.

   Whom thus the meager Shadow answerd soon.

Goe whither Fate and inclination strong

Leads thee, I shall not lag behinde, nor erre

The way, thou leading, such a sent I draw

Of carnage, prey innumerable, and taste

The savour of Death from all things there that live:

Nor shall I to the work thou enterprisest   270

Be wanting, but afford thee equal aid.

   So saying, with delight he snuff'd the smell

Of mortal change on Earth. As when a flock

Of ravenous Fowl, though many a League remote,

Against the day of Battel, to a Field,

Where Armies lie encampt, come flying, lur'd

With sent of living Carcasses design'd

For death, the following day, in bloodie fight.

So sented the grim Feature, and upturn'd

His Nostril wide into the murkie Air,   280

Sagacious of his Quarrey from so farr.

Then Both from out Hell Gates into the waste

Wide Anarchie of *Chaos* damp and dark

Flew divers, & with Power (thir Power was great)

Hovering upon the Waters; what they met

Solid or slimie, as in raging Sea

Tost up and down, together crowded drove

From each side shoaling towards the mouth of Hell.

As when two Polar Winds blowing adverse

Upon the *Cronian* Sea, together drive   290

Mountains of Ice, that stop th' imagin'd way

Beyond *Petsora* Eastward, to the rich

Cathaian Coast. The aggregated Soyle

Death with his Mace petrific, cold and dry,

As with a Trident smote, and fix't as firm

As *Delos* floating once; the rest his look

Bound with *Gorgonian* rigor not to move,

And with *Asphaltic* slime; broad as the Gate,

Deep to the Roots of Hell the gather'd beach

They fasten'd, and the Mole immense wraught on   300

Over the foaming deep high Archt, a Bridge

Of length prodigious joyning to the Wall

Immoveable of this now fenceless world

Forfeit to Death; from hence a passage broad,

Smooth, easie, inoffensive down to Hell.

So, if great things to small may be compar'd,

Xerxes, the Libertie of *Greece* to yoke,

From *Susa* his *Memnonian* Palace high

Came to the Sea, and over *Hellespont*

Bridging his way, *Europe* with *Asia* joyn'd,   310

And scourg'd with many a stroak th' indignant waves.

Now had they brought the work by wondrous Art

Pontifical, a ridge of pendent Rock
Over the vext Abyss, following the track
Of *Satan*, to the self same place where hee
First lighted from his Wing, and landed safe
From out of *Chaos* to the outside bare
Of this round World: with Pinns of Adamant
And Chains they made all fast, too fast they made
And durable; and now in little space   320
The Confines met of Empyrean Heav'n
And of this World, and on the left hand Hell
With long reach interpos'd; three sev'ral wayes
In sight, to each of these three places led.
And now thir way to Earth they had descri'd,
To Paradise first tending, when behold
Satan in likeness of an Angel bright
Betwixt the *Centaure* and the *Scorpion* stearing
His *Zenith*, while the Sun in *Aries* rose:
Disguis'd he came, but those this Childern dear   330
Thir Parent soon discern'd, though in disguise.
Hee, after *Eve* seduc't, unminded slunk
Into the Wood fast by, and changing shape
To observe the sequel, saw his guileful act
By *Eve*, though all unweeting, seconded
Upon her Husband, saw thir shame that sought
Vain covertures; but when he saw descend
The Son of God to judge them, terrifi'd
Hee fled, not hoping to escape, but shun
The present, fearing guiltie what his wrauth   340

Might suddenly inflict; that past, return'd
By Night, and listning where the hapless Paire
Sate in thir sad discourse, and various plaint,
Thence gatherd his own doom, which understood
Not instant, but of future time. With joy
And tidings fraught, to Hell he now return'd,
And at the brink of *Chaos*, neer the foot
Of this new wondrous Pontifice, unhop't
Met who to meet him came, his Ofspring dear.
Great joy was at thir meeting, and at sight   350
Of that stupendious Bridge his joy encreas'd.
Long hee admiring stood, till Sin, his faire
Inchanting Duaghter, thus the silence broke.
    O Parent, these are thy magnific deeds,
Thy Trophies, which thou view'st as not thine own,
Thou art thir Author and prime Architect:
For I no sooner in my Heart divin'd,
My Heart, which by a secret harmonie
Still moves with thine, joyn'd in connexion sweet,
That thou on Earth hadst prosper'd, which thy looks   360
Now also evidence, but straight I felt
Though distant from thee Worlds between, yet felt
That I must after thee with this thy Son;
Such fatal consequence unites us three:
Hell could no longer hold us in her bounds,
Nor this unvoyageable Gulf obscure
Detain from following thy illustrious track.
Thou hast atchiev'd our libertie, confin'd

Within Hell Gates till now, thou us impow'rd
To fortifie thus farr, and overlay   370
With this portentous Bridge the dark Abyss.
Thine now is all this World, thy vertue hath won
What thy hands builded not, thy Wisdom gain'd
With odds what Warr hath lost, and fully aveng'd
Our foile in Heav'n; here thou shalt Monarch reign,
There didst not; there let him still Victor sway,
As Battel hath adjudg'd, from this new World
Retiring, by his own doom alienated,
And henceforth Monarchie with thee divide
Of all things, parted by th' Empyreal bounds,   380
His Quadrature, from thy Orbicular World,
Or trie thee now more dang'rous to his Throne.
     Whom thus the Prince of Darkness answerd glad.
Fair Daughter, and thou Son and Grandchild both,
High proof ye now have giv'n to be the Race
Of *Satan* (for I glorie in the name,
Antagonist of Heav'ns Almightie King)
Amply have merited of me, of all
Th' Infernal Empire, that so neer Heav'ns dore
Triumphal with triumphal act have met,   390
Mine with this glorious Work, & made one Realm
Hell and this World, one Realm, one Continent
Of easie thorough-fare. Therefore while I
Descend through Darkness, on your Rode with ease
To my associate Powers, them to acquaint
With these succeses, and with them rejoyce,
You two this way, among those numerous Orbs

All yours, right down to Paradise descend;
There dwell & Reign in bliss, thence on the Earth
Dominion exercise and in the Aire,   400
Chiefly on Man, sole Lord of all declar'd,
Him first make sure your thrall, and lastly kill.
My Substitutes I send ye, and Create
Plenipotent on Earth, of matchless might
Issuing from mee: on your joynt vigor now
My hold of this new Kingdom all depends,
Through Sin to Death expos'd by my exploit.
If your joynt power prevaile, th' affaires of Hell
No detriment need feare, goe and be strong.
　So saying he dismiss'd them, they with speed   410
Thir course through thickest Constellations held
Spreading thir bane; the blasted Starrs lookt wan,
And Planets, Planet-strook, real Eclips
Then sufferd. Th' other way *Satan* went down
The Causey to Hell Gate; on either side
Disparted *Chaos* over built exclaimd,
And with rebounding surge the barrs assaild,
That scorn'd his indignation: throughout the Gate,
Wide open and unguarded, *Satan* pass'd,
And all about found desolate; for those   420
Appointed to sit there, had left thir charge,
Flown to the upper World; the rest were all
Farr to the in land retir'd, about the walls
Of *Pandæmonium*, Citie and proud seate
Of *Lucifer*, so by allusion calld,
Of that bright Starr to *Satan* paragond.

There kept thir Watch the Legions, while the Grand
In Council sate, sollicitous what chance
Might intercept thir Emperour sent, so hee
Departing gave command, and they observ'd.   430
As when the *Tartar* from his *Russian* Foe
By *Astracan* over the Snowie Plaines
Retires, or *Bactrian* Sophi from the hornes
Of *Turkish* Crescent, leaves all waste beyond
The Realme of *Aladule,* in his retreate
To *Tauris* or *Casbeen.* So these the late
Heav'n-banisht Host, left desert utmost Hell
Many a dark League, reduc't in careful Watch
Round thir Metropolis, and now expecting
Each hour their great adventurer from the search   440
Of Forrein Worlds: he through the midst unmarkt,
In shew plebeian Angel militant
Of lowest order, past; and from the dore
Of that *Plutonian* Hall, invisible
Ascended his high Throne, which under state
Of richest texture spred, at th' upper end
Was plac't in regal lustre. Down a while
He sate, and round about him saw unseen:
At last as from a Cloud his fulgent head
And shape Starr-bright appeer'd, or brighter, clad   450
With what permissive glory since his fall
Was left him, or false glitter: All amaz'd
At that so sudden blaze the *Stygian* throng
Bent thir aspect, and whom they wish'd beheld,
Thir mighty Chief returnd: loud was th' acclaime:

Forth rush'd in haste the great consulting Peers,
Rais'd from thir dark *Divan*, and with like joy
Congratulant approach'd him, who with hand
Silence, and with these words attention won.
    Thrones, Dominations, Princedoms, Vertues, Powers,   460
For in possession such, not onely of right,
I call ye and declare ye now, returnd
Successful beyond hope, to lead ye forth
Triumphant out of this infernal Pit
Abominable, accurst, the house of woe,
And Dungeon of our Tyrant: Now possess,
As Lords, a spacious World, to our native Heaven
Little inferiour, by my adventure hard
With peril great atchiev'd. Long were to tell
What I have don, what sufferd, with what paine   470
Voyag'd th' unreal, vast, unbounded deep
Of horrible confusion, over which
By Sin and Death a broad way now is pav'd
To expedite your glorious march; but I
Toild out my uncouth passage, forc't to ride
Th' untractable Abysse, plung'd in the womb
Of unoriginal *Night* and *Chaos* wilde,
That jealous of thir secrets fiercely oppos'd
My journey strange, with clamorous uproare
Protesting Fate supreame; thence how I found   480
The new created World, which fame in Heav'n
Long had foretold, a Fabrick wonderful
Of absolute perfection, therein Man
Plac't in a Paradise, by our exile

Made happie: Him by fraud I have seduc'd
From his Creator, and the more to increase
Your wonder, with an Apple; he thereat
Offended, worth your laughter, hath giv'n up
Both his beloved Man and all his World,
To Sin and Death a prey, and so to us,   490
Without our hazard, labour, or allarme,
To range in, and to dwell, and over Man
To rule, as over all he should have rul'd.
True is, mee also he hath judg'd, or rather
Mee not, but the brute Serpent in whose shape
Man I deceav'd: that which to mee belongs,
Is enmity, which he will put between
Mee and Mankinde; I am to bruise his heel;
His Seed, when is not set, shall bruise my head:
A World who would not purchase with a bruise,   500
Or much more grievous pain? Ye have th' account
Of my performance: What remaines, ye Gods,
But up and enter now into full bliss.
  So having said, a while he stood, expecting
Thir universal shout and high applause
To fill his eare, when contrary he hears
On all sides, from innumerable tongues
A dismal universal hiss, the sound
Of public scorn; he wonderd, but not long
Had leasure, wondring at himself now more;   510
His Visage drawn he felt to sharp and spare,
His Armes clung to his Ribs, his Leggs entwining
Each other, till supplanted down he fell

A monstrous Serpent on his Belly prone,
Reluctant, but in vaine, a greater power
Now rul'd him, punisht in the shape he sin'd,
According to his doom: he would have spoke,
But hiss for hiss returnd with forked tongue
To forked tongue, for now were all transform'd
Alike, to Serpents all as accessories   520
To his bold Riot: dreadful was the din
Of hissing through the Hall, thick swarming now
With complicated monsters, head and taile,
Scorpion and Asp, and *Amphisbæna* dire,
Cerastes hornd, *Hydrus*, and *Ellops* drear,
And *Dipsas* (Not so thick swarm'd once the Soil
Bedropt with blood of *Gorgon*, or the Isle
Ophiusa) but still greatest hee the midst,
Now Dragon grown, larger then whom the Sun
Ingenderd in the *Pythian* Vale on slime,   530
Hugh *Python*, and his Power no less he seem'd
Above the rest still to retain; they all
Him follow'd issuing forth to th' open Field,
Where all yet left of that revolted Rout
Heav'n-fall'n, in station stood or just array,
Sublime with expectation when to see
In Triumph issuing forth thir glorious Chief;
They saw, but other sight instead, a crowd
Of ugly Serpents; horror on them fell,
And horrid sympathie; for what they saw,   540
They felt themselvs now changing; down thir arms,
Down fell both Spear and Shield, down they as fast,

And the dire hiss renew'd, and the dire form
Catcht by Contagion, like in punishment,
As in their crime. Thus was th' applause they meant,
Turnd to exploding hiss, triumph to shame
Cast on themselves from thir own mouths. There stood
A Grove hard by, sprung up with this thir change,
His will who reigns above, to aggravate
Thir penance, laden with fair Fruit, like that   550
Which grew in Paradise, the bait of *Eve*
Us'd by the Tempter: on that prospect strange
Thir earnest eyes they fix'd, imagining
For one forbidden Tree a multitude
Now ris'n, to work them furder woe or shame;
Yet parcht with scalding thurst and hunger fierce,
Though to delude them sent, could not abstain,
But on they rould in heaps, and up the Trees
Climbing, sat thicker then the snakie locks
That curld *Megæra:* greedily they pluck'd   560
The Frutage fair to sight, like that which grew
Neer that bituminous Lake where *Sodom* flam'd;
This more delusive, not the touch, but taste
Deceav'd; they fondly thinking to allay
Thir appetite with gust, instead of Fruit
Chewd bitter Ashes, which th' offended taste
VVith spattering noise rejected: oft they assay'd,
Hunger and thirst constraining, drugd as oft,
VVith hatefullest disrelish writh'd thir jaws
VVith soot and cinders fill'd; so oft they fell   570

Into the same illusion, not as Man
Whom they triumph'd once lapst. Thus were they plagu'd
And worn with Famin, long and ceasless hiss,
Till thir lost shape, permitted, they resum'd,
Yearly enjoynd, some say, to undergo
This annual humbling certain number'd days,
To dash thir pride, and joy for Man seduc't.
However some tradition they dispers'd
Among the Heathen of thir purchase got,
And Fabl'd how the Serpent, whom they calld   580
Ophion with *Eurynome*, the wide-
Encroaching *Eve* perhaps, had first the rule
Of high *Olympus*, thence by *Saturn* driv'n
And *Ops*, ere yet *Dictæan Jove* was born.
Mean while in Paradise the hellish pair
Too soon arriv'd, *Sin* there in power before,
Once actual, now in body, and to dwell
Habitual habitant; behind her *Death*
Close following pace for pace, not mounted yet
On his pale Horse: to whom *Sin* thus began.   590
    Second of *Satan* sprung, all conquering *Death*,
What thinkst thou of our Empire now, though earnd
With travail difficult, not better farr
Then stil at Hels dark threshold to have sate watch,
Unnam'd, undreaded, and thy self half starv'd?
    Whom thus the Sin-born Monster answerd soon.
To mee, who with eternal Famin pine,
Alike is Hell, or Paradise, or Heaven,

There best, where most with ravin I may meet;
Which here, though plenteous, all too little seems   600
To stuff this Maw, this vast unhide-bound Corps.
   To whom th' incestuous Mother thus repli'd.
Thou therefore on these Herbs, and Fruits, & Flours
Feed first, on each Beast next, and Fish, and Fowle,
No homely morsels, and whatever thing
The Sithe of Time mowes down, devour unspar'd,
Till I in Man residing through the Race,
His thoughts, his looks, words, actions all infect,
And season him thy last and sweetest prey.
   This said, they both betook them several wayes,   610
Both to destroy, or unimmortal make
All kinds, and for destruction to mature
Sooner or later; which th' Almightie seeing,
From his transcendent Seat the Saints among,
To those bright Orders utterd thus his voice.
   See with what heat these Dogs of Hell advance
To waste and havoc yonder VVorld, which I
So fair and good created, and had still
Kept in that state, had not the folly of Man
Let in these wastful Furies, who impute   620
Folly to mee, so doth the Prince of Hell
And his Adherents, that with so much ease
I suffer them to enter and possess
A place so heav'nly, and conniving seem
To gratifie my scornful Enemies,
That laugh, as if transported with some fit
Of Passion, I to them had quitted all,

At random yeilded up to their misrule;
And know not that I call'd and drew them thither
My Hell-hounds, to lick up the draff and filth   630
Which mans polluting Sin with taint hath shed
On what was pure, till cramm'd and gorg'd, nigh burst
With suckt and glutted offal, at one sling
Of thy victorious Arm, well-pleasing Son,
Both *Sin*, and *Death*, and yawning *Grave* at last
Through *Chaos* hurld, obstruct the mouth of Hell
For ever, and seal up his ravenous Jawes.
Then Heav'n and Earth renewd shall be made pure
To sanctitie that shall receive no staine:
Till then the Curse pronounc't on both precedes.   640
    Hee ended, and the heav'nly Audience loud
Sung *Halleluia*, as the sound of Seas,
Through multitude that sung: Just are thy ways,
Righteous are thy Decrees on all thy Works;
Who can extenuate thee? Next, to the Son,
Destin'd restorer of Mankind, by whom
New Heav'n and Earth shall to the Ages rise,
Or down from Heav'n descend. Such was thir song,
While the Creator calling forth by name
His mightie Angels gave them several charge,   650
As sorted best with present things. The Sun
Had first his precept so to move, so shine,
As might affect the Earth with cold and heat
Scarce tollerable, and from the North to call
Decrepit Winter, from the South to bring
Solstitial summers heat. To the blanc Moone

Her office they prescrib'd, to th' other five
Thir planetarie motions and aspects
In *Sextile, Square,* and *Trine,* and *Opposite,*
Of noxious efficacie, and when to joyne   660
In Synod unbenigne, and taught the fixt
Thir influence malignant when to showre,
Which of them rising with the Sun, or falling,
Should prove tempestuous: To the Winds they set
Thir corners, when with bluster to confound
Sca, Aire, and Shoar, the Thunder when to rowle
With terror through the dark Aereal Hall.
Some say he bid his Angels turne ascanse
The Poles of Earth twice ten degrees and more
From the Suns Axle; they with labour push'd   670
Oblique the Centric Globe: Som say the Sun
Was bid turn Reines from th' Equinoctial Rode
Like distant breadth to *Taurus* with the Seav'n
Atlantick Sisters, and the *Spartan* Twins
Up to the *Tropic* Crab; thence down amaine
By *Leo* and the *Virgin* and the *Scales,*
As deep as *Capricorne,* to bring in change
Of Seasons to each Clime; else had the Spring
Perpetual smil'd on Earth with vernant Flours,
Equal in Days and Nights, except to those   680
Beyond the Polar Circles; to them Day
Had unbenighted shon, while the low Sun
To recompence his distance, in thir sight
Had rounded still th' *Horizon,* and not known
Or East or West, which had forbid the Snow

From cold *Estotiland,* and South as farr
Beneath *Magellan.* At that tasted Fruit
The Sun, as from *Thyestean* Banquet, turn'd
His course intended; else how had the World
Inhabited, though sinless, more then now,   690
Avoided pinching cold and scorching heate?
These changes in the Heav'ns, though slow, produc'd
Like change on Sea and Land, sideral blast,
Vapour, and Mist, and Exhalation hot,
Corrupt and Pestilent: Now from the North
Of *Norumbega,* and the *Samoed* shoar
Bursting thir brazen Dungeon, armd with ice
And snow and haile and stormie gust and flaw,
Boreas and *Cæcias* and *Argestes* loud
And *Thrascias* rend the Woods and Seas upturn;   700
With adverse blast up-turns them from the South
Notus and *Afer* black with thundrous Clouds
From *Serraliona;* thwart of these as fierce
Forth rush the *Levant* and the *Ponent* VVindes
Eurus and *Zephir* with thir lateral noise,
Sirocco, and *Libecchio.* Thus began
Outrage from liveless things; but Discord first
Daughter of Sin, among th' irrational,
Death introduc'd through fierce antipathie:
Beast now with Beast gan war, & Fowle with Fowle,   710
And Fish with Fish; to graze the Herb all leaving,
Devourd each other; nor stood much in awe
Of Man, but fled him, or with count'nance grim
Glar'd on him passing: these were from without

The growing miseries, which *Adam* saw
Alreadie in part, though hid in gloomiest shade,
To sorrow abandond, but worse felt within,
And in a troubl'd Sea of passion tost,
Thus to disburd'n sought with sad complaint.

   O miserable of happie! is this the end   720
Of this new glorious World, and mee so late
The Glory of that Glory, who now becom
Accurst of blessed, hide me from the face
Of God, whom to behold was then my highth
Of happiness: yet well, if here would end
The miserie, I deserv'd it, and would beare
My own deservings; but this will not serve;
All that I eate or drink, or shall beget,
Is propagated curse. O voice once heard
Delightfully, *Encrease and multiply,*   730
Now death to heare! for what can I encrease
Or multiplie, but curses on my head?
Who of all Ages to succeed, but feeling
The evil on him brought by me, will curse
My Head, Ill fare our Ancestor impure,
For this we may thank *Adam;* but his thanks
Shall be the execration; so besides
Mine own that bide upon me, all from mee
Shall with a fierce reflux on mee redound,
On mee as on thir natural center light   740
Heavie, though in thir place. O fleeting joyes
Of Paradise, deare bought with lasting woes!
Did I request thee, Maker, from my Clay

To mould me Man, did I sollicite thee

From darkness to promote me, or here place

In this delicious Garden? as my Will

Concurd not to my being, it were but right

And equal to reduce me to my dust,

Desirous to resigne, and render back

All I receav'd, unable to performe   750

Thy terms too hard, by which I was to hold

The good I sought not. To the loss of that,

Sufficient penaltie, why hast thou added

The sense of endless woes? inexplicable

Thy Justice seems; yet to say truth, too late,

I thus contest; then should have been refusd

Those terms whatever, when they were propos'd:

Thou didst accept them; wilt thou enjoy the good,

Then cavil the conditions? and though God

Made thee without thy leave, what if thy Son   760

Prove disobedient, and reprov'd, retort,

Wherefore didst thou beget me? I sought it not:

Wouldst thou admit for his contempt of thee

That proud excuse? yet him not thy election,

But Natural necessity begot.

God made thee of choice his own, and of his own

To serve him, thy reward was of his grace,

Thy puishment then justly is at his Will.

Be it so, for I submit, his doom is fair,

That dust I am, and shall to dust return: 770

O welcom hour whenever! why delayes

His hand to execute what his Decree

Fixd on this day? why do I overlive,
Why am I mockt with death, and length'nd out
To deathless pain? how gladly would I meet
Mortalitie my sentence, and be Earth
Insensible, how glad would lay me down
As in my Mothers lap? there I should rest
And sleep secure; his dreadful voice no more
Would Thunder in my ears, no fear of worse   780
To mee and to my ofspring would torment me
With cruel expectation. Yet one doubt
Pursues me still, least all I cannot die,
Least that pure breath of Life, the Spirit of Man
Which God inspir'd, cannot together perish
With this corporeal Clod; then in the Grave,
Or in some other dismal place, who knows
But I shall die a living Death? O thought
Horrid, if true! yet why? it was but breath
Of Life that sinn'd; what dies but what had life   790
And sin? the Bodie properly hath neither.
All of me then shall die: let this appease
The doubt, since humane reach no further knows.
For though the Lord of all be infinite,
Is his wrauth also? be it, man is not so,
But mortal doom'd. How can he exercise
Wrath without end on Man whom Death must end?
Can he make deathless Death? that were to make
Strange contradiction, which to God himself
Impossible is held, as Argument   800
Of weakness, not of Power. Will he, draw out,

For angers sake, finite to infinite

In punisht man, to satisfie his rigour

Satisfi'd never; that were to extend

His Sentence beyond dust and Natures Law,

By which all Causes else according still

To the reception of thir matter act,

Not to th' extent of thir own Spheare. But say

That Death be not one stroak, as I suppos'd,

Bereaving sense, but endless miserie   810

From this day onward, which I feel begun

Both in me, and without me, and so last

To perpetuitie; Ay me, that fear

Comes thundring back with dreadful revolution

On my defensless head; both Death and I

Am found Eternal, and incorporate both,

Nor I on my part single, in mee all

Posteritie stands curst: Fair Patrimonie

That I must leave ye, Sons; O were I able

To waste it all my self, and leave ye none!   820

So disinherited how would ye bless

Me now your curse! Ah, why should all mankind

For one mans fault thus guiltless be condemn'd,

If guiltless? but from mee what can proceed,

But all corrupt, both Mind and Will deprav'd,

Not to do onely, but to will the same

With me? how can they then acquitted stand

In sight of God? Him after all Disputes

Forc't I absolve: all my evasions vain

And reasonings, though through Mazes, lead me still   830

But to my own conviction: first and last
On mee, mee onely, as the sourse and spring
Of all corruption, all the blame lights due;
So might the wrauth. Fond wish! couldst thou support
That burden heavier then the Earth to bear,
Then all the World much heavier, though divided
With that bad Woman? Thus what thou desir'st,
And what thou fearst, alike destroyes all hope
Of refuge, and concludes thee miserable
Beyond all past example and future,   840
To *Satan* onely like both crime and doom.
O Conscience, into what Abyss of fears
And horrors hast thou driv'n me; out of which
I find no way, from deep to deeper plung'd!
   Thus *Adam* to himself lamented loud
Through the still Night, not now, as ere man fell,
Wholsom and cool, and mild, but with black Air
Accompanied, with damps and dreadful gloom,
Which to his evil Conscience represented
All things with double terror: On the ground   850
Outstretcht he lay, on the cold ground, and oft
Curs'd his Creation, Death as oft accus'd
Of tardie execution, since denounc't
The day of his offence. Why comes not Death,
Said hee, with one thrice acceptable stroke
To end me? Shall Truth fail to keep her word,
Justice Divine not hast'n to be just?
But Death comes not at call, Justice Divine
Mends not her slowest pace for prayers or cries.
O Woods, O Fountains, Hillocks, Dales and Bowrs,   860

VVith other echo late I taught your Shades
To answer, and resound farr other Song.
VVhom thus afflicted when sad *Eve* beheld,
Desolate where she sate, approaching nigh,
Soft words to his fierce passion she assay'd:
But her with stern regard he thus repell'd.

  Out of my sight, thou Serpent, that name best
Befits thee with him leagu'd, thy self as false
And hateful; nothing wants, but that thy shape,
Like his, and colour Serpentine may shew   870
Thy inward fraud, to warn all Creatures from thee
Henceforth; least that too heav'nly form, pretended
To hellish falshood, snare them. But for thee
I had persisted happie, had not thy pride
And wandring vanitie, when left was safe,
Rejected my forewarning, and disdain'd
Not to be trusted, longing to be seen
Though by the Devil himself, him overweening
To over-reach, but with the Serpent meeting
Fool'd and beguil'd, by him thou, I by thee,   880
To trust thee from my side, imagin'd wise,
Constant, mature, proof against all assaults,
And understood not all was but a shew
Rather then solid vertu, all but a Rib
Crooked by nature, bent, as now appears,
More to the part sinister from me drawn,
Well if thrown out, as supernumerarie
To my just number found. O why did God,
Creator wise, that peopl'd highest Heav'n
With Spirits Masculine, create at last   890

This noveltie on Earth, this fair defect

Of Nature, and not fill the World at once

With Men as Angels without Feminine,

Or find some other way to generate

Mankind? this mischief had not then befall'n,

And more that shall befall, innumerable

Disturbances on Earth through Femal snares,

And straight conjunction with this Sex: for either

He never shall find out fit Mate, but such

As some misfortune brings him, or mistake,   900

Or whom he wishes most shall seldom gain

Through her perverseness, but shall see her gaind

By a farr worse, or if she love, withheld

By Parents, or his happiest choice too late

Shall meet, alreadie linkt and Wedlock-bound

To a fell Adversarie, his hate or shame:

Which infinite calamitie shall cause

To Humane life, and houshold peace confound.

   He added not, and from her turn'd, but *Eve*

Not so repulst, with Tears that ceas'd not flowing,   910

And tresses all disorderd, at his feet

Fell humble, and imbracing them, besaught

His peace, and thus proceeded in her plaint.

   Forsake me not thus, *Adam*, witness Heav'n

What love sincere, and reverence in my heart

I beare thee, and unweeting have offended,

Unhappilie deceav'd; thy suppliant

I beg, and clasp thy knees; bereave me not,

Whereon I live, thy gentle looks, thy aid,

Thy counsel in this uttermost distress,   920

My onely strength and stay: forlorn of thee,

Whither shall I betake me, where subsist?

While yet we live, scarse one short hour perhaps,

Between us two let there be peace, both joyning,

As joyn'd in injuries, one enmitie

Against a Foe by doom express assign'd us,

That cruel Serpent: On me exercise not

Thy hatred for this miserie befall'n,

On me already lost, mee then thy self

More miserable; both have sin'd, but thou   930

Against God onely, I against God and thee,

And to the place of judgement will return,

There with my cries importune Heaven, that all

The sentence from thy head remov'd may light

On me, sole cause to thee of all this woe,

Mee mee onely just object of his ire.

    She ended weeping, and her lowlie plight,

Immoveable till peace obtain'd from fault

Acknowledg'd and deplor'd, in *Adam* wraught

Commiseration; soon his heart relented   940

Towards her, his life so late and sole delight,

Now at his feet submissive in distress,

Creature so faire his reconcilement seeking,

His counsel whom she had displeas'd, his aide;

As one disarm'd, his anger all he lost,

And thus with peaceful words uprais'd her soon.

Unwarie, and too desirous, as before,

So now of what thou knowst not, who desir'st

The punishment all on thy self; alas,

Beare thine own first, ill able to sustaine   950

His full wrauth whose thou feelst as yet lest part,

And my displeasure bearst so ill. If Prayers

Could alter high Decrees, I to that place

Would speed before thee, and be louder heard,

That on my head all might be visited,

Thy frailtie and infirmer Sex forgiv'n,

To me committed and by me expos'd.

But rise, let us no more contend, nor blame

Each other, blam'd enough elsewhere, but strive

In offices of Love, how we may light'n   960

Each others burden in our share of woe;

Since this days Death denounc't, if ought I see,

Will prove no sudden, but a slow-pac't evill,

A long days dying to augment our paine,

And to our Seed (O hapless Seed!) deriv'd.

To whom thus *Eve*, recovering heart, repli'd.

Adam, by sad experiment I know

How little weight my words with thee can finde,

Found so erroneous, thence by just event

Found so unfortunate; nevertheless,   970

Restor'd by thee, vile as I am, to place

Of new acceptance, hopeful to regaine

Thy Love, the sole contentment of my heart,

Living or dying from thee I will not hide

What thoughts in my unquiet brest are ris'n,

Tending to som relief of our extremes,

Or end, though sharp and sad, yet tolerable,

As in our evils, and of easier choice.

If care of our descent perplex us most,

Which must be born to certain woe, devourd   980

By Death at last, and miserable it is

To be to others cause of misery,

Our own begotten, and of our Loines to bring

Into this cursed World a woful Race,

That after wretched Life must be at last

Food for so foule a Monster, in thy power

It lies, yet ere Conception to prevent

The Race unblest, to being yet unbegot.

Childless thou art, Childless remaine: So Death

Shall be deceav'd his glut, and with us two   990

Be forc'd to satisfie his Rav'nous Maw.

But if thou judge it hard and difficult,

Conversing, looking, loving, to abstain

From Loves due Rites, Nuptial embraces sweet,

And with desire to languish without hope,

Before the present object languishing

With like desire, which would be miserie

And torment less then none of what we dread,

Then both our selves and Seed at once to free

From what we fear for both, let us make short,   1000

Let us seek Death, or hee not found, supply

With our own hands his Office on our selves;

Why stand we longer shivering under feares,

That shew no end but Death, and have the power,

Of many wayes to die the shortest choosing,

Destruction with destruction to destroy.

　She ended heer, or vehement despaire

Broke off the rest; so much of Death her thoughts

Had entertaind, as di'd her Cheeks with pale.

But *Adam* with such counsel nothing sway'd,   1010

To better hopes his more attentive minde

Labouring had rais'd, and thus to *Eve* repli'd.

　Eve, thy contempt of life and pleasure seems

To argue in thee somthing more sublime

And excellent then what thy minde contemnes;

But self-destruction therefore saught, refutes

That excellence thought in thee, and implies,

Not thy contempt, but anguish and regret

For loss of life and pleasure overlov'd.

Or if thou covet death, as utmost end   1020

Of miserie, so thinking to evade

The penaltie pronounc't, doubt not but God

Hath wiselier arm'd his vengeful ire then so

To be forestall'd; much more I fear least Death

So snatcht will not exempt us from the paine

We are by doom to pay; rather such acts

Of contumacie will provoke the highest

To make death in us live: Then let us seek

Som safer resolution, which methinks

I have in view, calling to minde with heed   1030

Part of our Sentence, that thy Seed shall bruise

The Serpents head; piteous amends, unless

Be meant, whom I conjecture, our grand Foe

Satan, who in the Serpent hath contriv'd
Against us this deceit: to crush his head
Would be revenge indeed; which will be lost
By death brought on our selves, or childless days
Resolv'd, as thou proposest; so our Foe
Shall scape his punishment ordain'd, and wee
Instead shall double ours upon our heads.   1040
No more be mention'd then of violence
Against our selves, and wilful barrenness,
That cuts us off from hope, and savours onely
Rancor and pride, impatience and despite,
Reluctance against God and his just yoke
Laid on our Necks. Remember with what mild
And gracious temper he both heard and judg'd
Without wrauth or reviling; wee expected
Immediate dissolution, which we thought
Was meant by Death that day, when lo, to thee   1050
Pains onely in Child-bearing were foretold,
And bringing forth, soon recompenc't with joy,
Fruit of thy Womb: On mee the Curse aslope
Glanc'd on the ground, with labour I must earne
My bread; what harm? Idleness had bin worse;
My labour will sustain me; and least Cold
Or Heat should injure us, his timely care
Hath unbesaught provided, and his hands
Cloath'd us unworthie, pitying while he judg'd;
How much more, if we pray him, will his ear   1060
Be open, and his heart to pitie incline,
And teach us further by what means to shun

Th' inclement Seasons, Rain, Ice, Hail and Snow,
Which now the Skie with various Face begins
To shew us in this Mountain, while the Winds
Blow moist and keen, shattering the graceful locks
Of these fair spreading Trees; which bids us seek
Som better shroud, som better warmth to cherish
Our Limbs benumm'd, ere this diurnal Starr
Leave cold the Night, how we his gather'd beams   1070
Reflected, may with matter sere foment,
Or by collision of two bodies grinde
The Air attrite to Fire, as late the Clouds
Justling or pusht with Winds rude in thir shock
Tine the slant Lightning, whose thwart flame driv'n down
Kindles the gummie bark of Firr or Pine,
And sends a comfortable heat from farr,
Which might supplie the Sun: such Fire to use,
And what may else be remedie or cure
To evils which our own misdeeds have wrought,   1080
Hee will instruct us praying, and of Grace
Beseeching him, so as we need not fear
To pass commodiously this life, sustain'd
By him with many comforts, till we end
In dust, our final rest and native home.
What better can we do, then to the place
Repairing where he judg'd us, prostrate fall
Before him reverent, and there confess
Humbly our faults, and pardon beg, with tears
VVatering the ground, and with our sighs the Air   1090

Frequenting, sent from hearts contrite, in sign
Of sorrow unfeign'd, and humiliation meek.
Undoubtedly he will relent and turn
From his displeasure; in whose look serene,
VVhen angry most he seem'd and most severe,
VVhat else but favor, grace, and mercie shon?

   So spake our Father penitent, nor *Eve*
Felt less remorse: they forthwith to the place
Repairing where he judg'd them prostrate fell
Before him reverent, and both confess'd   1100
Humbly thir faults, and pardon beg'd, with tears
VVatering the ground, and with thir sighs the Air
Frequenting, sent from hearts contrite, in sign
Of sorrow unfeign'd, and humiliation meek.

    The End of the Ninth Book.

PARADISE
LOST

BOOK X.

THus they in lowliest plight repentant stood
Praying, for from the Mercie-seat above
Prevenient Grace descending had remov'd
The stonie from thir hearts, and made new flesh
Regenerat grow instead, that sighs now breath'd
Unutterable, which the Spirit of prayer
Inspir'd, and wing'd for Heav'n with speedier flight
Then loudest Oratorie: yet thir port
Not of mean suiters, nor important less
Seem'd thir Petition, then when th' ancient Pair   10
In Fables old, less ancient yet then these,
Deucalion and chaste *Pyrrha* to restore
The Race of Mankind drownd, before the Shrine
Of *Themis* stood devout. To Heav'n thir prayers
Flew up, nor missd the way, by envious windes
Blow'n vagabond or frustrate: in they passd
Dimentionless through Heav'nly dores; then clad
With incense, where the Golden Altar fum'd,
By thir great Intercessor, came in sight
Before the Fathers Throne: Them the glad Son   20
Presenting, thus to intercede began.
　　See Father, what first fruits on Earth are sprung

From thy implanted Grace in Man, these Sighs
And Prayers, which in this Golden Censer, mixt
With Incense, I thy Priest before thee bring,
Fruits of more pleasing favour from thy seed
Sow'n with contrition in his heart, then those
Which his own hand manuring all the Trees
Of Paradise could have produc't, ere fall'n
From innocence. Now therefore bend thine eare   30
To supplication, heare his sighs though mute;
Unskilful with what words to pray, let mee
Interpret for him, mee his Advocate
And propitiation, all his works on mee
Good or not good ingraft, my Merit those
Shall perfet, and for these my Death shall pay.
Accept me, and in mee from these receave
The smell of peace toward Mankinde, let him live
Before thee reconcil'd, at least his days
Numberd, though sad, till Death, his doom (which I   40
To mitigate thus plead, not to reverse)
To better life shall yeeld him, where with mee
All my redeemd may dwell in joy and bliss,
Made one with me as I with thee am one.

   To whom the Father, without Cloud, serene.
All thy request for Man, accepted Son,
Obtain, all thy request was my Decree:
But longer in that Paradise to dwell,
The Law I gave to Nature him forbids:
Those pure immortal Elements that know   50
No gross, no unharmoneous mixture foule,

Eject him tainted now, and purge him off
As a distemper, gross to aire as gross,
And mortal food, as may dispose him best
For dissolution wrought by Sin, that first
Distemperd all things, and of incorrupt
Corrupted. I at first with two fair gifts
Created hm endowd, with Happiness
And Immortalitie: that fondly lost,
This other serv'd but to eternize woe;   60
Till I provided Death; so Death becomes
His final remedie, and after Life
Tri'd in sharp tribulation, and refin'd
By Faith and faithful works, to second Life,
Wak't in the renovation of the just,
Resignes him up with Heav'n and Earth renewd.
But let us call to Synod all the Blest
Through Heav'ns wide bounds; from them I will not hide
My judgments, how with Mankind I proceed,
As how with peccant Angels late they saw;   70
And in thir state, though firm, stood more confirmd.
   He ended, and the Son gave signal high
To the bright Minister that watchd, hee blew
His Trumpet, heard in *Oreb* since perhaps
When God descended, and perhaps once more
To sound at general Doom. Th' Angelic blast
Filld all the Regions: from thir blissful Bowrs
Of *Amarantin* Shade, Fountain or Spring,
By the waters of Life, where ere they sate
In fellowships of joy: the Sons of Light   80

Hasted, resorting to the Summons high,

And took thir Seats; till from his Throne supream

Th' Almighty thus pronounc'd his sovran Will.

   O Sons, like one of us Man is become

To know both Good and Evil, since his taste

Of that defended Fruit; but let him boast

His knowledge of Good lost, and Evil got,

Happier, had it suffic'd him to have known

Good by it self, and Evil not at all.

He sorrows now, repents, and prayes contrite,   90

My motions in him, longer then they move,

His heart I know, how variable and vain

Self-left. Least therefore his now bolder hand

Reach also of the Tree of Life, and eat,

And live for ever, dream at least to live

For ever, to remove him I decree,

And send him from the Garden forth to Till

The Ground whence he was taken, fitter soile.

   Michael, this my behest have thou in charge,

Take to thee from among the Cherubim   100

Thy choice of flaming Warriours, least the Fiend

Or in behalf of Man, or to invade

Vacant possession som new trouble raise:

Hast thee, and from the Paradise of God

Without remorse drive out the sinful Pair,

From hallowd ground th' unholie, and denounce

To them and to thir Progenie from thence

Perpetual banishment. Yet least they faint

At the sad Sentence rigorously urg'd,

For I behold them soft'nd and with tears   101

Bewailing thir excess, all terror hide.

If patiently thy bidding they obey,

Dismiss them not disconsolate; reveale

To *Adam* what shall come in future dayes,

As I shall thee enlighten, intermix

My Cov'nant in the Womans seed renewd;

So send them forth, though sorrowing, yet in peace:

And on the East side of the Garden place,

Where entrance up from *Eden* easiest climbes,

Cherubic watch, and of a Sword the flame   120

Wide waving, all approach farr off to fright,

And guard all passage to the Tree of Life:

Least Paradise a receptacle prove

To Spirits foule, and all my Trees thir prey,

With whose stol'n Fruit Man once more to delude.

    He ceas'd; and th' Archangelic Power prepar'd

For swift descent, with him the Cohort bright

Of watchful Cherubim; four faces each

Had, like a double *Janus*, all thir shape

Spangl'd with eyes more numerous then those   130

Of *Argus*, and more wakeful then to drouze,

Charm'd with *Arcadian* Pipe, the Pastoral Reed

Of *Hermes*, or his opiate Rod. Mean while

To resalute the World with sacred Light

Leucothea wak'd, and with fresh dews imbalmd

The Earth, when *Adam* and first Matron *Eve*

Had ended now thir Orisons, and found,

Strength added from above, new hope to spring

Out of despaire, joy, but with fear yet linkt;

Which thus to *Eve* his welcome words renewd.   140

  Eve, easily may Faith admit, that all

The good which we enjoy, from Heav'n descends

But that from us ought should ascend to Heav'n

So prevalent as to concerne the mind

Of God high-blest, or to incline his will,

Hard to belief may seem; yet this will Prayer,

Or one short sigh of humane breath, up-borne

Ev'n to the Seat of God. For since I saught

By Prayer th' offended Deitie to appease,

Kneel'd and before him humbl'd all my heart,   150

Methought I saw him placable and mild,

Bending his eare; perswasion in me grew

That I was heard with favour; peace returnd

Home to my brest, and to my memorie

His promise, that thy Seed shall bruise our Foe;

Which then not minded in dismay, yet now

Assures me that the bitterness of death

Is past, and we shall live. Whence Haile to thee,

Eve rightly call'd, Mother of all Mankind,

Mother of all things living, since by thee   160

Man is to live, and all things live for Man.

  To whom thus *Eve* with sad demeanour meek.

Ill worthie I such title should belong

To me transgressour, who for thee ordaind

A help, became thy snare; to mee reproach

Rather belongs, distrust and all dispraise:

But infinite in pardon was my Judge,

That I who first brought Death on all, am grac't

The sourse of life; next favourable thou,
Who highly thus to entitle me voutsaf'st,   170
Farr other name deserving. But the Field
To labour calls us now with sweat impos'd,
Though after sleepless Night; for see the Morn,
All unconcern'd with our unrest, begins
Her rosie progress smiling; let us forth,
I never from thy side henceforth to stray,
Wherere our days work lies, though now enjoind
Laborious, till day droop; while here we dwell,
What can be toilsom in these pleasant Walkes?
Here let us live, though in fall'n state, content.   180
    So spake, so wish'd much-humbl'd *Eve*, but Fate
Subscrib'd not; Nature first gave Signs, imprest
On Bird, Beast, Aire, Aire suddenly eclips'd
After short blush of Morn; nigh in her sight
The Bird of *Jove*, stoopt from his aerie tour,
Two Birds of gayest plume before him drove:
Down from a Hill the Beast that reigns in Woods,
First Hunter then, pursu'd a gentle brace,
Goodliest of all the Forrest, Hart and Hinde;
Direct to th' Eastern Gate was bent thir flight.   190
Adam observ'd, and with his Eye the chase
Pursuing, not unmov'd to *Eve* thus spake.
    O *Eve*, some furder change awaits us nigh,
Which Heav'n by these mute signs in Nature shews
Forerunners of his purpose, or to warn
Us haply too secure of our discharge

From penaltie, because from death releast
Some days; how long, and what til then our life,
Who knows, or more then this, that we are dust,
And thither must return and be no more.   200
VVhy else this double object in our sight
Of flight pursu'd in th' Air and ore the ground
One way the self-same hour? why in the East
Darkness ere Dayes mid-course, and Morning light
More orient in yon VVestern Cloud that draws
O're the blew Firmament a radiant white,
And slow descends, with somthing heav'nly fraught.
   He err'd not, for by this the heav'nly Bands
Down from a Skie of Jasper lighted now
In Paradise, and on a Hill made alt,   210
A glorious Apparition, had not doubt
And carnal fear that day dimm'd *Adams* eye.
Not that more glorious, when the Angels met
Jacob in *Mahanaim*, where he saw
The field Pavilion'd with his Guardians bright;
Nor that which on the flaming Mount appeerd
In *Dothan*, cover'd with a Camp of Fire,
Against the *Syrian* King, who to surprize
One man, Assassin-like had levied Warr,
Warr unproclam'd. The Princely Hierarch   220
In thir bright stand, there left his Powers to seise
Possession of the Garden; hee alone,
To finde where *Adam* shelterd, took his way,
Not unperceav'd of *Adam*, who to *Eve*,
While the great Visitant approachd, thus spake.

Eve, now expect great tidings, which perhaps
Of us will soon determin, or impose
New Laws to be observ'd; for I descrie
From yonder blazing Cloud that veils the Hill
One of the heav'nly Host, and by his Gate   230
None of the meanest, some great Potentate
Or of the Thrones above, such Majestie
Invests him coming; yet not terrible,
That I should fear, nor sociably mild,
As *Raphael*, that I should much confide,
But solemn and sublime, whom not to offend,
With reverence I must meet, and thou retire.
He ended; and th' Arch-Angel soon drew nigh,
Not in his shape Celestial, but as Man
Clad to meet Man; over his lucid Armes   240
A militarie Vest of purple flowd
Livelier then *Melibæan*, or the graine
Of *Sarra*, worn by Kings and Hero's old
In time of Truce; *Iris* had dipt the wooff;
His starrie Helme unbuckl'd shew'd him prime
In Manhood where Youth ended; by his side
As in glistering *Zodiac* hung the Sword,
Satans dire dread, and in his hand the Spear.
Adam bowd low, hee Kingly from his State
Inclin'd not, but his coming thus declar'd.   250
    Adam, Heav'ns high behest no Preface needs:
Sufficient that thy Prayers are heard, and Death,
Then due by sentence when thou didst transgress,
Defeated of his seisure many dayes

Giv'n thee of Grace, wherein thou may'st repent,
And one bad act with many deeds well done
Mayst cover: well may then thy Lord appeas'd
Redeem thee quite from Deaths rapacious claime;
But longer in this Paradise to dwell
Permits not; to remove thee I am come, 260
And send thee from the Garden forth to till
The ground whence thou wast tak'n, fitter Soile.

   He added not, for *Adam* at the newes
Heart-strook with chilling gripe of sorrow stood,
That all his senses bound; *Eve,* who unseen
Yet all had heard, with audible lament
Discover'd soon the place of her retire.

   O unexpected stroke, worse then of Death!
Must I thus leave thee Paradise? thus leave
Thee Native Soile, these happie Walks and Shades, 270
Fit haunt of Gods? where I had hope to spend,
Quiet though sad, the respit of that day
That must be mortal to us both. Of flours,
That never will in other Climate grow,
My early visitation, and my last
At Eev'n, which I bred up with tender hand
From the first op'ning bud, and gave ye Names,
Who now shall reare ye to the Sun, or ranke
Your Tribes, and water from th' ambrosial Fount?
Thee lastly nuptial Bowre, by mee adornd 280
With what to sight or smell was sweet; from thee
How shall I part, and whither wander down
Into a lower World, to this obscure

And wilde, how shall we breath in other Aire
Less pure, accustomd to immortal Fruits?
  Whom thus the Angel interrupted milde.
Lament not *Eve,* but patiently resigne
What justly thou hast lost; nor set thy heart,
Thus over fond, on that which is not thine;
Thy going is not lonely, with thee goes   290
Thy Husband, him to follow thou art bound;
Where he abides, think there thy native soile.
  Adam by this from the cold sudden damp
Recovering, and his scatterd spirits returnd,
To *Michael* thus his humble words addressd.
  Celestial, whether among the Thrones, or nam'd
Of them the Highest, for such of shape may seem
Prince above Princes, gently hast thou tould
Thy message, which might else in telling wound,
And in performing end us; what besides   300
Of sorrow and dejection and despair
Our frailtie can sustain, thy tidings bring,
Departure from this happy place, our sweet
Recess, and onely consolation left
Familiar to our eyes, all places else
Inhospitable appeer and desolate,
Nor knowing us nor known: and if by prayer
Incessant I could hope to change the will
Of him who all things can, I would not cease
To wearie him with my assiduous cries: 310
But prayer against his absolute Decree
No more availes then breath against the winde,

Blown stifling back on him that breaths it forth:
Therefore to his great bidding I submit.
This most afflicts me, that departing hence,
As from his face I shall be hid, deprivd
His blessed count'nance; here I could frequent,
With worship, place by place where he voutsaf'd
Presence Divine, and to my Sons relate;
On this Mount he appeerd, under this Tree   320
Stood visible, among these Pines his voice
I heard, here with him at this Fountain talk'd:
So many grateful Altars I would reare
Of grassie Terfe, and pile up every Stone
Of lustre from the brook, in memorie,
Or monument to Ages, and thereon
Offer sweet smelling Gumms & Fruits and Flours:
In yonder nether World where shall I seek
His bright appearances, or footstep trace?
For though I fled him angrie, yet recall'd   330
To life prolongd and promisd Race, I now
Gladly behold though but his utmost skirts
Of glory, and farr off his steps adore.
    To whom thus *Michael* with regard benigne.
Adam, thou know'st Heav'n his, and all the Earth,
Not this Rock onely; his Omnipresence fills
Land, Sea, and Aire, and every kinde that lives,
Fomented by his virtual power and warmd:
All th' Earth he gave thee to possess and rule,
No despicable gift; surmise not then   340

His presence to these narrow bounds confin'd
Of Paradise or *Eden:* this had been
Perhaps thy Capital Seate, from whence had spred
All generations, and had hither come
From all the ends of th' Earth, to celebrate
And reverence thee thir great Progenitor.
But this præeminence thou hast lost, brought down
To dwell on eeven ground now with thy Sons:
Yet doubt not but in Vallie and in Plaine
God is as here, and will be found alike   350
Present, and of his presence many a signe
Still following thee, still compassing thee round
With goodness and paternal Love, his Face
Express, and of his steps the track Divine.
Which that thou mayst beleeve, and be confirmd,
Ere thou from hence depart, know I am sent
To shew thee what shall come in future dayes
To thee and to thy Ofspring; good with bad
Expect to hear, supernal Grace contending
With sinfulness of Men; thereby to learn   360
True patience, and to temper joy with fear
And pious sorrow, equally enur'd
By moderation either state to beare,
Prosperous or adverse: so shalt thou lead
Safest thy life, and best prepar'd endure
Thy mortal passage when it comes. Ascend
This Hill; let *Eve* (for I have drencht her eyes)
Here sleep below while thou to foresight wak'st,

As once thou slepst, while Shee to life was formd.

   To whom thus *Adam* gratefully repli'd.   370

Ascend, I follow thee, safe Guide, the path

Thou lead'st me, and to the hand of Heav'n submit,

However chast'ning, to the evil turne

My obvious breast, arming to overcom

By suffering, and earne rest from labour won,

If so I may attain. So both ascend

In the Visions of God: It was a Hill

Of Paradise the highest, from whose top

The Hemisphere of Earth in cleerest Ken

Stretcht out to amplest reach of prospect lay.   380

Nor higher that Hill nor wider looking round,

Whereon for different cause the Tempter set

Our second *Adam* in the Wilderness,

To shew him all Earths Kingdomes and thir Glory.

His Eye might there command wherever stood

City of old or modern Fame, the Seat

Of mightiest Empire, from the destind Walls

Of *Cambalu*, seat of *Cathaian Can*

And *Samarchand* by *Oxus*, *Temirs* Throne,

To *Paquin* of *Sinæan* Kings, and thence   390

To *Agra* and *Lahor* of great *Mogul*

Down to the golden *Chersonese*, or where

The *Persian* in *Ecbatan* sate, or since

In *Hispahan*, or where the *Russian Ksar*

In *Mosco*, or the Sultan in *Bizance*,

Turchestan-born; nor could his eye not ken

Th' Empire of *Negus* to his utmost Port

Ercoco and the less Maritine Kings
Mombaza, and *Quiloa,* and *Melind,*
And *Sofala* thought *Ophir,* to the Realme   400
Of *Congo,* and *Angola* fardest South;
Or thence from *Niger* Flood to *Atlas* Mount
The Kingdoms of *Almansor, Fez* and *Sus,*
Marocco and *Algiers,* and *Tremisen;*
On *Europe* thence, and where *Rome* was to sway
The VVorld: in Spirit perhaps he also saw
Rich *Mexico* the seat of *Motezume,*
And *Cusco* in *Peru,* the richer seat
Of *Atabalipa,* and yet unspoil'd
Guiana, whose great Citie *Geryons* Sons   410
Call *El Dorado:* but to nobler sights
Michael from *Adams* eyes the Filme remov'd
VVhich that false Fruit that promis'd clearer sight
Had bred; then purg'd with Euphrasie and Rue
The visual Nerve, for he had much to see;
And from the VVell of Life three drops instill'd.
So deep the power of these Ingredients pierc'd,
Eevn to the inmost seat of mental sight,
That *Adam* now enforc't to close his eyes,
Sunk down and all his Spirits became intranst: 420
But him the gentle Angel by the hand
Soon rais'd, and his attention thus recall'd.
    Adam, now ope thine eyes, and first behold
Th' effects which thy original crime hath wrought
In some to spring from thee, who never touch'd
Th' excepted Tree, nor with the Snake conspir'd,

Nor sinn'd thy sin, yet from that sin derive
Corruption to bring forth more violent deeds.

   His eyes he op'nd, and beheld a field,
Part arable and tilth, whereon were Sheaves   430
New reapt, the other part sheep-walks and foulds;
Ith' midst an Altar as the Land-mark stood
Rustic, of grassie sord; thither anon
A sweatie Reaper from his Tillage brought
First Fruits, the green Eare, and the yellow Sheaf,
Uncull'd, as came to hand; a Shepherd next
More meek came with the Firstlings of his Flock
Choicest and best; then sacrificing, laid
The Inwards and thir Fat, with Incense strew'd,
On the cleft Wood, and all due Rites perform'd.   440
His Offring soon propitious Fire from Heav'n
Consum'd with nimble glance, and grateful steame;
The others not, for his was not sincere;
Whereat hee inlie rag'd, and as they talk'd,
Smote him into the Midriff with a stone
That beat out life; he fell, and deadly pale
Groand out his Soul with gushing bloud effus'd.
Much at that sight was *Adam* in his heart
Dismai'd, and thus in haste to th' Angel cri'd.

   O Teacher, some great mischief hath befall'n   450
To that meek man, who well had sacrific'd;
Is Pietie thus and pure Devotion paid?

   T' whom *Michael* thus, hee also mov'd, repli'd.
These two are Brethren, *Adam,* and to come
Out of thy loyns; th' unjust the just hath slain,

For envie that his Brothers Offering found
From Heav'n acceptance; but the bloodie Fact
Will be aveng'd, and th' others Faith approv'd
Loose no reward, though here thou see him die,
Rowling in dust and gore. To which our Sire.   460
   Alas, both for the deed and for the cause!
But have I now seen Death? Is this the way
I must return to native dust? O sight
Of terrour, foul and ugly to behold,
Horrid to think, how horrible to feel!
   To whom thus *Michael*. Death thou hast seen
In his first shape on man; but many shapes
Of Death, and many are the wayes that lead
To his grim Cave, all dismal; yet to sense
More terrible at th' entrance then within.   470
Some, as thou saw'st, by violent stroke shall die,
By Fire, Flood, Famin, by Intemperance more
In Meats and Drinks, which on the Earth shal bring
Diseases dire, of which a monstrous crew
Before thee shall appear; that thou mayst know
What miserie th' inabstinence of *Eve*
Shall bring on men. Immediately a place
Before his eyes appeard, sad, noysom, dark,
A Lazar-house it seemd, wherein were laid
Numbers of all diseas'd, all maladies   480
Of gastly Spasm, or racking torture, qualmes
Of heart-sick Agonies, all feavorous kinds,
Convulsions, Epilepsies, fierce Catarrhs,
Intestin Stone and Ulcer, Colic pangs,

Dropsies, and Asthma's, and Joint-racking Rheums.
Dire was the tossing, deep the groans, despair
Tended the sick busiest from Couch to Couch;
And over them triumphant Death his Dart
Shook, but delaid to strike, though oft invok't
With vows, as thir chief good, and final hope.   490
Sight so deform what heart of Rock could long
Drie-ey'd behold? *Adam* could not, but wept,
Though not of Woman born; compassion quell'd
His best of Man, and gave him up to tears
A space, till firmer thoughts restraind excess,
And scarce recovering words his plaint renew'd.
   O miserable Mankind, to what fall
Degraded, to what wretched state reserv'd!
Better end heer unborn. Why is life giv'n
To be thus wrested from us? rather why   500
Obtruded on us thus? who if we knew
What we receive, would either not accept
Life offer'd, or soon beg to lay it down,
Glad to be so dismist in peace. Can thus
Th' Image of God in man created once
So goodly and erect, though faultie since,
To such unsightly sufferings be debas't
Under inhuman pains? Why should not Man,
Retaining still Divine similitude
In part, from such deformities be free,   510
And for his Makers Image sake exempt?
   Thir Makers Image, answerd *Michael*, then
Forsook them, when themselves they villifi'd

To serve ungovern'd appetite, and took
His Image whom they serv'd, a brutish vice,
Inductive mainly to the sin of *Eve*.
Therefore so abject is thir punishment,
Disfiguring not Gods likeness, but thir own,
Or if his likeness, by themselves defac't
While they pervert pure Natures healthful rules   520
To loathsom sickness, worthily, since they
Gods Image did not reverence in themselves.
    I yeild it just, said *Adam*, and submit.
But is there yet no other way, besides
These painful passages, how we may come
To Death, and mix with our connatural dust?
    There is, said *Michael*, if thou well observe
The rule of not too much, by temperance taught
In what thou eatst and drinkst, seeking from thence
Due nourishment, not gluttonous delight,   530
Till many years over thy head return:
So maist thou live, till like ripe Fruit thou drop
Into thy Mothers lap, or be with ease
Gatherd, not harshly pluckt, for death mature:
This is old age; but then thou must outlive
Thy youth, thy strength, thy beauty, which will change
To witherd weak & gray; thy Senses then
Obtuse, all taste of pleasure must forgoe,
To what thou hast, and for the Aire of youth
Hopeful and cheerful, in thy blood will reigne   540
A melancholy damp of cold and dry
To waigh thy spirits down, and last consume

The Balme of Life. To whom our Ancestor.

   Henceforth I flie not Death, nor would prolong
Life much, bent rather how I may be quit
Fairest and easiest of this combrous charge,
Which I must keep till my appointed day
Of rendring up. *Michael* to him repli'd.

   Nor love thy Life, not hate; but what thou livst
Live well, how long or short permit to Heav'n: 550
And now prepare thee for another sight.

   He lookd and saw a spacious Plaine, whereon
Were Tents of various hue; by some were herds
Of Cattel grazing: others, whence the sound
Of Instruments that made melodious chime
Was heard, of Harp and Organ; and who moovd
Thir stops and chords was seen: his volant touch
Instinct through all proportions low and high
Fled and pursu'd transverse the resonant fugue.
In other part stood one who at the Forge   560
Labouring, two massie clods of Iron and Brass
Had melted (whether found where casual fire
Had wasted woods on Mountain or in Vale,
Down to the veins of Earth, thence gliding hot
To som Caves mouth, or whether washt by stream
From underground) the liquid Ore he dreind
Into fit moulds prepar'd; from which he formd
First his own Tooles; then, what might else be wrought
Fusil or grav'n in mettle. After these,
But on the hether side a different sort   570

From the high neighbouring Hills, which was thir Seat,
Down to the Plain descended: by thir guise
Just men they seemd, and all thir study bent
To worship God aright, and know his works
Not hid, nor those things last which might preserve
Freedom and Peace to men: they on the Plain
Long had not walkt, when from the Tents behold
A Beavie of fair Women, richly gay
In Gems and wanton dress; to the Harp they sung
Soft amorous Ditties, and in dance came on: 580
The Men though grave, ey'd them, and let thir eyes
Rove without rein, till in the amorous Net
Fast caught, they lik'd, and each his liking chose;
And now of love they treat till th' Eevning Star
Loves Harbinger appeerd; then all in heat
They light the Nuptial Torch, and bid invoke
Hymen, then first to marriage Rites invok't;
With Feast and Musick all the Tents resound.
Such happy interview and fair event
Of love & youth not lost, Songs, Garlands, Flours,   590
And charming Symphonies attach'd the heart
Of *Adam*, soon enclin'd to admit delight,
The bent of Nature; which he thus express'd.

   True opener of mine yes, prime Angel blest,
Much better seems this Vision, and more hope
Of peaceful dayes portends, then those two past;
Those were of hate and death, or pain much worse,
Here Nature seems fulfilld in all her ends.

To whom thus *Michael*. Judg not what is best
By pleasure, though to Nature seeming meet,   600
Created, as thou art, to nobler end
Holie and pure, conformitie divine.
Those Tents thou sawst so pleasant, were the Tents
Of wickedness, wherein shall dwell his Race
Who slew his Brother; studious they appere
Of Arts that polish Life, Inventers rare,
Unmindful of thir Maker, though his Spirit
Taught them, but they his gifts acknowledg'd none.
Yet they a beauteous ofspring shall beget;
For that fair femal Troop thou sawst, that seemd   610
Of Goddesses, so blithe, so smooth, so gay,
Yet empty of all good wherein consists
Womans domestic honour and chief praise;
Bred onely and completed to the taste
Of lustful appetence, to sing, to dance,
To dress, and troule the Tongue, and roule the Eye.
To these that sober Race of Men, whose lives
Religious titl'd them the Sons of God,
Shall yeild up all thir vertue, all thir fame
Ignobly, to the traines and to the smiles   620
Of these fair Atheists, and now swim in joy,
(Erelong to swim at larg) and laugh; for which
The world erelong a world of tears must weepe.
    To whom thus *Adam* of short joy bereft.
O pittie and shame, that they who to live well
Enterd so faire, should turn aside to tread
Paths indirect, or in the mid way faint!

But still I see the tenor of Mans woe
Holds on the same, from Woman to begin.
    From Mans effeminate slackness it begins,   630
Said th' Angel, who should better hold his place
By wisdome, and superiour gifts receavd.
But now prepare thee for another Scene.
    He lookd and saw wide Territorie spred
Before him, Towns, and rural works between,
Cities of Men with lofty Gates and Towrs,
Concours in Arms, fierce Faces threatning Warr,
Giants of mightie Bone, and bould emprise;
Part wield thir Arms, part courb the foaming Steed,
Single or in Array of Battel rang'd   640
Both Horse and Foot, nor idely mustring stood;
One way a Band select from forage drives
A herd of Beeves, faire Oxen and faire Kine
From a fat Meddow ground; or fleecy Flock,
Ewes and thir bleating Lambs over the Plaine,
Thir Bootie; scarce with Life the Shepherds flye,
But call in aide, which tacks a bloody Fray;
With cruel Tournament the Squadrons joine;
Where Cattel pastur'd late, now scatterd lies
With Carcasses and Arms th' ensanguind Field   650
Deserted: Others to a Citie strong
Lay Siege, encampt; by Batterie, Scale, and Mine,
Assaulting; others from the Wall defend
With Dart and Jav'lin, Stones and sulfurous Fire;
On each hand slaughter and gigantic deeds.
In other part the scepter'd Haralds call

To Council in the Citie Gates: anon
Grey-headed men and grave, with Warriours mixt,
Assemble, and Harangues are heard, but soon
In factious opposition, till at last 660
Of middle Age one rising, eminent
In wise deport, spake much of Right and Wrong,
Of Justice, of Religion, Truth and Peace,
And Judgement from above: him old and young
Exploded, and had seiz'd with violent hands,
Had not a Cloud descending snatch'd him thence
Unseen amid the throng: so violence
Proceeded, and Oppression, and Sword-Law
Through all the Plain, and refuge none was found.
Adam was all in tears, and to his guide 670
Lamenting turnd full sad; O what are these,
Deaths Ministers, not Men, who thus deal Death
Inhumanly to men, and multiply
Ten thousand fould the sin of him who slew
His Brother; for of whom such massacher
Make they but of thir Brethren, men of men?
But who was that Just Man, whom had not Heav'n
Rescu'd, had in his Righteousness bin lost?
To whom thus *Michael*; These are the product
Of those ill-mated Marriages thou saw'st; 680
Where good with bad were matcht, who of themselves
Abhor to joyn; and by imprudence mixt,
Produce prodigious Births of bodie or mind.
Such were these Giants, men of high renown;
For in those dayes Might onely shall be admir'd,

And Valour and Heroic Vertu call'd;
To overcome in Battel, and subdue
Nations, and bring home spoils with infinite
Man-slaughter, shall be held the highest pitch
Of human Glorie, and for Glorie done   690
Of triumph, to be styl'd great Conquerours,
Patrons of Mankind, Gods, and Sons of Gods,
Destroyers rightlier call'd and Plagues of men.
Thus Fame shall be achiev'd, renown on Earth,
And what most merits fame in silence hid.
But hee the seventh from thee, whom thou beheldst
The onely righteous in a World perverse,
And therefore hated, therefore so beset
With Foes for daring single to be just,
And utter odious Truth, that God would come   700
To judge them with his Saints: Him the most High
Rapt in a balmie Cloud with winged Steeds
Did, as thou sawst, receave, to walk with God
High in Salvation and the Climes of bliss,
Exempt from Death; to shew thee what reward
Awaits the good, the rest what punishment;
Which now direct thine eyes and soon behold.
     He look'd, & saw the face of things quite chang'd;
The brazen Throat of Warr had ceast to roar,
All now was turn'd to jollitie and game,   710
To luxurie and riot, feast and dance,
Marrying or prostituting, as befell,
Rape or Adulterie, where passing faire
Allurd them; thence from Cups to civil Broiles.

At length a Reverend Sire among them came,
And of thir doings great dislike declar'd,
And testifi'd against thir wayes; hee oft
Frequented thir Assemblies, whereso met,
Triumphs or Festivals, and them preachd
Conversion and Repentance, as to Souls   720
In prison under Judgements imminent:
But all in vain: which when he saw, he ceas'd
Contending, and remov'd his Tents farr off;
Then from the Mountain hewing Timber tall,
Began to build a Vessel of huge bulk,
Measur'd by Cubit, length, & breadth, and highth,
Smeard round with Pitch, and in the side a dore
Contriv'd, and of provisions laid in large
For Man and Beast: when loe a wonder strange!
Of everie Beast, and Bird, and Insect small   730
Came seavens, and pairs, and enterd in, as taught
Thir order; last the Sire, and his three Sons
With thir four Wives; and God made fast the dore.
Meanwhile the Southwind rose, & with black wings
Wide hovering, all the Clouds together drove
From under Heav'n; the Hills to their supplie
Vapour, and Exhalation dusk and moist,
Sent up amain; and now the thick'nd Skie
Like a dark Ceeling stood; down rush'd the Rain
Impetuous, and continu'd till the Earth   740
No more was seen; the floating Vessel swum
Uplifted; and secure with beaked prow
Rode tilting o're the Waves, all dwellings else

Flood overwhelmd, and them with all thir pomp
Deep under water rould; Sea cover'd Sea,
Sea without shoar; and in thir Palaces
Where luxurie late reign'd, Sea-monsters whelp'd
And stabl'd; of Mankind, so numerous late,
All left, in one small bottom swum imbark't.
How didst thou grieve then, *Adam*, to behold   750
The end of all thy Ofspring, end so sad,
Depopulation; thee another Floud,
Of tears and sorrow a Floud thee also drown'd,
And sunk thee as thy Sons; till gently reard
By th' Angel, on thy feet thou stoodst at last,
Tough comfortless, as when a Father mourns
His Childern, all in view destroyd at once;
And scarce to th' Angel utterdst thus thy plaint.

   O Visions ill foreseen! better had I
Liv'd ignorant of future, so had borne   760
My part of evil onely, each dayes lot
Anough to bear; those now, that were dispenst
The burd'n of many Ages, on me light
At once, by my foreknowledge gaining Birth
Abortive, to torment me ere thir being,
With thought that they must be. Let no man seek
Henceforth to be foretold what shall befall
Him or his Childern, evil he may be sure,
Which neither his foreknowing can prevent,
And hee the future evil shall no less   770
In apprehension then in substance feel
Grievous to bear: but that care now is past,

Man is not whom to warne: those few escap't

Famin and anguish will at last consume

Wandring that watrie Desert: I had hope

When violence was ceas't, and Warr on Earth,

All would have then gon well, peace would have crownd

With length of happy days the race of man;

But I was farr deceav'd; for now I see

Peace to corrupt no less then Warr to waste.   780

How comes it thus? unfould, Celestial Guide,

And whether here the Race of man will end.

To whom thus *Michael*. Those whom last thou sawst

In triumph and luxurious wealth, are they

First seen in acts of prowess eminent

And great exploits, but of true vertu void;

Who having spilt much blood, and don much waste

Subduing Nations, and achievd thereby

Fame in the World, high titles, and rich prey,

Shall change thir course to pleasure, ease, and sloth,   790

Surfet, and lust, till wantonness and pride

Raise out of friendship hostil deeds in Peace.

The conquerd also, and enslav'd by Warr

Shall with thir freedom lost all vertu loose

And feare of God, from whom their pietie feign'd

In sharp contest of Battel found no aide

Against invaders; therefore coold in zeale

Thenceforth shall practice how to live secure,

Worldlie or dissolute, on what thir Lords

Shall leave them to enjoy; for th' Earth shall bear   800

More then anough, that temperance may be tri'd:

So all shall turn degenerate, all deprav'd,
Justice and Temperance, Truth and Faith forgot;
One Man except, the onely Son of light
In a dark Age, against example good,
Against allurement, custom, and a World
Offended; fearless of reproach and scorn,
Or violence, hee of thir wicked wayes
Shall them admonish, and before them set
The paths of righteousness, how much more safe,   810
And full of peace, denouncing wrauth to come
On thir impenitence; and shall returne
Of them derided, but of God observd
The one just Man alive; by his command
Shall build a wondrous Ark, as thou beheldst,
To save himself and houshold from amidst
A World devote to universal rack.
No sooner hee with them of Man and Beast
Select for life shall in the Ark be lodg'd,
And shelterd round, but all the Cataracts   820
Of Heav'n set open on the Earth shall powre
Raine day and night, all fountaines of the Deep
Broke up, shall heave the Ocean to usurp
Beyond all bounds, till inundation rise
Above the highest Hills: then shall this Mount
Of Paradise by might of Waves be moovd
Out of his place, pushd by the horned floud,
With all his verdure spoil'd, and Trees adrift
Down the great River to the op'ning Gulf,
And there take root an Iland salt and bare,   830

The haunt of Seales and Orcs, and Sea-mews clang.
To teach thee that God attributes to place
No sanctitie, if none be thither brought
By Men who there frequent, or therein dwell.
And now what further shall ensue, behold.

   He lookd, and saw the Ark hull on the floud,
Which now abated, for the Clouds were fled,
Drivn by a keen North-winde, that blowing drie
Wrinkl'd the face of Deluge, as decai'd;
And the cleer Sun on his wide watrie Glass   840
Gaz'd hot, and of the fresh Wave largely drew,
As after thirst, which made thir flowing shrink
From standing lake to tripping ebbe, that stole
With soft foot towards the deep, who now had stopt
His Sluces, as the Heav'n his windows shut.
The Ark no more now flotes, but seems on ground
Fast on the top of som high mountain fixt.
And now the tops of Hills as Rocks appeer;
With clamor thence the rapid Currents drive
Towards the retreating Sea thir furious tyde.   850
Forthwith from out the Arke a Raven flies,
And after him, the surer messenger,
A Dove sent forth once and agen to spie
Green Tree or ground whereon his foot may light;
The second time returning, in his Bill
An Olive leafe he brings, pacific signe:
Anon drie ground appeers, and from his Arke
The ancient Sire descends with all his Train;
Then with uplifted hands, and eyes devout,
Grateful to Heav'n, over his head beholds   860

A dewie Cloud, and in the Cloud a Bow
Conspicuous with three lifted colours gay,
Betok'ning peace from God, and Cov'nant new.
Whereat the heart of *Adam* erst so sad
Greatly rejoyc'd, and thus his joy broke forth.
   O thou who future things canst represent
As present, Heav'nly instructer, I revive
At this last sight, assur'd that Man shall live
With all the Creatures, and thir seed preserve.
Farr less I now lament for one whole World   870
Of wicked Sons destroyd, then I rejoyce
For one Man found so perfet and so just,
That God voutsafes to raise another World
From him, and all his anger to forget.
But say, what mean those colourd streaks in Heavn,
Distended as the Brow of God appeas'd,
Or serve they as a flourie verge to binde
The fluid skirts of that same watrie Cloud,
Least it again dissolve and showr the Earth?
   To whom th' Archangel. Dextrously thou aim'st;   880
So willingly doth God remit his Ire,
Though late repenting him of Man deprav'd,
Griev'd at his heart, when looking down he saw
The whole Earth fill'd with violence, and all flesh
Corrupting each thir way; yet those remoov'd,
Such grace shall one just Man find in his sight,
That he relents, not to blot out mankind,
And makes a Covenant never to destroy
The Earth again by flood, nor let the Sea
Surpass his bounds, nor Rain to drown the World   890

With Man therein or Beast; but when he brings
Over the Earth a Cloud, will therein set
His triple-colour'd Bow, whereon to look
And call to mind his Cov'nant: Day and Night,
Seed time and Harvest, Heat and hoary Frost
Shall hold thir course, till fire purge all things new,
Both Heav'n and Earth, wherein the just shall dwell.
Thus thou hast seen one World begin and end;
And Man as from a second stock proceed.
Much thou hast yet to see, but I perceave   900
Thy mortal sight to faile; objects divine
Must needs impaire and wearie human sense:
Henceforth what is to com I will relate,
Thou therefore give due audience, and attend.
This second sours of Men, while yet but few,
And while the dread of judgement past remains
Fresh in thir mindes, fearing the Deitie,
With some regard to what is just and right
Shall lead thir lives, and multiplie apace,
Labouring the soile, and reaping plenteous crop,   910
Corn wine and oyle; and from the herd or flock,
Oft sacrificing Bullock, Lamb, or Kid,
With large Wine-offerings pour'd, and sacred Feast
Shal spend thir dayes in joy unblam'd, and dwell
Long time in peace by Families and Tribes
Under paternal rule; till one shall rise
Of proud ambitious heart, who not content
With fair equalitie, fraternal state,

Will arrogate Dominion undeserv'd
Over his brethren, and quite dispossess   920
Concord and law of Nature from the Earth;
Hunting (and Men not Beasts shall be his game)
With Warr and hostile snare such as refuse
Subjection to his Empire tyrannous:
A mightie Hunter thence he shall be styl'd
Before the Lord, as in despite of Heav'n,
Or from Heav'n claming second Sovrantie;
And from Rebellion shall derive his name,
Though of Rebellion others he accuse.
Hee with a crew, whom like Ambition joyns   930
With him or under him to tyrannize,
Marching from *Eden* towards the West, shall finde
The Plain, wherein a black bituminous gurge
Boiles out from under ground, the mouth of Hell;
Of Brick, and of that stuff they cast to build
A Citie & Towre, whose top may reach to Heav'n;
And get themselves a name, least far disperst
In foraign Lands thir memorie be lost,
Regardless whether good or evil fame.
But God who oft descends to visit men   940
Unseen, and through thir habitations walks
To mark thir doings, them beholding soon,
Comes down to see thir Citie, ere the Tower
Obstruct Heav'n Towrs, and in derision sets
Upon thir Tongues a various Spirit to rase
Quite out thir Native Language, and instead

To sow a jangling noise of words unknown:
Forthwith a hideous gabble rises loud
Among the Builders; each to other calls
Not understood, till hoarse, and all in rage,   950
As mockt they storm; great laughter was in Heav'n
And looking down, to see the hubbub strange
And hear the din; thus was the building left
Ridiculous, and the work Confusion nam'd.
   Whereto thus *Adam* fatherly displeas'd.
O execrable Son so to aspire
Above his Brethren, to himself assuming
Authoritie usurpt, from God not giv'n:
He gave us onely over Beast, Fish, Fowl
Dominion absolute; that right we hold   960
By his donation; but Man over men
He made not Lord; such title to himself
Reserving, human left from human free.
But this Usurper his encroachment proud
Stayes not on Man; to God his Tower intends
Siege and defiance: Wretched man! what food
Will he convey up thither to sustain
Himself and his rash Armie, where thin Aire
Above the Clouds will pine his entrails gross,
And famish him of Breath, if not of Bread?   970
   To whom thus *Michael*. Justly thou abhorr'st
That Son, who on the quiet state of men
Such trouble brought, affecting to subdue
Rational Libertie; yet know withall,
Since thy original lapse, true Libertie

Is lost, which alwayes with right Reason dwells
Twinn'd, and from her hath no dividual being:
Reason in man obscur'd, or not obeyd,
Immediately inordinate desires
And upstart Passions catch the Government   980
From Reason, and to servitude reduce
Man till then free. Therefore since hee permits
Within himself unworthie Powers to reign
Over free Reason, God in Judgement just
Subjects him from without to violent Lords;
Who oft as undeservedly enthrall
His outward freedom: Tyrannie must be,
Though to the Tyrant thereby no excuse.
Yet somtimes Nations will decline so low
From vertue, which is reason, that no wrong,   900
But Justice, and some fatal curse annext
Deprives them of thir outward libertie,
Thir inward lost: Witness th' irreverent Son
Of him who built the Ark, who for the shame
Don to his Father, heard this heavie curse,
Servant of Servants, on his vitious Race.
Thus will this latter, as the former World,
Still tend from bad to worse till God at last
Wearied with their iniquities, withdraw
His presence from among them, and avert   1000
His holy Eyes; resolving from thenceforth
To leave them to thir own polluted wayes;
And one peculiar Nation to select
From all the rest, of whom to be invok'd,

A Nation from one faithful man to spring:
Him on this side *Euphrates* yet residing,
Bred up in Idol-worship; O that men
(Canst thou believe?) should be so stupid grown,
While yet the Patriark liv'd, who scap'd the Flood,
As to forsake the living God, and fall   1010
To worship thir own work in Wood and Stone
For Gods! yet him God the most High voutsafes
To call by Vision from his Fathers house,
His kindred and false Gods, into a Land
Which he will shew him, and from him will raise
A mightie Nation, and upon him showre
His benediction so, that in his Seed
All Nations shall be blest; hee straight obeys,
Not knowing to what Land, yet firm believes:
I see him, but thou canst not, with what Faith   1020
He leaves his Gods, his Friends, and native Soile
Ur of *Chaldæa*, passing now the Ford
To *Haran*, after him a cumbrous Train
Of Herds and Flocks, and numerous servitude;
Not wandring poor, but trusting all his wealth
With God, who call'd him, in a land unknown.
Canaan he now attains, I see his Tents
Pitcht about *Sechem*, and the neighbouring Plaine
Of *Moreh*; there by promise he receaves
Gift to his Progenie of all that Land;   1030
From *Hamath* Northward to the Desert South
(Things by thir names I call, though yet unnam'd)
From *Hermon* East to the great Western Sea,

Mount *Hermon*, yonder Sea, each place behold
In prospect, as I point them; on the shoare
Mount *Carmel*; here the double-founted stream
Jordan, true limit Eastward; but his Sons
Shall dwell to *Senir*, that long ridge of Hills.
This ponder, that all Nations of the Earth
Shall in his Seed be blessed; by that Seed   1040
Is meant thy great deliverer, who shall bruise
The Serpents head; whereof to thee anon
Plainlier shall be reveald. This Patriarch blest,
Whom *faithful Abraham* due time shall call,
A Son, and of his Son a Grand-childe leaves,
Like him in faith, in wisdom, and renown;
The Grandchilde with twelve Sons increast, departs
From *Canaan*, to a Land hereafter call'd
Egypt, divided by the River *Nile*;
See where it flows, disgorging at seaven mouthes   1050
Into the Sea: to sojourn in that Land
He comes invited by a yonger Son
In time of dearth, a Son whose worthy deeds
Raise him to be the second in that Realme
Of *Pharao:* there he dies, and leaves his Race
Growing into a Nation, and now grown
Suspected to a sequent King, who seeks
To stop thir overgrowth, as inmate guests
Too numerous; whence of guests he makes them slaves
Inhospitably, and kills thir infant Males: 1060
Till by two brethren (those two brethren call
Moses and *Aaron*) sent from God to claime

His people from enthralment, they return
With glory and spoile back to thir promis'd Land.
But first the lawless Tyrant, who denies
To know thir God, or messge to regard,
Must be compelld by Signes and Judgements dire;
To blood unshed the Rivers must be turnd,
Frogs, Lice and Flies must all his Palace fill
With loath'd intrusion, and fill all the land;   1070
His Cattel must of Rot and Murren die,
Botches and blaines must all his flesh imboss,
And all his people; Thunder mixt with Haile,
Haile mixt with fire must rend th' *Egyptian* Skie
And wheel on th' Earth, devouring where it rouls;
What it devours not, Herb, or Fruit, or Graine,
A darksom Cloud of Locusts swarming down
Must eat, and on the ground leave nothing green:
Darkness must overshadow all his bounds,
Palpable darkness, and blot out three dayes;   1080
Last with one midnight stroke all the first-born
Of *Egypt* must lie dead. Thus with ten wounds
The River-dragon tam'd at length submits
To let his sojourners depart, and oft
Humbles his stubborn heart, but still as Ice
More hard'nd after thaw, till in his rage
Pursuing whom he late dismissd, the Sea
Swallows him with his Host, but them lets pass
As on drie land between two christal walls,
Aw'd by the rod of *Moses* so to stand   1090

Divided, till his rescu'd gain thir shoar:
Such wondrous power God to his Saint will lend,
Though present in his Angel, who shall goe
Before them in a Cloud, and Pillar of Fire,
By day a Cloud, by night a pillar of Fire,
To guide them in thir journey, and remove
Behinde them, while th' obdurat King pursues:
All night he will pursue, but his approach
Darkness defends between till morning Watch;
Then through the Firey Pillar and the Cloud   1100
God looking forth will trouble all his Host
And craze thir Chariot wheels: when by command
Moses once more his potent Rod extends
Over the Sea; the Sea his Rod obeys;
On thir imbattelld ranks the Waves return,
And overwhelm thir Warr: the Race elect
Safe towards *Canaan* from the shoar advance
Through the wilde Desert, not the readiest way,
Least entring on the *Canaanite* allarmd
Warr terrifie them inexpert, and feare   1110
Return them back to *Egypt*, choosing rather
Inglorious life with servitude; for life
To noble and ignoble is more sweet
Untraind in Armes, where rashness leads not on.
This also shall they gain by thir delay
In the wide Wilderness, there they shall found
Thir government, and thir great Senate choose
Through the twelve Tribes, to rule by Laws ordaind:

God from the Mount of *Sinai*, whose gray top

Shall tremble, he descending, will himself   1120

In Thunder Lightning and loud Trumpets sound

Ordaine them Lawes: part such as appertaine

To civil Justice, part religious Rites

Of sacrifice, informing them, by types

And shadowes, of that destind Seed to bruise

The Serpent, by what meanes he shall achieve

Mankinds deliverance. But the voice of God

To mortal eare is dreadful; they beseech

That *Moses* might report to them his will,

And terror cease; he grants them thir desire,   1130

Instructed that to God is no access

Without Mediator, whose high Office now

Moses in figure beares, to introduce

One greater, of whose day he shall foretell,

And all the Prophets in thir Age the times

Of great *Messiah* shall sing. Thus Laws and Rites

Establisht, such delight hath God in Men

Obedient to his will, that he voutsafes

Among them to set up his Tabernacle,

The holy One with mortal Men to dwell: 1140

By his prescript a Sanctuary is fram'd

Of Cedar, overlaid with Gold, therein

An Ark, and in the Ark his Testimony,

The Records of his Cov'nant, over these

A Mercie-seat of Gold between the wings

Of two bright Cherubim, before him burn

Seaven Lamps as in a Zodiac representing

The Heav'nly fires; over the Tent a Cloud
Shall rest by Day, a fierie gleame by Night,
Save when they journie, and at length they come,   1150
Conducted by his Angel to the Land
Promisd to *Abraham* and his Seed: the rest
Were long to tell, how many Battels fought,
How many Kings destroyd, and Kingdoms won,
Or how the Sun shall in mid Heav'n stand still
A day entire, and Nights due course adjourne,
Mans voice commanding, Sun in *Gibeon* stand,
And thou Moon in the vale of *Aialon*,
Till *Israel* overcome; so call the third
From *Abraham*, Son of *Isaac*, and from him   1160
His whole descent, who thus shall *Canaan* win.
    Here *Adam* interpos'd. O sent from Heav'n,
Enlightner of my darkness, gracious things
Thou hast reveald, those chiefly which concerne
Just *Abraham* and his Seed: now first I finde
Mine eyes true op'ning, and my heart much eas'd,
Erwhile perplext with thoughts what would becom
Of mee and all Mankind; but now I see
His day, in whom all Nations shall be blest,
Favour unmerited by me, who sought   1170
Forbidd'n knowledge by forbidd'n means.
This yet I apprehend not, why to those
Among whom God will deigne to dwell on Earth
So many and so various Laws are giv'n;
So many Laws argue so many sins
Among them; how can God with such reside?

To whom thus *Michael*. Doubt not but that sin
Will reign among them, as of thee begot;
And therefore was Law given them to evince
Thir natural pravitie, by stirring up 1180
Sin against Law to fight; that when they see
Law can discover sin, but not remove,
Save by those shadowie expiations weak,
The bloud of Bulls and Goats, they may conclude
Some bloud more precious must be paid for Man,
Just for unjust, that in such righteousness
To them by Faith imputed, they may finde
Justification towards God, and peace
Of Conscience, which the Law by Ceremonies
Cannot appease, nor Man the moral part 1190
Perform, and not performing cannot live.
So Law appears imperfet, and but giv'n
With purpose to resign them in full time
Up to a better Cov'nant, disciplin'd
From shadowie Types to Truth, from Flesh to Spirit,
From imposition of strict Laws, to free
Acceptance of large Grace, from servil fear
To filial, works of Law to works of Faith.
And therefore shall not *Moses*, though of God
Highly belov'd, being but the Minister 1200
Of Law, his people into *Canaan* lead;
But *Joshua* whom the Gentiles *Jesus* call,
His Name and Office bearing, who shall quell
The adversarie Serpent, and bring back
Through the worlds wilderness long wanderd man

Safe to eternal Paradise of rest.
Meanwhile they in thir earthly *Canaan* plac't
Long time shall dwell and prosper, but when sins
National interrupt thir public peace,
Provoking God to raise them enemies: 1210
From whom as oft he saves them penitent
By Judges first, then under Kings; of whom
The second, both for pietie renownd
And puissant deeds, a promise shall receive
Irrevocable, that his Regal Throne
For ever shall endure; the like shall sing
All Prophecie, That of the Royal Stock
Of *David* (so I name this King) shall rise
A Son, the Womans Seed to thee foretold,
Foretold to *Abraham*, as in whom shall trust   1220
All Nations, and to Kings foretold, of Kings
The last, for of his Reign shall be no end.
But first a long succession must ensue,
And his next Son for Wealth and Wisdom fam'd,
The clouded Ark of God till then in Tents
Wandring, shall in a glorious Temple enshrine.
Such follow him, as shall be registerd
Part good, part bad, of bad the longer scrowle,
Whose foul Idolatries, and other faults
Heapt to the popular summe, will so incense   1230
God, as to leave them, and expose thir Land,
Thir Citie, his Temple, and his holy Ark
With all his sacred things, a scorn and prey
To that proud Citie, whose high Walls thou saw'st

Left in confusion, *Babylon* thence call'd.

There in captivitie he lets them dwell

The space of seventie years, then brings them back,

Remembring mercie, and his Cov'nant sworn

To *David*, stablisht as the dayes of Heav'n.

Returnd from *Babylon* by leave of Kings   1240

Thir Lords, whom God dispos'd, the house of God

They first re-edifie, and for a while

In mean estate live moderate, till grown

In wealth and multitude, factious they grow;

But first among the Priests dissension springs,

Men who attend the Altar, and should most

Endeavour Peace: thir strife pollution brings

Upon the Temple it self: at last they seise

The Scepter, and regard not *Davids* Sons,

Then loose it to a stranger, that the true   1250

Anointed King *Messiah* might be born

Barr'd of his right; yet at his Birth a Starr

Unseen before in Heav'n proclaims him com,

And guides the Eastern Sages, who enquire

His place, to offer Incense, Myrrh, and Gold;

His place of birth a solemn Angel tells

To simple Shepherds, keeping watch by night;

They gladly thither haste, and by a Quire

Of squadrond Angels hear his Carol sung.

A Virgin is his Mother, but his Sire   1260

The Power of the most High; he shall ascend

The Throne hereditarie, and bound his Reign

With earths wide bounds, his glory with the Heav'ns.

He ceas'd, discerning *Adam* with such joy
Surcharg'd, as had like grief bin dew'd in tears,
Without the vent of words, which these he breathd.
    O Prophet of glad tidings, finisher
Of utmost hope! now clear I understand
What oft my steddiest thoughts have searcht in vain,
Why our great expectation should be call'd   1270
The seed of Woman: Virgin Mother, Haile,
High in the love of Heav'n, yet from my Loynes
Thou shalt proceed, and from thy Womb the Son
Of God most High; So God with man unites.
Needs must the Serpent now his capital bruise
Expect with mortal paine: say where and when
Thir fight, what stroke shall bruise the Victors heel.
    To whom thus *Michael*. Dream not of thir fight,
As of a Duel, or the local wounds
Of head or heel: not therefore joynes the Son   1280
Manhood to God-head, with more strength to foil
Thy enemie; nor so is overcome
Satan, whose fall from Heav'n, a deadlier bruise,
Disabl'd not to give thee thy deaths wound:
Which hee, who comes thy Saviour, shall recure,
Not by destroying *Satan*, but his works
In thee and in thy Seed: nor can this be,
But by fulfilling that which thou didst want,
Obedience to the Law of God, impos'd
On penaltie of death, and suffering death,   1290
The penaltie to thy transgression due,
And due to theirs which out of thine will grow:

So onely can high Justice rest appaid.

The Law of God exact he shall fulfill

Both by obedience and by love, though love

Alone fulfill the Law; thy punishment

He shall endure by coming in the Flesh

To a reproachful life and cursed death,

Proclaming Life to all who shall believe

In his redemption, and that his obedience   1300

Imputed becomes theirs by Faith, his merits

To save them, not thir own, though legal works.

For this he shall live hated, be blasphem'd,

Seis'd on by force, judg'd, and to death condemnd

A shameful and accurst, naild to the Cross

By his own Nation, slaine for bringing Life;

But to the Cross he nailes thy Enemies,

The Law that is against thee, and the sins

Of all mankinde, with him there crucifi'd,

Never to hurt them more who rightly trust   1310

In this his satisfaction; so he dies,

But soon revives, Death over him no power

Shall long usurp; ere the third dawning light

Returne, the Starres of Morn shall see him rise

Out of his grave, fresh as the dawning light,

Thy ransom paid, which Man from death redeems,

His death for Man, as many as offerd Life

Neglect not, and the benefit imbrace

By Faith nor void of workes: this God-like act

Annuls thy doom, the death thou shouldst have dy'd,   1320

In sin for ever lost from life; this act
Shall bruise the head of *Satan*, crush his strength
Defeating Sin and Death, his two maine armes,
And fix farr deeper in his head thir stings
Then temporal death shall bruise the Victors heel,
Or theirs whom he redeems, a death like sleep,
A gentle wafting to immortal Life.
Nor after resurrection shall he stay
Longer on Earth then certaine times to appeer
To his Disciples, Men who in his Life   1330
Still follow'd him; to them shall leave in charge
To teach all nations what of him they learn'd
And his Salvation, them who shall beleve
Baptizing in the profluent streame, the signe
Of washing them from guilt of sin to Life
Pure, and in mind prepar'd, if so befall,
For death, like that which the redeemer dy'd.
All Nations they shall teach; for from that day
Not onely to the Sons of *Abrahams* Loines
Salvation shall be Preacht, but to the Sons   1340
Of *Abrahams* Faith wherever through the world;
So in his seed all Nations shall be blest.
Then to the Heav'n of Heav'ns he shall ascend
With victory, triumphing through the aire
Over his foes and thine; there shall surprise
The Serpent, Prince of aire, and drag in Chaines
Through all his realme, & there confounded leave;
Then enter into glory, and resume

His Seat at Gods right hand, exalted high
Above all names in Heav'n; and thence shall come,   1350
When this worlds dissolution shall be ripe,
With glory and power to judge both quick & dead,
To judge th' unfaithful dead, but to reward
His faithful, and receave them into bliss,
Whether in Heav'n or Earth, for then the Earth
Shall all be Paradise, far happier place
Then this of *Eden*, and far happier daies.
   So spake th' Archangel *Michael*, then paus'd,
As at the Worlds great period; and our Sire
Replete with joy and wonder thus repli'd.   1360
   O goodness infinite, goodness immense!
That all this good of evil shall produce,
And evil turn to good; more wonderful
Then that which by creation first brought forth
Light out of darkness! full of doubt I stand,
Whther I should repent me now of sin
By mee done and occasiond, or rejoyce
Much more, that much more good thereof shall spring,
To God more glory, more good will to Men
From God, and over wrauth grace shall abound.   1370
But say, if our deliverer up to Heav'n
Must reascend, what will betide the few
His faithful, left among th' unfaithful herd,
The enemies of truth; who then shall guide
His people, who defend? will they not deale
Wors with his followers then with him they dealt?
   Be sure they will, said th' Angel; but from Heav'n

Hee to his own a Comforter will send,
The promise of the Father, who shall dwell
His Spirit within them, and the Law of Faith   138•
Working through love, upon thir hearts shall write,
To guide them in all truth, and also arme
With spiritual Armour, able to resist
Satans assaults, and quench his fierie darts,
What Man can do against them, not affraid,
Though to the death, against such cruelties
With inward consolations recompenc't,
And oft supported so as shall amaze
Thir proudest persecuters: for the Spirit
Powrd first on his Apostles, whom he sends   139•
To evangelize the Nations, then on all
Baptiz'd, shall them with wondrous gifts endue
To speak all Tongues, and do all Miracles,
As did thir Lord before them. Thus they win
Great numbers of each Nation to receave
With joy the tidings brought from Heav'n: at length
Thir Ministry perform'd, and race well run,
Thir doctrine and thir story written left,
They die; but in thir room, as they forewarne,
Wolves shall succeed for teachers, grievous Wolves,   140•
Who all the sacred mysteries of Heav'n
To thir own vile advantages shall turne
Of lucre and ambition, and the truth
With superstitions and traditions taint,
Left onely in those written Records pure,
Though not but by the Spirit understood.

Then shall they seek to avail themselves of names,
Places and titles, and with these to joine
Secular power, though feigning still to act
By spiritual, to themselves appropriating   1410
The Spirit of God, promisd alike and giv'n
To all Beleevers; and from that pretense,
Spiritual Lawes by carnal power shall force
On every conscience; Laws which none shall finde
Left them inrould, or what the Spirit within
Shall on the heart engrave. What will they then
But force the Spirit of Grace it self, and binde
His consort Libertie; what, but unbuild
His living Temples, built by Faith to stand,
Thir own Faith not anothers: for on Earth   1420
Who against Faith and Conscience can be heard
Infallible? yet many will presume:
Whence heavie persecution shall arise
On all who in the worship persevere
Of Spirit and Truth; the rest, farr greater part,
Will deem in outward Rites and specious formes
Religion satisfi'd; Truth shall retire
Bestuck with slandrous darts, and works of Faith
Rarely be found: so shall the World goe on,
To good malignant, to bad men benigne,   1430
Under her own waight groaning, till the day
Appeer of respiration to the just,
And vengeance to the wicked, at return
Of him so lately promiss'd to thy aid,
The Womans seed, obscurely then foretold,

Now amplier known thy Saviour and thy Lord,
Last in the Clouds from Heav'n to be reveald
In glory of the Father, to dissolve
Satan with his perverted World, then raise
From the conflagrant mass, purg'd and refin'd,   1440
New Heav'ns, new Earth, Ages of endless date
Founded in righteousness and peace and love,
To bring forth fruits Joy and eternal Bliss.
He ended; and thus *Adam* last reply'd.
How soon hath thy prediction, Seer blest,
Measur'd this transient World, the Race of time,
Till time stand fixt: beyond is all abyss,
Eternitie, whose end no eye can reach.
Greatly instructed I shall hence depart,
Greatly in peace of thought, and have my fill   1450
Of knowledge, what this vessel can containe;
Beyond which was my folly to aspire.
Henceforth I learne, that to obey is best,
And love with feare the onely God, to walk
As in his presence, ever to observe
His providence, and on him sole depend,
Merciful over all his works, with good
Still overcoming evil, and by small
Accomplishing great things, by things deemd weak
Subverting worldly strong, and worldly wise   1460
By simply meek; that suffering for Truths sake
Is fortitude to highest victorie,
And to the faithful Death the Gate of Life;
Taught this by his example whom I now

Acknowledge my Redeemer ever blest.

   To whom thus also th' Angel last repli'd:

This having learnt, thou hast attaind the summe

Of wisdom; hope no higher, though all the Starrs

Thou knewst by name, and all th' ethereal Powers,

All secrets of the deep, all Natures works,   1470

Or works of God in Heav'n, Air, Earth, or Sea,

And all the riches of this World enjoydst,

And all the rule, one Empire; onely add

Deeds to thy knowledge anwerable, add Faith,

Add Vertue, Patience, Temperance, add Love,

By name to come call'd Charitie, the soul

Of all the rest: then wilt thou not be loath

To leave this Paradise, but shalt possess

A Paradise within thee, happier farr.

Let us descend now therefore from this top   1480

Of Speculation; for the hour precise

Exacts our parting hence; and see the Guards,

By mee encampt on yonder Hill, expect

Thir motion, at whose Front a flaming Sword,

In signal of remove, waves fiercely round;

We may no longer stay: go, waken *Eve*;

Her also I with gentle Dreams have calm'd

Portending good, and all her spirits compos'd

To meek submission: thou at season fit

Let her with thee partake what thou hast heard,   1490

Chiefly what may concern her Faith to know,

The great deliverance by her Seed to come

(For by the Womans Seed) on all Mankind.

That ye may live, which will be many dayes,
Both in one Faith unanimous though sad,
With cause for evils past, yet much more cheer'd
With meditation on the happie end.
　　He ended, and they both descend the Hill;
Descended, *Adam* to the Bowre where *Eve*
Lay sleeping ran before, but found her wak't;   1500
And thus with words not sad she him receav'd.
　　Whence thou returnst, & whither wentst, I know;
For God is also in sleep, and Dreams advise,
Which he hath sent propitious, some great good
Presaging, since with sorrow and hearts distress
VVearied I fell asleep: but now lead on;
In mee is no delay; with thee to goe,
Is to stay here; without thee here to stay,
Is to go hence unwilling; thou to mee
Art all things under Heav'n, all places thou,   1510
VVho for my wilful crime art banisht hence.
This further consolation yet secure
I carry hence; though all by mee is lost,
Such favour I unworthie am voutsaft,
By mee the Promis'd Seed shall all restore.
　　So spake our Mother *Eve,* and *Adam* heard
VVell pleas'd, but answer'd not; for now too nigh
Th' Archangel stood, and from the other Hill
To thir fixt Station, all in bright array
The Cherubim descended; on the ground   1520
Gliding meteorous, as Ev'ning Mist
Ris'n from a River o're the marish glides,

And gathers ground fast at the Labourers heel
Homeward returning. High in Front advanc't,
The brandisht Sword of God before them blaz'd
Fierce as a Comet; which with torrid heat,
And vapour as the *Libyan* Air adust,
Began to parch that temperate Clime; whereat
In either hand the hastning Angel caught
Our lingring Parents, and to th' Eastern Gate   1530
Led them direct, and down the Cliff as fast
To the subjected Plaine; then disappeer'd.
They looking back, all th' Eastern side beheld
Of Paradise, so late thir happie seat,
Wav'd over by that flaming Brand, the Gate
With dreadful Faces throng'd and fierie Armes:
Som natural tears thy drop'd, but wip'd them soon;
The World was all before them, where to choose
Thir place of rest, and Providence thir guide:
They hand in hand with wandring steps and slow,   1540
Through *Eden* took thir solitarie way.

THE END.

Discussion of the Edited Text

Changes and Lack of Changes Made

Line numbers are given on the right side of the text rather than on alternate right and left sides of a page. Long printed ∫, which looks like an f, is not reproduced; however, typographic puns may exist as possibly in 3.6: "Bright effluence of bright e∫∫ence increate." For references here, see "Textual Variants" (for states of the text), and "Errors." Brackets indicate no change from that state of the copy-text.

Book 1

1.25: th' deleted; erratum
1.159: ought > aught; error
1.173: The > This; error
1.377: the > thir; error
1.409: Heronaim > Horonaim; erratum
1.432: those > these; error
[1.530: no change, but see "Errors"]
[1.603: no change, but see "Errors"]
1.710: A non > Anon; error
1.737: Herarchie > Hierarchie; error
1.758: and Band > Band and; erratum
1.760: hundreds > hunderds; erratum

Book 2

[2.4: state 2]
[2.15: state 2]
[2.143: state 2, although state 1 "appeer" (?) and "exasperat" conform to Milton's spelling.]

2.329: What > Why; error
2.360: 366 > 360; error
[2.414: no change despite erratum]
2.422: red > read; error
2.790: 900 > 790 [state 2]
[2.819: state 2]
2.881: great > grate; erratum
[2.986: state 3]
[2.1009: state 3]

Book 3

[3.40: state 2]
[3.50, 60, 70, 80: state 2 of line numbers]
[3.61: state 2]
[3.97: state 2]
3.329: What > Why; error.
3.530: 5 0 > 530; error.
3.580: Sarry > Starry; error.
3.592: Medal > Metal; error.
3.594: Which > With; error.
3.600 through 740: numbers and placement corrected.
[3.630: state 2]
[3.653: state 2]
[3.655: state 2]
[3.679: state 2]
[3.690: state 2]
3.741: with > in; erratum

Book 4

[4.41: state 2]
[4.83: state 2/3]
[4.88: state 2/3]
[4.90, line number: state 3]
[4.90: state 2/3]
[4.91: state 2/3]

[4.100, line number: state 3]
[4.100: state 2/3]
[4.110, line number : state 3]
4.627: walks > walk; error (?), changed in 1674
[4.660, 670, 680: state 2]
4.760–1010: placement of numbers corrected
[4.810, line number: state 2]

Book 5

[5.121: state 3]
[5.133: state 3]
[5.150: states 2, 3]
[5.151: states 2, 3]
[5.153: state 3]
[5.154: states 2, 3]
[5.156: states 1, 3]
[5.160: state 3 and states 2, 3]
[5.161: state 3]
5.193: Breath > Breathe; erratum
[5.240: states 2, 3 and state 3]
[5.251: states 2, 3]
[5.257: state 3 and state 3]
[5.258: states 2, 3 and states 2, 3]
[5.259: states 2, 3]
[5.269: states 2, 3]
[5.271: states 2, 3]
[5.273: states 2, 3]
[5.277: states 2, 3]
[5.287: state 3]
[5.292: states 2, 3]
[5.297: state 3 and states 2, 3]
[5.301: state 3]
[5.302: states 2, 3]
5.361: indented > not indented; error
[5.510: state 2]

5.598: whoseop > whose top; erratum
[5.609: state 2]
[5.616: state 2]
5.627: "now" added; error
5.656: "in" added; erratum
[5.710: state 2]
[5.725: state 2]
[5.743: state 2]
[5.827: state 2]

Book 6

6.115: realtie > fealtie; error
6.184: blessed > blest; erratum
6.215: Sounder > So under; erratum
6.352: Limb > limn; error
6.405: mov'd^ > mov'd.; error
[6.521: day-spring; various copies do not show the hyphen but
    Fletcher treats it as a problem of inking rather than as a change]
[6.749: whirl- / wind found > whirlwind found; spelling uncertain]
6.817: assig'n'd > assign'd; error

Book 7

First printing, lines 1–236
[7.1: *Urania,*]
[7.3: Following,]
[7.7: Heav'nlie]
[7.9: Eternal]
[7.11: Almightie Father,]
[7.13: Heav'ns]
[7.15: safetie]
[7.19: Discounted,]
[7.21: remaines]
[7.24: Sing]
[7.25: dayes,]
7.27: rouud > round; error

[7.30: still]

[7.34: wilde]

[7.36: rapture,]

7.39: "Heav'n lie", > "Heav'nlie"; error [second printing, "Heav'nlie" without comma]

[7.40: Goddess,]

[7.41: Arch-angel,]

[7.48: obeyd]

[7.49: tasts]

[7.52: admiration,]

[7.56: confusion:]

[7.57: Driv'n]

[7.60, 70: placed correctly]

[7.71: Farr]

[7.76: infinitly]

[7.78: solemne]

[7.80: voutsaf't]

[7.83: knowing,]

[7.85: availe]

[7.89: Aire]

[7.90, 100, 110: placed correctly]

[7.92: Eternitie]

[7.93: begun,]

[7.97: works,]

[7.100: heares]

[7.101: heare]

[7.104: Starr]

[7.104: Eevning]

[7.106: Sleep]

[7.109: illustrous]

[7.110: answerd]

[7.122: King,]

[7.126: Knowledge]

[7.126: as food]

[7.130, 140: placed correctly]

[7.135: returnd]

[7.136: th ' Omnipotent]
[7.138: spake.]
[7.139: envious]
[7.139: Foe]
[7.139: fail'd,]
[7.142: Deitie]
[7.144: many,]
[7.151: done,]
[7.156: innumerable,]
[7.158: length]
[7.160: (first) Heavn]
[7.162: Heav'n,]
[7.171: goodness,]
[7.172: Necessitie]
[7.177: human]
[7.181: Almightie's]
[7.182: most High, good]
[7.183: peace:]
[7.184: Glorie]
[7.185: driven]
[7.189: maligne]
[7.190: diffuse]
[7.191: Worlds]
[7.194: Omnipotence]
[7.195: Majestie]
[7.201: brazen]
[7.205: op'nd]
[7.207: moving,]
[7.210, 220, 230: placed correctly]
[7.210: heav'nly]
[7.212: wasteful]
[7.215: highth]
[7.216: troubl'd]
[7.218: Wings]
[7.220: *Chaos,*]
[7.223: Creation,]

[7.224: the]
[7.224: Wheeles]
[7.225: golden]
[7.234: watrie]
[7.236: infus'd,]
7.321: smelling > swelling; error
7.366: his > her; error
7.451: Fowle > Soul; error
7.494: Needlest > Needless; error
7.494: repeaed > repeated; error
7.588: Father (for > Father, for; error
7.906 [8.269]: as > and; error?
[7.1035 (8.398): not indented although 1674 indents]
[7.end notation: missing; the only book with no *finis* line.]

Book 8

8.186: Not > Nor; error?
8.632: make > made; error
8.1183: Women > Woman; error

Book 9

[9.47: state 2, even > eevn]
9.230: line number corrected (2g0 > 230); error
9.240: line number added; error
9.241: Avenger > Avengers; error
9.250, 260, 270: position of line numbers corrected; error
9.510: line number corrected (570 > 510); error
[9.820–870: state 2 of line numbers]
9.827: "then" added as in Second edition; error, line metrically deficient
[9.940–1000: state 2 of line numbers]
[9.968: state 2, Words > words]
[9.982: state 2, misery. > misery,]
9.989–90: "So Death" erroneously placed on line 990 (with lowercase "shall"); moved to line 989 and "Shall" capitalized

[9.1010: state 2, line number corrected]

[9.1078: state 2, supply > supplie]

Book 10

10.32 [11.32]: state 2, pray let me, > pray, let mee

10.76 [11.76]: state 2, doom > Doom

10.101 [11.101]: state 2, warriours > Warriours

10.139 [11.139]: state 2, linkt, > linkt;

10.150, 160, 170 [11.150, 160, 170]: Position of line numbers corrected

10.575 [11.579]: lost > last; errata

10.866 [11.870]: that > who; error

10.880–1540 [11.884–12.649]: position of line numbers corrected

[10.905 (12.13): what looks like "few;" in some copies is apparently "few," with an extraneous mark making it look like a semicolon; see Fletcher, 2.612n. The second edition in 1674, however, gives "few;"'.]

10.1083 [12.191]: This > The; error

10.1110: corrected and repositioned from "1100" given alongside 1111.

10.1130 [12.238]: no change, since the line is not deficient.

10.1424–1541 [12.532–649]: first printing

The First Edition of *Paradise lost*
(With Comment on the
Second Edition and the Manuscript)

The text of *Paradise lost* 1667, its textual variants, the reissues and changes made in 1667–1669, and the text of *Paradise Lost* 1674 will be found in Harris F. Fletcher's facsimile edition of John Milton's "Poetical Works," vols. 2 and 3. References in the following discussions are to the authoritative text of the first issue in 1667 as reproduced in this edition; changes are recorded immediately following the text. Errors in line numbers occur frequently in the original issue. The line number given in all textual discussions will cite the correct number as given in this edition, but followed (1) by the original line number in parentheses when differences occur, or (2) by the revised line numbers of the second 1674 edition in brackets when differences have been created. For example, "The present misery, and render Hell," which is given as line 460, book 2, from the 1667 edition, will be cited as "459 (460)" because the line number is misplaced in the first edition by one line. Line 652 in book 7, "When I behold this goodly Frame, this World," undergoes a changed reference in the 1674 edition and will be cited as "652 [8.15]." However, because all the lines of 10.880–1541, are wrong by being one line too low (that is, 880 is alongside 881 and 1540 is alongside 1541), a constant notation of original numbering in these lines is not made.

Fletcher's Facsimile Edition

Fletcher's facsimile edition prints most photographs from the University of Illinois copy 36, that is, from a copy of 1669[1] rather than from a copy of 1667[1]. He does not indicate which facsimile pages are from a different copy except that he sometimes notes one or more copies where a variant "state" of a page may be found. Concluding that the printing process was an ongoing act, Fletcher argues (2.212) that "There is only an accidental connection between any given title page and any given textual variant or variants, although it is probable that the first copies bound would tend to contain the sheets last printed, hence with the changes made." Implied is that a first "state" of a page may have appeared in later issues only, not in 1667[1]: "It is profitless to describe textual variants in terms of the title pages with which they are *accidentally* bound" (our emphasis). His lack of identification of the sources for his facsimiles can be understood under that belief. "[I]t is probable that no two extant copies are exactly alike in their texts." See also our remarks on his use of the term "state" in our section "Textual Variants" below.

Nineteenth Century Editions

There were two editions of the 1667 text in the nineteenth century and two notices of the second of these, and a facsimile edition by The Scolar Press. The first of these was *Paradise Lost In Ten Books. The TEXT exactly reproduced from the first edition of 1667 With an APPENDIX containing the Additions made in Later Issues and a Monograph on the Original Publication of the Poem* (London: Basil Montagu Pickering, 1873). The preliminary sheets were also reproduced from a 1668 issue, presumably 1668[2]. Neither copy is specifically identified. See the Newberry Library copy, shelfmark Y/185/.M6587. The monograph (17 unpaged pages) was written by Richard Herne Shepherd and discusses orthography, with a general biographical comment. A tabulation of variants in the last signature of book 10 drawn from Lowndes's bibliographic catalog; the April 27, 1668, contract for printing with Samuel Simmons; and the April 26, 1669, receipt of payment are included. Following Lowndes (or rather Bohn), Shepherd refers to eight issues for the first edition, and the copy used as text is identified as Lowndes's No. 1. Some variants, which are noted in "Textual Variants," indicate that this is not an exact facsimile of the 1667 text but one that has had some alteration before the photographic process was used. The volume is no. 734 in Stevens's *Reference Guide to Milton.*

References to Lowndes are not exact. William Thomas Lowndes produced *The Bibliographer's Manual of English Literature* (1834) in which he cited five title pages for the first edition of *Paradise Lost* (3:1268–69). The correspondence is as follows: his issue 1 = issue 1; issue 2 = issue 3; issue 3 = issue 4; issue 4 = issue 5; issue 5 = issue 6. The volume was republished as a *New Edition, Revised, Corrected and Enlarged* [etc.]. *By Henry G. Bohn* (1858); the Milton entries appear in volume 2 (1860), 1557–58. This edition was republished with the legend "London: Henry G. Bohn, 1857," the Milton entries appearing in part 6 (1861), 1557–58. Bohn revised the entries to eight issues, his fourth having a "fleur-de-lis ornament" under Milton's name, his fifth having "stars before and after John Milton," and his sixth omitting the stars and having a different "Printer to the Reader." No copy with stars before and after the name is known, and the sixth is inaccurately dated 1668. As Fletcher remarks (2:162), "Bohn in his revision of Lowndes then went on to list and describe eight different title pages for the first edition, some of which no one has since been able to verify."

The second edition is (reversed italics) *PARADISE LOST, as Originally Published By John Milton, Being a Facsimile Reproduction of the* First Edition. *With an Introduction by David Masson, M.A., LL.D.* (London: Elliot Stock, 1877). It is listed as no. 735 in Stevens. A paragraph review in an anonymous column, "Our Library Table," appeared in *The Athenæum* in 1877. The reviewer remarks that "The blunders of Milton's printer and his deficiencies have been copied with laudable accuracy. The facsimile printer's own faults are not numerous, but sufficient to mar the idea of perfect imitation." The reviewer is concerned with the correction of spacing ("children-scries" in 1.395 and "I n" in 2.558, for example). There are various other differences between this alleged facsimile and all examined copies of the original. Some comments reveal that the reviewer was not aware of the multiple changes in issues, of which the review states, "no less than nine distinct title-pages were affixed to the copies as they were successively sold, viz., two with the date 1667, four with the date 1668, and three with the date 1669." A second review was by R. C. Browne, who published an edition of *English Poems by John Milton* in 1866; its second edition (*New Edition, with Etymological Notes Revised by Henry Bradley*) appeared in 1894 and was frequently reprinted. The review, part of a composite review, was published in *The Academy* in 1877; the single paragraph appears on page 83. Browne is positive toward such an edition: "We are glad to be familiar with the very look of favourite passages, and these things help thereto—though they are, after all, matters of liking and luxury, unessential, not to be dwelt on over-much." But Browne's remarks are more concerned with Masson's attempt "to preserve the last home which Milton's eyes beheld" and with the lack of a standard for spelling in the seventeenth century.

The copy reproduced is not identified, but presumably is the first issue of 1667 as the title page seems to indicate. The introduction, pages [v]–xviii, reviews what was known of the provenance of writing the epic and of its publication, but it thus includes the inaccuracies of late-nineteenth-century scholarship. Masson notes that states of pages exist because of "the detection of errors in time to correct them for a portion of the impression. Thus several of the sheets, as kept in bales for binding, might be in different states of correctness, and a later-bound copy might have one of these sheets in its first or less correct state" (xiii). Despite that statement and his implied attention to the text, Masson invalidly remarks, "All in All, the First Edition of *Paradise Lost* was a very carefully printed book" (xiv). We report the Newberry Library copy, shelfmark Y/185/.M6566, checked with the copy owned by the University of North Carolina at Pembroke; and the reprint by the Folcroft Library Edition (Folcroft, Pa: 1972), owned by the University of Illinois at Chicago, shelfmark PR/3560/1877a (but misbound). This Folcroft reprint was republished in 1976 and in Philadelphia by R. West in 1978. As noted later, this so-called facsimile has been altered in a number of places; for one example note the line number for book 10, 1450, which is given as 1045, a variation not reported by Fletcher and not found in any copy of a 1667 issue that we have examined. It is certainly not a "facsimile"; comparisons with original copies indicate that the types are *not* the same.

Scolar Facsimile Edition

The Scolar Press (1968) presents a copy from its own holdings. The copies listed in the appendix from which the title pages of the six issues are there reproduced include its own copy last, thus indicating (but with some uncertainty) that its copy is the sixth issue 1669^2. This text is supplemented by about 86 pages drawn from five other copies of the text in the British Library ([iii]). Substitute pages are taken from British Library copies G.11558 (issue 5, 1669^1); C.57.3.20 (issue 6, 1669^2); C.59.b.1 (issue 3, 1668^1); 684.d.30 (issue 5, 1669^1); C.14.a.10 (issue 4, 1668^2). The title pages reproduced in the appendix are, in order, from British Library copies C.14.a.9 (issue 1); C.69.ff.5 (issue 2); C.59.b.1(issue 3); C.14.a.11 (issue 4); G.11558 (issue 5); Scolar copy (issue 6). The preliminary leaves are taken from copy 684.d.30 (issue 5) with two substitutions from copy G.11558 (issue 5). Scolar lists only the call numbers, not the issue numbers or dates. Hereafter the abbreviation BL will be used in reference to these copies. References to these substituted sheets in the Scolar material are sometimes incomplete and sometimes confused.

A first issue of this facsimile owned by the University of Kentucky (Special Collections, *821.47/O-P2274/1968) does not include the extended note detailing which pages are substituted. Indeed, no published citation of the Scolar edition seems to be aware that it appears in two issues (amounting to almost two *editions*), reference consistently being to the second without notation. For this information on substituted pages see a different (second) issue, which is the one reported in *Milton Newsletter* 2 (1968) and *Seventeenth-Century News* 28 (1970), although neither periodical indicates that it is reviewing a second edition, which, as it turns out, is at times different from the first. This second edition is also owned by the University of Kentucky (PR / 3560 / 1667a), and both issues are collated here. The original note and the extended note in issue 2 are

confused and state, erroneously, that the title page (1667[1]) comes from
BL copy G.11558 (which is 1669[1]). The title page of the Scolar
facsimile given at the beginning of the facsimile edition is different
(in inking, marks on the page, and the like) from the first title page
given in the appendix to that edition, apparently from BL copy
C.14.1.10. The substitutions have been necessary "because of the
thin paper, irregular inking, and occasional bad press-work in the
original edition." Attention is not paid to states of the text, but corrected pages are presented when the occasion arises, and thus this
is *not* a facsimile of the first issue of the first edition, but a composite (as is Fletcher's) of different issues of the first edition. Scolar
gives the title pages of all six issues and the preliminary leaves
added in the fourth issue (1668[2]) in an appendix. The comment that
"the sheets of the poem . . . are identical in all copies of the first edition, apart from the inevitable press corrections and minor alterations
made within the impression" must derive from the import of
Fletcher's work. It is not an adequate or valid statement. The copy-
text may be uncertain because the facsimile does not reproduce the
second printing of sigs. Z or Vv, which printing often appears with
1669[2]. Either Scolar's copy is a sixth issue copy but with the first
printing of sigs. Z and Vv, which are found in other copies, or it has
substituted such pages although they are not listed among the
acknowledged substitutions. Discrepancies between the two editions
and pages that are questionable as to inclusion in a 1669[2] copy,
although such pages are not listed as substitutions, are pointed out
in our later discussion.

Electronic Editions

An electronic version of the 1667 edition employs the Scolar Press
publication, transcribed by Judy Boss and available from the Electronic
Text Center, University of Virginia Library (1999): <http://etext.lib.vir-
ginia.edu>. The Internet site prints out the HTML conversion with
corrections by various people at different times. "The Scolar Press
edition is a 'hybrid' facsimile: it is neither a diplomatic facsimile of
one copy nor an eclectic facsimile of an 'ideal copy.'" Alterations in
the electronic text occur; for example, the line numbers given are

added and italics are rendered as capital letters. The copy used was that of the second issue of Scolar.

Second Edition, 1674

The second edition of 1674 adds a total of fifteen lines, three of which result from the division of book 7 into books 7 and 8, and five of which result from the division of book 10 into books 11 and 12. The change from ten books into twelve causes original book 7 to become books 7 and 8, book 8 to become book 9, book 9 to become book 10, and book 10 to become books 11 and 12. The line additions in 1674 are: 5.636; 5.638–39; 8.1–3; 11.485–87; 11.551–52, created from one line in 1667 (10.548); and 12.1–5. The Arguments are now distributed before their respective books, with each of those for 1667's books 7 and 10 now divided with some changes into books 7 and 8 and books 11 and 12. Preliminary materials in the second edition of 1674 are S. B.'s poem "In Paradisum Amissam Summi Poetæ Johannis Miltoni," Andrew Marvell's poem "On Paradise Lost," and "The Verse," thus omitting "The Printer to the Reader" (also deleted in 1669²). Corrections of the "Errata" were made in the 1674 edition except for reading "wee" in place of "we" in 2.414 (discussed later).

Manuscript, Book 1

A manuscript of book 1 in the hand of an unknown amanuensis with numerous corrections by various hands is owned by the Pierpont Morgan Library, New York City. This scribe is designated Amanuensis D by James Holly Hanford in his work on Milton's Commonplace Book, which has two entries by this same scribe. Notations on the manuscript show that it was the copy source for the first edition, even though the printed text is frequently different. The manuscript was probably preserved because the verso of its outside leaf holds the imprimatur of Richard Royston allowing it to be printed. Helen Darbishire edited and discussed *The Manuscript of Paradise Lost. Book I* in 1931, with a facsimile, transcription, and notes, and Fletcher likewise includes a facsimile, transcription, notes, and discussion in volume 2 of his facsimile edition of the poetic works.

Issues of the First Edition

There were six issues of the first edition in 1667–69 with six different title pages, two issues in each year. However, "issue" in this sentence indicates only the six different title pages since the texts do *not* evidence distinct issuing. The authoritative text of this edition has been collated with the text of the Newberry Library's 1667^1 issue; the text of the preliminary leaves is that of the University of Kentucky's 1668^2 issue. All textual remarks have been checked against at least one additional copy of each issue of the first edition and one copy of the second edition. These copies are: ***1667^1, British Library (issue 1, C.14.a.9) and Newberry Library (issue 1, Case / 4A /909); 1667^2, Huntington Library (issue 2) and Newberry Library (issue 2 but with preliminary leaves added, Case/Y/185/.M6565); 1668^{1A}, Huntington Library (issue 3); 1668^2, University of Kentucky (issue 4, Special Collections, PR 3560 .A1), Huntington Library (issue 4), and Newberry Library (issue 4, Case/Y/185/.M65663); 1669^1, University of Kentucky (issue 5, Special Collections, PR 3560/1669), Huntington Library (issue 5), and Newberry Library (issue 5, Case/3A/629); 1669^2, University of Kentucky (issue 6, Special Collections, PR 3560/1669/Copy 3) and Huntington Library (issue 6); 1674, University of Kentucky and Huntington Library. Also consulted: University of Kentucky copy with issue 3 title page, a composite text from the fourth, fifth, and sixth issues, and second printing of preliminary leaves (Special Collections, PR 3560 1668b), here designated UK 1669^x since it usually has the fifth issue text but with a third issue title page. Composite texts may be common, often with earlier title pages attached. BL hereafter refers to British Library copies; HEH to Henry E. Huntington Library copies; and UK to University of Kentucky copies.

Another, earlier title page (1668¹) for the third issue (1668¹ᴬ) errs by omission of a period after "BOOKS"; see Stephen B. Dobranski's essay, "Simmons' Shell Game: The Six Title Pages of *Paradise Lost*," in *"Paradise Lost: A Poem Written in Ten Books": Essays on the 1667 Edition*, for discussion of these issues. The omission of the period follows its absence in issues 1 and 2, but the alteration of the following line ("By *JOHN MILTON*." > "The Author *J. M.*") necessitated a period after "BOOKS" as in 1668², 1669¹, 1669². (The order of the printing of the issues is thus reasserted; for Hugh Amory's speculation regarding which title page issue was published first, see his "'Things Unattempted Yet'" in which he argues that 1668¹ was the first published title page "issue," largely on the basis of the initials "*J. M.*" on the title page rather than the full name, which is given on the 1667, 1668², and 1669 issues. The lack of a period after "BOOKS" in the 1667 issues is continued, incorrectly, on the 1668¹ title page despite the alteration of the line concerning authorship. Demanded by that alteration is the addition of a period after "BOOKS" as given in 1668¹ᴬ and 1668², as well as both 1669 issues. Amory ignores the evidence of this period as well as the date 1668 as printed. Textual alterations made in the five additional "issues" are collated against the authoritative transcription of the first issue given here (see "Textual Variants"). These issues were created by reassembling pages printed for the first issue but not used, or by deletion and replacement of the original title page on existing unsold copies of a previous issue, or under Fletcher's scenario through stop-press variant pages that were not used at the time of such stop-press action in 1667. Indeed, none of his "first state" pages appears in copies of 1667¹. In other words, the term "issue" is inaccurate for the text and applies only to the title page accompanying whatever text was assembled. Added in the second issue of 1668 (that is, the fourth issue of the text) are preliminary pages that include "The Printer to the Reader" (in both a four- and a six-line version), "The Arguments" to the ten books (gathered together), "The Verse," and "Errata." A second reset and printed version of the preliminary matter for the sixth issue, 1669, does not include "The Printer to the Reader," and various changes occur.

Apparently around the same time that 1669[2] was being readied, sufficient copies of signatures Z and Vv did not exist for this sixth issue and thus they were reset and reprinted, creating additional textual variants therein. The changes from the reset signatures of the text are recorded under "Textual Variants." Significant variants in the preliminary leaves among the last three issues of the first edition of *Paradise Lost* are also listed and discussed. The frequent poor spacing of words and lines, turned letters, and the anomalies of types and fonts are omitted from citation here, as are the resetting of lines creating hyphenation in the second printing of the preliminary leaves or deleting hyphenation from the first printing. In all, the reset second printing is inferior to the first and points to a different compositor from the original one for the preliminary leaves.

Textual Variants

In the course of printing, changes may be made to a text as a result of recognition of an error by the compositor, disruption of a letter or letters in the mechanical operation of printing or making changes, and sometimes because of a deliberate change by the author. The first two reasons yield some significance for the authorial text, although they basically comment upon the printer's work and conditions of work. Yet some of these alterations do tell us about the "authorial" copy-text, and these will be discussed below. At times changes necessitate an adjustment of spacing, and often these printing changes occur on conjugate leaves, suggesting the nature of the compositor's working habits and attentiveness. Stop-press variants, which created different states of a page, corrected errors made in the course of setting type and printing, resulting usually in a stoppage of printing, correction, and then continued printing. Probably many of the textual variants recorded here are of that nature. Fletcher's assignment of states is based on such stop-press changes. The pages of the 1667 edition of Milton's poem evidence the following textual and press variants, listed here as state 1, state 2, state 3, and state 4 when such states occur.

Fletcher's citations do not identify in which copies the states occur (with the exception of a few variations, as noted below), a situation that therefore does not allow us to determine whether states of the text reported are related to issues of the text. We do not know, that is, whether there are true press variants for the 1667[1] text, thus creating state 2 of a page, or whether the resultant so-called states were created when new issues were produced. However, the mixture of states that exists in some copies of later issues but not in all copies of those same issues points to the contention which Fletcher posits, that a state did not come into existence because a new issue was being produced but rather that such states existed earlier than the new issue, which mixed such states at random with other states of the text, thus affecting some but not all copies of an issue. Fletcher treats the issues aside from the sixth as being the same printing as the first except for the title page; that is, the only new printing for an issue was the title page (but see textual variants for book 5 below). For the sixth issue, 1669[2], signatures Z and Vv were reset; one concludes that this occurred because not enough copies of those signatures existed for the full sixth issue when that issue was produced. Other pages do not evidence resetting even though variants may appear on them.

Generally it has been thought that either copies of the 1667[1] text had the title page removed and a new title page added for the successive five issues (a very common practice), or a new issue was created by taking signatures from a pile of previously printed signatures (printed in 1667 when the first issue was being produced) but that had not yet been used (in the first issue). Probably both possibilities are correct. This would demand the maintenance of such piles of unused pages from August(?) 1667 through perhaps April(?) 1669. Such piles of signatures would, under the conclusion to which the evidence points, include first, second, and third states, thus accounting for the *accidental* use of "inaccurate" pages in later issues. It is most curious that almost none of the variant pages appears in copies of 1667[1]. (See the variants below for book 1, however.) Fletcher seems to base his opinion for calling a page state 1 or state 2 on what he believed were or were not Miltonic practices of spelling and other mechanics of writing, and upon variants that are adjudged corrections, thus being labeled state 2. Further, whenever a reading is not the better reading or is a clear error (this happens particularly when line numbering errors occur), he calls it state 1 and the "better" reading or "correction," state 2. We may thus find Fletcher's ordering of states questionable and even unacceptable, since neither possibility is consistently true. The term "state" *should* mean that the text designated state 1 was set first and that changes to that text (particularly changes made while printing is taking place) thus become state 2, whether the changes are corrections or errors or simply alterations created in resetting a word, a line, or a page by the compositor. Fletcher's use of the term "state," it will be found, is sometimes faulty. Thus, we should not assume that changes in a "second" state are necessarily correct; they may be the compositor's mechanics of language (for example, in book 2, the changes from "appeer" to "appear" [2.15] and from "exasperat" to "exasperate" [2.143]).

Book 1

1.530, line number: 3 0 / 530
1.563, 566: a piece of type set for "A" and "A" / not present
1.569: views; / views,
1.682: gold / Gold
1.696: out done (or) out-done / outdone
After 1.718, catchword: Equall'd / Equal'd (as given in 719 in all copies)

All first state items above occur only in copy number 12, which is a copy of 1669[1], in signature C. Fletcher remarks: it "was probably printed first, perhaps as a proof sheet. Then later it was used either deliberately to make up needed copies, or inadvertently" (2.238). (Variants in copy 12 against all other copies will be cited again in other books.) The state 2 readings do not disagree with what might have been Milton's text, but the readings of lines 569, 682, 696 (out don), and the catchword (but not 719) all agree with the manuscript. In other words, the state 2 readings for book 1 can be assigned to the compositor, not to Milton's text, and the state 1 readings would seem indeed to be state 1 and derived from the manuscript copy-text that is still extant. However, both issues of the Scolar facsimile read with state 2 for the first five items above, including "outdone" on the same page as the catchword, but with state 1 for the catchword. The page is C_4r but this is not listed as a substitute page in the Scolar note, and thus we must assign it to the Scolar issue reported (apparently but not certainly 1669[2]). In any case this is a separate, "new" state of the page not discovered by Fletcher, existing between state 1 and state 2, unless someone has tampered with the "facsimile." A like problem also exists with the Masson "facsimile" in line 359, which clearly reads "Exeelling." The type "c" is frequently battered in the 1667 edition, but all copies examined read "Excelling" when carefully scrutinized. Did someone tamper with the "facsimile" printed under Masson's name? (We refer to the 1877 publication as the Masson facsimile although the variants in the text are probably the result of the printer who made alterations.)

Conclusion: Issue 1 of *Paradise Lost* in 1667, therefore, has only state 2 pages for book 1, and what is construed as state 1 has been discovered in only one copy. But an interim state, not previously recognized, also exists between state 1 and state 2 if the Scolar facsimile has not been tampered with.

Book 2

2.4: Barbaric / *Barbaric*
2.15: appeer / appear
2.D3v, head: Book 1. / Book 2.
2.D4r, head: Book 1. / Book 2.
2.143: exasperat / exasperate
2.714: other / other
2.790: 900 / 790
2.819: Heavn' / Heav'n
2.980, 990, 1000: alongside 981, 991, 1001 / corrected, states 2 and 3
2.986: standerd / standerd / Standerd
2.1009: Havook / Havook / Havock
2.1010, 1020, 1030, 1040: alongside 1011, 1021, 1031, 1041 / corrected, state 2 and 3

Questions of which state of a page precedes another emerge with the variants above. Fletcher writes that state 2 of the first five items above appears in all copies except 4, 7, 127, 131, 133, 176. All additional copies of all issues that we have checked show only state 2. Fletcher does not relate the six copies he cites to any other alterations. Three of these copies are issues 4, two are issues 5, and the last is not listed in the sigla. One of the items raises the possibility that the second state may not be faithful to Milton's text, whereas the first state may be, for Milton would have spelled "exasperat," and it does appear in the second edition (1644) of *Doctrine and Discipline of Divorce*. One cannot be sure about "appeer" (the most frequent spelling in the epic), for it does emerge in *Il Penseroso*, 122, although in extant holograph Milton spelled only "appear." These five items as state 1 of the signatures bear out Fletcher's contention that first printings sometimes were used in later issues though they seem not to have been used earlier when actually printed.

The printing errors in lines 714, 790, and 819 are assigned to state 1 although these do not exist in signature D in Fletcher's copies noted above. For line 790 he writes, "In some copies, notably copies 9, 10, and 26, this is 900" and at line 714, "The first [state] printed it **other,** and the second printed it **other,** It belongs with the change in line number 790 from 900 three pages later and on the same side of the sheet" (2, 282, 278–79). But the copies cited are of the fifth and sixth issues, not what copies of the first and other earlier issues given by Fletcher evidence. However, the first issue, 1667[1], in the Newberry Library gives "900" for 790, but otherwise has state 2 for lines 4–819, including "other," and state 3 for lines 980–1040, including "other." This makes Fletcher's remark most dubious. Fletcher's assignment of states is thus, as in some other cases, questionable. The variant lines 714 through 819 given above are found in signature G (G$_{1r}$, G$_{2v}$, G$_{3r}$). The other readings ("other," "790," "Heav'n") are given by Fletcher as state 2, and they all appear with the previous five labeled state 2 items in all copies of 1667[1] (except the Newberry and Masson copies), 1667[2], 1668[1], 1669[1], and 1669[2] examined, with one exception: the University of Kentucky (UK) copy of 1669[2] has "other," "900," and "Heavn'." What we find—if indeed the scenario of keeping inaccurate printings in the compositor's shop for two years, perhaps mixed in with corrected printings, is valid as it seems to be—is a matter of haphazard picking up a signature from this pile or that, or from mixed piles of signatures, as new issues are put together in 1667, 1668, and 1669.

The copy of 1668² shows the four state 2 readings above in lines 714, 721, 790, 819, and the correct placement of numbers in 980, and so on, and 1010, and so on, but it also has "standerd" and "Havook" in both copies of this issue examined, as well as UK 1669ˣ and issue 1 of the Scolar facsimile, both of which thus are seen to employ pages also found in 1668². That is, these copies show state 2 only, not state 3 as might be expected in a 1669² issue. (Here we have further evidence of unacknowledged change in the Scolar facsimile in sig. H₁ᵥ, which in the second issue of Scolar is a substitute page from BL copy 684.d.30, a copy of issue 5. The first Scolar issue apparently was reproduced from a copy of 1669² in the possession of the press with a different page from that in the second Scolar issue, but we are not told what issue of *Paradise Lost* is for that page.) This therefore defines a state 2 for the line numbers 986, 1009, and the further line numbers. All other copies are of state 3. The last four items are not assigned by Fletcher to any specific copies for the three states. The fourth issue (1668²) often shows variations, suggesting that "corrected" signatures were reduced in availability and "uncorrected" ones were picked up at that time, thus not only through a matter of happenstance.

Two anomalous and unique printings occur in the Masson facsimile where *Tartarean*, 69, is given as *Tartarcan* and no comma follows "remov'd" in line 321.

Conclusion: States 2 and 3 should be followed from 1667¹, with correction of "900," except that "exasperat," 143 (state 1), may reflect Milton's preference.

Book 3

3.40: year / Year
3.60, 70, 80: alongside 50, 60, 70, and with no 50 and no number alongside 80 / correct line numbers in correct position.
3.61: siight / sight
3.97: me / mee
3.630 (640): impure∧ / impure;
3.653 (663): accostes; / accostes.

3.655 (665): God's / Gods
3.679 (689): race / Race
3.690 (700): regent / Regent

The last page of book 3 prints lines 721–42, but line numbering gives 740–61 (states 1 and 2) and [730]–751 (state 3): 3.740 given alongside 721, and numbers 750 and 760 thus alongside 731 and 741 in states 1 and 2. Numbers 740 and 750 given alongside 731 and 741, with no line number alongside 721 in state 3. (Thus, in addition to the ten-line error in line numbers from 600 [610] forward [listed here under "Errors"], the last page of book 3 creates an additional one-line error, ending with line 761 or line 751 instead of line 742.)

3.729 (748/738): renewing, / renewing_∧_ / renewing_∧_
3.729 (748/738): Heav'n; / Heav'n, / Heav'n,
3.731 (750/740): th' Earth / the Earth / the Earth
3.737 (756/746): Heaven / Heav'n / Heav'n
3.741 (760/750): with / in / in [Errata, in fourth, fifth, and sixth
    issues, reads "Lib 3. V. 760. for *with* r. *in*."]

State 2 of the first four items (sig. H) appears in all copies examined (including the first issue) except for Newberry 1669[1], which has state 1. Fletcher does not indicate which copies or how many exhibit state 1. State 1 variants in 630, 653, 655 (sig. L) are found in issues 1 (both copies), 3, 4 (both copies), Newberry fifth issue, HEH sixth issue, and Scolar; state 2, in issues 2, 4 (Newberry), 5 (HEH and UK copies), UK sixth issue, and UK 1669[x], as well as the Shepherd facsimile. Again Masson is different from every copy examined, giving "impure_∧_", "accostes.", and "God's". State 1 variants in 679 and 690 ("race" and "regent") appear only in Fletcher's copy 12. Issues 1667[1] (BL and Newberry), 1667[2] (HEH), 1668[1], UK copy of 1668[2], and HEH copy of 1669[2], and both issues of the Scolar facsimile show state 1 of numbering of lines 721–42 (740, 750, 760, and "with"). Newberry copy of 1667[2], HEH and Newberry copies of 1668[2], Newberry, UK, and HEH copies of 1669[1], and UK copy of 1669[2] evidence state 3 of lines 721–42 (740, 750, and "in"). No copy consulted has state 2 (740, 750, 760, and "in"); Fletcher does not specify which copy (or copies) does. The final five variants are all state 1 in 1667[1], 1667[2], 1668[1], UK 1668[2], HEH 1669[2], and Scolar. States 2 and 3 of these final five variants (being the same) are found in HEH 1668[2], UK and HEH 1669[1], UK 1669[2], but since numbering on the last page of book 3 is the third state for all of these copies, they would be assigned as state 3. UK copy 1669[x] agrees with UK copies of the fifth and sixth issues. However, Newberry issue 2 has state 3 for all variants except for "with" in line 741 (changed later by an erratum); Newberry issue 4 has state 2 for all variants, and Newberry issue 5 has state 1. Shepherd has only state 3, whereas Masson has state 1 for numbering and lines 729 (two instances) and 741 but state 2–3 for lines 731 and 737. Also, Masson uniquely prints a capitalized "Posteritie" in line 209 and deletes the hyphen in "First-seen" in line 549. Fletcher has missed a variation in line 204 where the BL 1667[1] copy has "feältie" (also found in Masson). We do not find the dieresis in any other copy.

Conclusion: Issue one of *Paradise Lost* has state 1 of the above variants except for lines 40, 60, 61, 97, 679, 690 (sigs. H$_3$v, H$_4$r, H$_4$v, L$_1$v, L$_2$r), which variants have been observed only in Newberry 1669[1]. Fletcher does not give any information about copies with state 1 in signatures H and L; is he perhaps reporting only a few copies? Are those copies all found in issue 5? (See comment for books 1, 2, 4.)

Book 4

4.41: (King: [below the line] / King: [on line]
4.52: immence / immense
4.83 (73, 73, 83): spirits / Spirits / Spirits
4.88 (78, 78, 88): groane; / groane: / groane:
4.90: 80 / 80 / 90
4.90 (80, 80, 90): advanc'd / advanc't / advanc't
4.91 (81, 81, 91): Supream / supream / supream
4.100: 90 / 90 / 100
4.100 (90, 90, 100): relapse$_\wedge$ / relapse, / relapse,
4.110: 100 / 100 / 110
4.660, 670, 680 placed between 660–61, 670–71, 680–81 / [adjusted] (Numbers from 760 to the end of the book are placed one line too high; thus, 760 alongside 759 through 1010 alongside 1009.)
4.alongside 809: 381 / 810

The first state of lines 41 and 52 appears only in copy 12. Variants in lines 90–110 above appear in different states in various issues: issue 1 has state 1; issue 2, state 3; issue 3, state 1; issue 4, UK copy state 1 and HEH copy state 2; issue 5, state 1 in Newberry but state 3 in HEH and UK copies examined; issue 6, UK copy state 2 and HEH copy state 1. UK's third title page copy has state 3, and both Scolar facsimiles give state 1. The first state of the numbers for 660ff. and 809 appears in UK issues 4, 5, and 1669^x, and BL and Huntington copies of issues 1, 5, 6; the second state in Newberry issues 1 and 5, UK issue 6, and HEH copies of issues 2 and 3. Newberry issues 2 and 5, HEH issue 4, and both Scolar facsimiles show state 1 for 660ff. and state 2 for 809. These two variants appear on signatures O$_1$v and O$_3$r, suggesting that signature O appears in an intermediate state rather than only two states as Fletcher records and discusses them. Scolar again does not list either of these pages as a substitute page. The Shepherd facsimile gives state 3 for lines 83–110 and state 1 of the numbers for 660–809; the Masson facsimile gives state 1 for those lines except in line 100 ("relapse,") which is apparently another change made in the so-called facsimile, and state 1 of the numbers. BL 1667[1] and the Masson facsimile print a dieresis in "Preëminent" in line 447.

Conclusion: The first issue of *Paradise Lost* has state 1 of these variants in book 4 except for those at line 41 and 52. Line numbering for the first issue should be corrected.

Book 5

See note on states immediately following.
5.121: do: / do: / do.
5.133: he / he / hee
5.150: their / thir / thir
5.151: Harp, / Harp$_\wedge$ / Harp$_\wedge$
5.153: works$_\wedge$ / works$_\wedge$ / works,
5.154: frame / Frame / Frame
5.156: Heavens$_\wedge$ / Heavens, / Heavens$_\wedge$

5.160: Speak ye / Speak ye / Speak yee
5.161: ye / ye / yee
catchword: Moon∧ / Moon∧ / Moon, [line 175, Moon,]
5.240: fal'n / falln / falln
5.240: Heaven / Heaven / Heav'n
5.251: quires / Quires / Quires
5.257: [indented] / [indented] / [not indented]
5.257: cloud∧ / cloud∧ / cloud,
5.258: interposd / interpos'd / interpos'd
5.258: how ever / however / however
5.259: unconforme / unconform / unconform
5.269: Fanne / Fann / Fann
5.271: fowles / Fowles / Fowles
5.273: Sunn's / Sun's / Sun's
5.277: *Seraph* / Seraph / Seraph
5.287: bands / bands / Bands
5.292: blisul / blissful / blissful
5.297: art / art / Art
5.297: blisse / bliss / bliss
5.301: raies, / Raies, / Raies∧
5.302: need[s]∧ / need[s]; / need[*s*]; [the s prints only as a mark]
5.510: 150 / 510
5.608: Lord, / Lord:
5.616: [not indented] / [indented]
5.713 [710]: within, / within∧
5.728 [725]: battel∧ / battel,
5.746 [743]: Morning∧ / Morning,
5.830 [827]: our / one

States given above are those recorded in Fletcher; however, states 1 and 3 for lines 121–302 should be reversed. State 2 exhibits both state 1 and state 3 variants as well as its own different variants. The reading of 1667[1] (see BL and Newberry copies) for line 121 through line 302 is consistently that given by Fletcher as state 3, and the reading of 1669[2] is consistently that given by Fletcher as state 1. Such an ordering of states as Fletcher presents is untenable. Issues 3, 4, and 5 in the Huntington and the Newberry issues 2 and 4 are also consistently state 3 (that is, 1); and HEH issue 2 is state 2, as is Newberry issue 5. UK's copy 1669^x is state 2, and Scolar is state 3 (that is, 1) in the first issue, but there has been a change in sig. Q4r in the second issue, which gives state 2 of this page. According to the bibliographic note, this page is substituted by one from BL C.59.b.1, which is issue 3, giving state 3 (that is, 1), as in the first edition; therefore, this additional substitution in issue 2 of Scolar has not been recorded. Of the copies examined, it is only issues HEH 2, Newberry 5, UK 4, UK 5, and UK 1669^x that are state 2. We suspect that Fletcher gives the order that he does because he finds no evidence of a resetting of sig. Q although he notes numerous movements of types (2.375) while saying, "The page [Q$_1$v] has not been reset," and because the variants in his state 1 are sometimes so clearly wrong (like "interposd"). (Fletcher's ordering of states in his edition apparently is consistently based on his judgment that what are viewed as errors constitute state 1 and "corrections" constitute a later state.) Instead, it would seem that we have another example of revision made for the sixth issue, the only one showing his state 1 (state 3), like the resetting of sigs. Z and Vv. In all three sets of pages, sigs. Q, Z, Vv, a plethora of errors and bad composing occur, which one does not find in the rest of the signatures, despite their poor workmanship. While Fletcher finds no evidence of resetting any signatures in book 5, the evidence otherwise points to changes being made for the sixth issue of 1669^2, and so we posit reordering of the above states for lines 121–302, with state 1 replacing state 3, and state 3 replacing state 1. The Masson facsimile is consistently state 1 (that is, state 3) for lines 121–302, and state 2 for lines 510–830.

The "s" in line 302 ("needs;") prints only as a mark and may thus not be recognized when looking at the page swiftly. Tampering, rather than an actual facsimile of Q4r, seems to have occurred in the Shepherd and Masson facsimiles, which clearly show only a space: "need ;". The Shepherd facsimile also prints "battel$_\wedge$" (state 1), line 728, amid other variants of state 2, the only copy we have found with this anomaly. It occurs on the same page as "Morning," (state 2), line

746, but in all other copies where that page reads "Morning," (state 2), the reading is "battel," (state 2).

Of the numbering error of "150" for "510," Fletcher simply says that the error appears in many copies. We find it in the BL copy of 1668[1], the Newberry 1667[1] and 1667[2], the UK and HEH copies of 1669[1], and the UK copies of 1669[2] and 1669[x]; all the others have the correct number. This is sig. R$_3$v, and seems to be an isolated change because the HEH third issue, the Newberry first issue, the UK fifth issue, and UK 1669[x] show state 2 for the remaining variants (lines 608–827, sig. S); but the HEH fifth issue, the Newberry second issue, and the UK sixth issue give only state 1 for those variants. We are therefore again suspicious that Fletcher's states for lines 608–827 might be reversed, unless there are two cases where an erroneous early printing accidentally found use in two later issues, one of them the sixth issue, which required some resetting in other signatures.

Conclusion: Fletcher's states for variants in book 5 would seem to be wrong; rather, state 1 in lines 121–302 should be state 3, and state 3 should be state 1. Line 510 is problematic, and lines 608–827 may be questionable as to states. The text of the first issue of 1667 thereby should present ("new") state 1 of variants in lines 121–302, and state 2 for the remaining variants, including line 510.

Book 6

No variants. However, Shepherd deletes the hyphen in "day-spring," line 521.

Book 7

Signature Z, printing lines 1–238, was reset. These reset pages are found in Nos. 40 and 185, as well as a copy in the Berg Collection, New York Public Library. No. 40 is listed by Fletcher as being a copy of 1669[1] and 1669[2], which he explains on page 441: "the Z Signature" was "reprinted at about the same time that the 1669[2] title page was printed, and, because in the IU copy 40 it is on paper containing the same watermark (number 17–18), at the same time as the half sheet

Vv was reprinted." No. 185 is a copy of 1669². He remarks that copies with reprinted signature Z are "very rare," and this implies that at least most other copies of the sixth issue he has seen do not have the reprinted form. Variants in this reprinting are numerous. Most turned letters, bad spacing, nonprinting letters, and the like are omitted from the following list; some are included to indicate the nature of the sloppy and inaccurate work of the second compositor.

7.1: *Urania,* / *Urania*ᴧ
7.3: Following, / Followingᴧ
7.9: Eternal / eternal
7.11: Almightie / Almighty
7.11: Father, / Fatherᴧ
7.15: safetie / safety
7.19: Dismounted, / Dismountedᴧ
7.21: remaines / remains
7.24: Sing / sing
7.25: dayes, / tongues;
7.30: still / Still
7.34: wilde / wild
7.36: rapture, / raptureᴧ
7.36: clamor / clamour
7.39: Heav'n lie, / Heav'nlieᴧ
7.40: Goddess, / Goddessᴧ
7.41: Arch-angel, / Arch-Angel
7.48: obeyd / obey'd
7.49: tasts / tastes
7.52: admiration, / admirationᴧ
7.52: Muse / muse
7.56: confusion: / confusion,
7.57: Driv'n / Driven
7.60, 70: placed correctly / alongside 61, 71
7.71: Farr / Far
7.76: infinitly / Infinitely
7.78: solemne / solemn
catchword: Immu- / Im-

7.80: voutsaf't / vouchsaf't

7.83: knowing, / knowing‿

7.85: availe / avail

7.88: yeelds / yields

7.89: Aire / Air

7.90, 100, 110: 90 and 110 placed correctly but 100 placed alongside
99 / printed between lines 89–90, 98–99, 109–110

7.92: Eternitie / Eternity

7.93: begun, / begun‿

7.97: works, / works‿

7.100: heares / hears

7.101: heare / hear

7.104: Starr / Star

7.104: Eevning / Evening

7.106: Sleep / sleep

7.109: illustrous / illustrious

7.110: answerd / answered

7.122: King, / King‿

7.126: Knowledge / knowledge

7.126: as food / a food

7.130, 140: placed correctly / alongside 132, 141

7.135: returnd / teturnd

7.136: th' Omnipotent / the Omnipotent

7.138: spake. / spake‿

7.139: envious / invious

7.139: Foe / foe

7.139: fail'd, / fail'd‿

7.142: Deitie / Deity

7.144: many, / many‿

7.151: done, / done‿

7.156: innumerable, / innumerable‿

7.158: length / lenghth

7.160: [first] Heavn / Heav'n

7.162: Heav'n, / Heav'n;

7.171: goodness, / goodness‿

7.172: Necessitie / Necessity

7.177: human / humane
7.181: Almightie's / Almigties
7.182: most High, good / mst hgood
7.183: peace: / peace;
7.184: Glorie / Glory
7.185: driven / driv'n ("driven" is prosodically correct)
7.189: maligne / malign
7.190: diffuse / dffuse
7.191: Worlds / World
7.194: Omnipotence / On nipotence
7.195: Majestie / Majesty
7.201: brazen / Brazen
7.205: op'nd / open'd
7.207: moving, / moving∧
7.210, 220, 230: placed correctly / alongside 211, between 220 and
    221, alongside 232
7.210: heav'nly / Heav'nly
7.212: wasteful / wastful
7.215: Heav'ns / Hcav'ns
7.215: highth / hight
7.216: troubl'd / troubled
7.218: Wings / wings
7.220: *Chaos,* / *Chaos*∧
7.223: Creation, / Creation∧
7.224: the / his
7.224: Wheeles / Wheels
7.225: golden / Golden
7.234: watrie / watery
7.236: infus'd, / infus'd∧

Printing 1 is the text of all issues of all copies examined except for
HEH 1669[2], which has printing 2. The catchword for line 79 in
printing 1 is printed "Immu-" in copies of 1667[1], 1667[2], 1668[1], but
(suggesting some disruption in the plate) "Im mu-" in 1668[2], 1669[1],
UK 1669[2], UK 1669[x], and both Scolar issues. Again, the Masson facsimile, while presenting state 1 of the above lines, has altered the

placement of number 100 to its correct position; this occurs in no other copy reported or examined. The Masson facsimile incorrectly alters the period (which is broken) to a comma (after "Winde" in line 130. Furthermore, the facsimile printed "recevaes" in line 726; a displacement of lines at this point in the printing is in evidence in original copies.

Conclusion: Printing 1 provides the text for 1667, first issue.

(Lines 239–1290 are found as the first and only printing in book 7. There are no variants. Lines 641–1290 were separated from book 7 in 1674 and became book 8.)

Book 8 (that is, book 9 in 1674)

No variants.

Book 9 (that is, book 10 in 1674)

9.47: even / eevn
9.820, 830, 840, 850, 860, 870, 940, 950, 960, 970, 980, 990, 1000 misplaced alongside 824, 834, 844, 854, 864, 874, 944, 954, 964, 975, 984, 994, 1004 / correct
9.968: Words / words
9.982: misery. / misery,
9.1010: 0110 / 1010
9.1078: supply / supplie

Some of the copies are composites of state 1 and state 2 readings, making classification uncertain. Miltonic spelling would have been "eevn," according to Fletcher, the spelling of "most" copies examined. "Even" appears in Fletcher's copies 22, 32, and 33, respectively 1669[2], 1669[1], 1669[2]; but it also is found in BL 1667[1] and HEH 1669[2]. Fletcher's ordering of that variant state (that is, as a correction) seems to be accurate. The correct numbers appear in "most" copies, thus accounting for Fletcher's ordering of states; the incorrect placements are found in copy 23 (1669[1]) and apparently others. We also find the incorrect numbering in Newberry 1667[2], Newberry 1669[1], HEH 1668[2], and HEH 1669[2]. Likewise, uppercase "Words" occurs in Newberry 1667², Newberry 1669¹, HEH 1668², and HEH 1669². Fletcher does not indicate specific copies. The Newberry copies of the second and fifth issues, and the Huntington copies of the fourth and sixth issues have the incorrect numbering, "Words", and "misery."—all state 1. Of the additional copies examined the Newberry fifth issue and the HEH sixth issue are the only ones in which "0110" is given; Fletcher does not cite any copy but he does say that this error is not connected with the incorrect numbering in 980ff. In the BL first issue, "supply" certainly seems to be the first state; it is repeated in the Newberry first and second, HEH second, HEH and UK fourth, and UK 1669ˣ copies. Fletcher cites it from copy 17, a fifth issue text. We are told that "supplie" appears in "many" copies. The Newberry fifth issue gives all state 1 readings except for "supplie". The Shepherd facsimile has state 2 except for "even", line 47, and the Masson facsimile has state 1 for lines 47, 982, and 1078, and state 2 for other variants. We must consider that there may have been some tampering with these facsimiles.

Conclusion: Only the variants listed as state 1 in lines 47 and 1078 are both found in the BL 1667¹ (as well as the Masson facsimile), all the other variants in that copy being state 2. Milton would have spelled "eevn" and either "supplie" or "supply," suggesting that both state 2 variants should be adopted for the authoritative text of issue 1 printed here, despite the appearance of "even" and "supply" in BL 1667¹.

Book 10 (lines 1–897 became book 11 in 1674)

10.32: pray let me, / pray, let mee
10.76: doom / Doom
10.101: warriours / Warriours
10.139: linkt, / linkt;

From line 880 to the end of the book line numbers are placed one line too high (that is, at 881, 891, and so on). The above four items are the only variants recorded for lines in the section that became book 11. The first state of line 32 appears only in Fletcher's copies 10, 23, and 31, all of which are 1669¹; we find it also in Newberry 1669¹, HEH 1668¹, and 1669². Fletcher connects "doom" with copies that read "supply" in 9.1078, where he cites copy "17," 1669[1], but here he instances copy "11," 1667[2], seemingly (but erroneously?) meaning the same copy. The readings "supply" and "doom" appear in BL 1667[1], Newberry 1667[1] and 1668[2], HEH 1667[2], UK and HEH 1668[2], and UK 1669[x]. HEH 1668[1], UK and HEH 1669[1], UK and HEH 1669[2], and Scolar editions have "supplie" and "Doom." In agreement as to states are "doom" and "warriours" (Fletcher cites copy 11), and "Doom" and "Warriours" in all issues. Similarly, "pray let me," and "linkt," and "pray, let mee" and "linkt;" are in agreement as to states in all issues. Fletcher makes no connection between these last two variants, saying only that the semicolon of "linkt;" appears in "many copies" and the comma "in copy 23 *inter alia*"; copy 23 is issue 5. But as these data show only UK copies of 1669[1] and 1669[2], Newberry copy 1668[2], and Scolar are consistent in having one state (state 2). The Shepherd facsimile agrees with Newberry 1669[1]. The Masson facsimile, on the other hand, has clearly been altered: line 32 has, uniquely: "pray, let mee,"; it also is the only copy examined that shows state 1 for line 76 but state 2 for both line 101 and line 139.

Book 10 (lines 898–1541 became book 12 in 1674)

Line numbers are placed one line too low in all these lines. For example, 1430 is printed alongside 1431, and thus 1425, the correct line number, appears to be 1426 in the original printing, and so on. References here, therefore, are to the correct line number but, *in this case only*, without indication of the original numbering. As noted above, the half sheet, signature Vv, lines 1424–1541, was reset and reprinted for the sixth issue in 1669, creating numerous variants in at least three states. Fletcher cites the first printing and the second printing employing copy 34 as state 1, copy 33 as state 2, and copy 185 as state 3. That is, "state" here now means the altered pages of reset signature Vv, not of the primary text. The lefthand item below is the reading of the first printing (there is one copy showing one previously unreported state) and it occurs in all copies examined, including UK 1669[2] but excepting HEH 1669[2], which has the second printing, state 3. There are no variants recorded for lines 898–1423.

10.1425 [12.533]: farr / far / far/ far
10.1426 [12.534]: Rites / Rights / Rites / Rites
10.1429 [12.537]: goe / go / go/ go
10.1429 [12.537]: on, / on / on / on
10.1434 [12.542]: promiss'd / promis'd / promis'd / promis'd
10.1437 [12.545]: reveald / reveal'd / reveal'd / reveal'd
10.1438 [12.546]: glory / glorie / glorie / glorie
10.1438 [12.546]: Father / Fathe / Father / Father
10.1439 [12.547]: World, / world$_\wedge$ / world, / world,
10.1439 [12.547]: raise$_\wedge$ / raise, / raise$_\wedge$ / raise$_\wedge$
10.1442 [12.550]: righteousness / Righteousness / Righteousness / Righteousness
10.1442 [12.550]: peace / Peace / Peace / Peace
10.1442 [12.550]: love / Love / Love / Love
10.1446 [12.554]: this / thi; / this / this
10.1447 [12.555]: fixt: / fixt; / fixt; / fixt;
10.1451 [12.559]: knowledge / Knowledge / Knowledge / Knowledge
10.1451 [12.559]: containe / contain / contain / contain
10.1454 [12.562]: feare / fear / fear / fear
catchword: His / his / His / His
running head: Book 10. / Book 7. / Book 7. / Book 7.
10.1456 [12.564]: providence / Providence / Providence / Providence
10.1469 [12.577]: ethereal / Ethereal / Ethereal / Ethereal
10.1479 [12.587]: thee, / thee$_\wedge$ / thee$_\wedge$ / thee$_\wedge$
10.1483 [12.591]: mee / me / me / me
10.1491 [12.599]: Chiefly / Cheifly / Cheifly / Cheifly
10.1492 [12.600]: her / ber / ber / ber
10.1493 [12.601]: Seed) / seed) / seed) / seed)
10.1493 [12.601]: Mankind. / Mankind, / Mankind, / Mankind,
10.1495 [12.603]: unanimous$_\wedge$ / unanimous, / unanimous, / unanimous,
10.1497 [12.605]: happie / happy / happy / happy
10.1499 [12.607]: Descended, / Descended$_\wedge$ / Descended$_\wedge$ / Descended^
10.1499 [12.607]: Bowre / Bower / Bower / Bower

10.1507 [12.615]: mee / me / me / me
10.1507 [12.615]: goe / go / go / go
10.1511 [12.619]: banisht / banish't / banish't / banish't
10.1513 [12.621]: mee / me / me / me
10.1514 [12.622]: voutsaft / vouchsaft / vouchsaft / vouchsaft
10.1515 [12.623]: mee / me / me / me
10.1518 [12.626]: Archangel / ArchAngel / ArchAngel / ArchAngel
10.1521 [12.629]: meteorous / Meteorous / Meteorous / Meteorous
10.1522 [12.630]: marish / Marish / Marish / Marish
10.1524 [12.632]: Front / front / front / front
10.1525 [12.633]: brandisht / brandish't / brandish't / brandish't
10.1525 [12.633]: Sword / sword / sword / sword
10.1526 [12.634]: heat, / heat, / heat$_\wedge$ / heat,
10.1537 [12.645]: Som / Some / Some / Some
10.1540 [12.648]: slow, / slow$_\wedge$ / slow$_\wedge$ / slow$_\wedge$
10.1541 [12.649]: thir / their / thir / thir
THE END. /THE END. / THE EN / THE END.

Previously unreported is a second state of the first printing; see X, 1439, in HEH 1668[1], which clearly has "World;". Fletcher suggests that state 1 of the second printing was a proof sheet for the reset Vv signature. The Huntington copy of the sixth issue examined is the same copy as 185 employed by Fletcher, that is, state 3. Another unique reading in the Masson facsimile is line number 1450, which is printed as 1045.

Conclusion: The reset Vv signature indicates the incompetent work of the compositor in 1669, and thus the diplomatic text presented here follows the "original" text of 1667, issue 1.

Textual Errors

Considered here are verbal errors and some textual difficulties—like indentation and punctuation—that appear in issues of the first edition and that are not included as errata or above under "Textual Variants." Not included are spacing problems, upside-down letters, font or type differences, capitalization, italicization, spelling variations, or some line numbers.

1.159: ought
> Manuscript has the correct "aught"; 1674 does not correct.

1.173: The
> Manuscript has "This"; 1674 does not alter.

1.377: the
> A meaningless reading of the manuscript, 1667, and 1674; intended would have been "thir" as Richard Bentley suggested.

catchword, 1.494/495: With
> Should be "Turns"; "With" refers to 1.496.

1.432: those
> Manuscript has "these"; 1674 does not alter.

1.530: fainted
> Uncertain since the manuscript also has "fainted." However, 1674 alters to "fanting", and "fainting" has been construed as the intended adjective modifying "courage."

1.603: courage
> Rather than an error, this may be a deliberate revision from the manuscript's "valour."

1.710: A non
> Manuscript and 1674 have "Anon."

1.737: Herarchie

Manuscript has "hierarchy" and 1674, "Hierarchie."

2.329: What

This should read "Why" ("What sit we then projecting Peace and Warr?"); it is unchanged in 1674 despite two states of this page in the second edition.

2.353: whol

Not corrected in 1674.

2.360: line number given as 366.

2.422: red

Corrected in 1674.

2.536: Pric

Corrected in 1674.

2.720: misplaced alongside 721, both states, all copies.

3.530: line number, 5 0

Error or nonprinting problem.

3.580: Sarry

Corrected to "Starry" in 1674.

3.592: Medal

Should be "Metal," generally spelled "mettal" in Milton's texts, as in 3.595. Unchanged in 1674.

3.594: Which

Corrected to "With" in 1674.

3.600: numbered 610; error continues through book 3 in all copies.

4.627: walks

Uncertain, but 1674 "walk" is more logical within this passage.

4.759 (760) through 1009 (1010): numbers placed one line too high through the end of the book.

5.361: indented

A questionable indentation because this curious line is a continuation of line 360, yet it becomes Adam's speech to Raphael, which would produce indentation.

5.627: defective line

1674 corrects by insertion of "now."

6.115: realtie
>   Should be "fealtie" as John Shawcross argues.

6.352: Limb
>   Should be "limn" as Shawcross argues.

6.405: period omitted
>   1674 corrects.

7.27: rouud
>   Should be "round".

7.39: Heav'n lie
>   Should be "Heav'nlie".

7.321: smelling
>   Should be "swelling" as Richard Bentley argued.

7.366: his
>   The reference to the "Morning Planet" is to Venus, not to Lucifer, as Fletcher construes it; thus, the change to "her" in 1674 is correct.

7.451: Fowle
>   Should be "Soul" as Bentley argued; 1674 gives "Foul."

7.494: Needlest
>   Should be "Needless"; not corrected in 1674.

7.494: repeaed
>   Should be "repeated".

7.524 forn d
>   Fletcher's note seems to be incorrect; "n" does not seem to be a broken "m". Corrected to "formd" in 1674.

7.588: Father (for
>   Should be "Father, for".

7.906 (8.269): as
>   Apparently should be "and".

[7.1035 (8.398): Is there an error here? Not indented, although 1674 indents.]

8.186 [9.186]: Not
>   1674 changes to "Nor", which seems better; the 1667 compositor perhaps simply repeated the first word of line 185.

8.632 [9.632]: make
>   1674 changes to the preterite "made," which is correct.

8.1183 [9.1183]: Women
> The use of "her," "she," "her self," and "Shee" in the same sentence in the next three lines calls for an emendation to "Woman." Not changed in 1674.

9.230: line number given as "2g0".

9.240: line number missing.

9.241 [10.241]: Avenger
> Should be "Avengers" to agree with "their," line 242. Corrected in 1674.

9.250, 260, 270: line numbers misplaced.

9.827 (10.827): defective line
> 1674 adds "then" ("With me? how can they then acquitted stand").

9.989–90 [10.989–90]: "So Death"
> misplaced on line 990; not corrected in 1674.

10.866 [11.870]: that
> This pronoun is not really correct; 1674 changes it to "who."

10.880ff.: line numbers placed one line too high to the end of the book (that is, 881, 891, and so on).

10.1083 [12.91]: This
> 1674 changes to "The"; the River-dragon (Pharaoh) has been introduced before as "the lawless Tyrant," making this a toss-up, not necessarily an error.

10.1131 (1130) [12.238]: them thir desire
> In 1674 this is altered to "what they besaught." Fletcher (3.443) makes the incomprehensible statement, "For meter, 1667 is one syllable deficient, and the 1674 form of the line must be preferred." The line in 1667 is *not* deficient: "And terror cease; he grants them thir desire"; 1674 is "And terror cease; he grants what they besaught." This is not an "error" in 1667, but the reason for the revision is not evidential.

Added Preliminary
Material, 1668–69

Added to the 1668^2 issue and later issues were a statement from the printer, arguments for the ten books, "The Verse," and "Errata." A revision in the printer's statement also exists for some copies of the 1668^2 issue (the fourth) and a second reset printing of the two signatures occurred with the 1669^2 issue (the sixth). See later for variants. Line numbers are added for the arguments and the verse. Hyphenations and the running head ("The Argument.") are not reproduced.

The Printer to the Reader.

COurteous Reader, There was no Argument at first
intended to the Book, but for the satisfaction of many
that have desired it, is procured.   *S. Simmons.*

The Printer to the Reader.

COurteous Reader, There was no Argument at first
intended to the Book, but for the satisfaction of many
that have desired it, I have procured it, and withall a reason
of that which stumbled many others, why the Poem Rimes
not.

S. Simmons.

THE
ARGUMENT:
Of the
FIRST BOOK.

THe first Book proposes first in brief the whole Subject, *Mans disobedience, and the loss thereupon of Paradise wherein he was plac't:* Then touches *the prime cause of his fall, the Serpent, or rather* Satan *in the Serpent; who revolting from God, and drawing to his side many Legions of Angels, was by the command of God driven out of Heaven with all his Crew into the great Deep.* Which action past over, the Poem hasts into the midst of things, presenting *Satan with his Angels now fallen into Hell,* describ'd here, *not in the Center* (for Heaven and Earth may be suppos'd as yet not made, certainly not yet accurst) *but in a place of utter darknesse, fitliest call'd* Chaos: *Here* Satan *with his Angels lying on the burning Lake, thunderstruck and astonisht, after a certain space recovers, as from confusion, calls up him who next in Order and Dignity lay by him; they confer of thir miserable fall.* Satan *awakens all his Legions, who lay till then in the same manner confounded; They rise, thir Numbers, array of Battel, thir chief Leaders nam'd, according to the Idols known afterwards in* Canaan *and the Countries adjoyning. To these* Satan *directs his Speech, comforts them with hope yet of regaining Heaven, but tells them lastly of a new World and new kind of Creature to be created, according to an*

5

10

15

20

ancient Prophesie or report in Heaven; for that Angels were long
before this visible Creation, was the opinion of many ancient Fathers.
To find out the truth of this Prophesie, and what to determin thereon
he refers to a full Councell. What his Associates thence
attempt. Pandemonium *the Palace of* Satan *rises, suddenly built*   25
out of the Deep: The infernal Peers there sit in Counsel.

Of the
SECOND BOOK.

THe Consultation begun, Satan *debates whether another*
Battel be to be hazarded for the recovery of Heaven: some advise it,
others dissuade: A third proposal is prefer'd, mention'd before by
Satan, *to search the truth of that Prophesie or Tradition in Heaven*
concerning another world and another kind of creature equall or not much   5
inferiour to themselves about this time to be created: Thir
doubt who shall be sent on this difficult search: Satan *thir chief*
undertakes alone the voyage, is honourd and applauded. The Councel
thus ended, the rest betake them several wayes & to several
imployments, as thir inclinations lead them, to entertain the time   10
till Satan *return. He passes on his Journey to Hell Gates, finds them*
shut, and who sat there to guard them, by whom at length they are
op'nd, and discover to him the great Gulf between Hell and Heaven;
with what difficulty he passes through, directed by Chaos, *the Power*
of that place, to the sight of this new World which he sought.   15

Of the
THIRD BOOK[.]

God *sitting on his Throne sees* Satan *flying towards this world, then*
newly created; shews him to the Son who sat at his right hand; foretells
the success of Satan *in perverting mankind; clears his own Justice and*
VVisdom from all imputation, having created Man free and able enough
to have withstood his Tempter; yet declares his purpose of grace   5
towards him, in regard he fell not of his own malice, as did Satan, *but*
by him seduc't. The Son of God renders praises to his Father for the
manifestation of his gracious purpose towards Man; but God again
declares, that Grace cannot be extended towards Man without the
satisfaction of divine Justice; Man hath offended the majesty of God by   10
aspiring to Godhead, and therefore with all his Progeny devoted to
death must dye, unless some one can be found sufficient to answer
for his offence, and undergoe his Punishment. The Son of God freely
offers himself a Ransome for Man: the Father accepts him, ordains his
incarnation, pronounces his exaltation above all Names in Heaven and   15
Earth; commands all the Angels to adore him; they obey: and hymning
to thir Harps in full Quire, celebrate the Father and the Son. Mean while
Satan *alights upon the bare convex of this VVorlds outermost Orb; where*
wandring he first finds a place since call'd The Lymbo of Vanity; what
persons and things fly up thither; thence comes to the Gate of Heaven,   20

describ'd ascending by stairs, and the waters above the Firmament that
flow about it: His passage thence to the Orb of the Sun; he finds there
Uriel *the Regent of that Orb, but first changes himself into the shape*
of a meaner Angel [;] *and pretending a zealous desire to behold the*
new Creation and Man whom God had plac't here, inquires of him the place   25
of his habitation, and is directed; alights first on Mount Niphates.

Of the
FOURTH BOOK.

SAtan *now in prospect of* Eden, *and nigh the place where he must*
now attempt the bold enterprize which he undertook alone against
God and Man, falls into many doubts with himself, and many passions,
fear, envy, and despare; but at length confirms himself in evil, journeys
on to Paradise, whose outward prospect and scituation is described, over-   5
leaps the bounds, sits in the shape of a Cormorant on the Tree
of life, as highest in the Garden to look about him. The Garden
describ'd; Satans *first sight of* Adam *and* Eve; *his wonder at thir*
excellent form and happy state, but with resolution to work thir
fall; overhears thir discourse, thence gathers that the Tree of   10
knowledge was forbidden them to eat of, under penalty of death; and
thereon intends to found his temptation, by seducing them to
transgress: then leaves them a while, to know further of thir state by
some other means. Mean while Uriel *descending on a Sun-beam warns*
Gabriel, *who had in charge the Gate of Paradise, that some evil spirit had*   15
escap'd the Deep, and past at Noon by his Sphere in the shape of a
good Angel down to Paradise, discovered after by his furious gestures
in the Mount. Gabriel *promises to find him out ere morning. Night coming*
on, Adam *and* Eve *discourse of going to thir rest: thir Bower describ'd;*
thir Evening worship. Gabriel *drawing forth his Bands of Night-watch to*   20

walk the round of Paradise, appoints two strong Angels to Adams
Bower, *least the evill spirit should be there doing some harm to* Adam
or Eve *sleeping; there they find him at the ear of* Eve, *tempting her in
a dream, and bring him, though unwilling, to* Gabriel; *by whom question'd,
he scornfully answers, prepares resistance, but hinder'd by a Sign*   25
from Heaven, flies out of Paradise.

Of the
FIFTH BOOK.

MOrning approach't, Eve *relates to* Adam *her troublesome dream; he*
likes it not, yet comforts her: They come forth to thir day labours: Thir
Morning Hymn at the Door of thir Bower. God *to render Man inexcusable*
sends Raphael *to admonish him of his obedience, of his free estate, of*
his enemy near at hand; who he is, and why his enemy, and whatever else   5
may avail Adam *to know.* Raphael *comes down to Paradise, his appear-*
ance describ'd, his coming discern'd by Adam *afar off sitting*
at the door of his Bower; he goes out to meet him, brings him to his
lodge, entertains him with the choycest fruits of Paradise got together
by Eve; *thir discourse at Table:* Raphael *performs his message, minds*   10
Adam *of his state and of his enemy; relates at* Adams *request who that*
enemy is, and how he came to be so, beginning from his first revolt in Heaven,
and the occasion thereof; how he drew his Legions after him to
the parts of the North, and there incited them to rebel with him,
perswading all but only Abdiel *a Seraph, who in Argument dissuades and*   15
opposes him, then forsakes him.

Of the
SIXTH BOOK.

RAphael *continues to relate how* Michael *and* Gabriel *were sent forth to Battel against* Satan *and his Angels. The first Fight describ'd:* Satan *and his Powers retire under Night: He calls a Councel, invents devilish Engines, which in the second dayes Fight put* Michael *and his Angels to some disorder; but they at length pulling up Mountains overwhelm'd both the force and Machins of* Satan: *Yet the Tumult not so ending, God on the third day sends* Messiah *his Son, for whom he had reserv'd the glory of that Victory: Hee in the Power of his Father coming to the place, and causing all his Legions to stand still on either side, with his Chariot and Thunder driving into the midst of his Enemies, pursues them unable to resist towards the wall of Heaven; which opening, they leap down with horrour and confusion into the place of punishment prepar'd for them in the Deep:* Messiah *returns with triumph to his Father.*

5

10

Of the
SEAVENTH BOOK.

RAphael *at the request of* Adam *relates how and wherefore this*
World was first created; that God, after the expelling of Satan
and his Angels out of Heaven, declar'd his pleasure to create another
World and other Creatures to dwell therein; sends his Son with Glory
and attendance of Angels to perform the work of Creation in six   5
dayes: the Angels celebrate with Hymns the performance thereof,
and his reascention into Heaven. Adam *then inquires concerning*
celestial Motions, is doubtfully answer'd, and exhorted to search
rather things more worthy of knowledg: Adam *assents, and still*
desirous to detain Raphael, *relates to him what he remember'd*   10
since his own Creation, his placing in Paradise, his talk with God
concerning solitude and fit society, his first meeting and Nuptials
with Eve, *his discourse with the Angel thereupon; who after*
admonitions repeated departs.

Of the
EIGHTH BOOK.

SAtan *having compast the Earth, with meditated guile returns as a*
mist by Night into Paradise, enters into the Serpent sleeping. Adam
and Eve *in the Morning go forth to thir labours, which* Eve *proposes to*
divide in several places, each labouring apart: Adam *consents not,*
alledging the danger, lest that Enemy, of whom they were forewarn'd,   5
should attempt her found alone: Eve *loath to be thought not circumspect*
or firm enough, urges her going apart, the rather desirous to make tryal
of her strength; Adam *at last yields: The Serpent finds her alone; his*
subtle approach, first gazing, then speaking, with much flattery
extolling Eve *above all other Creatures.* Eve *wondring to hear the*   10
Serpent speak, asks how he attain'd to human speech and such
understanding not till now; the Serpent answers, that by tasting of a
certain Tree in the Garden he attain'd both to Speech and Reason, till
then void of both: Eve *requires him to bring her to that Tree, and finds*
it to be the Tree of Knowledge forbidden: The Serpent now grown bolder,   15
with many wiles and arguments induces her at length to eat; she pleas'd with
the taste deliberates a while whether to impart thereof to
Adam *or not, at last brings him of the Fruit, relates what perswaded her*
to eat thereof: Adam *at first amaz'd, but perceiving her lost, resolves*

through vehemence of love to perish with her; and extenuating the   20
trespass, eats also of the Fruit: The Effects thereof in them both;
they seek to cover thir nakedness; then fall to variance and accusation
of one another.

Of the
NINTH BOOK.

MAns transgression known, the Guardian Angels forsake Paradise, and
return up to Heaven to approve thir vigilance, and are approv'd, God
declaring that the entrance of Satan could not be by them prevented.
He sends his Son to judge the Transgressors, who descends and
gives Sentence accordingly; then in pity cloaths them both, and
reascends. Sin and Death sitting till then at the Gates of Hell, by
wondrous sympathie feeling the success of Satan in this new World,
and the sin by Man there committed, resolve to sit no longer confin'd
in Hell, but to follow Satan thir Sire up to the place of Man: To make
the way easier from Hell to this World to and fro, they pave a broad
Highway or Bridge over Chaos, according to the Track that Satan first
made; then preparing for Earth, they meet him proud of his
success returning to Hell; thir mutual gratulation. Satan arrives
at Pandemonium, in full assembly relates with boasting his success
against Man; instead of applause is entertained with a general hiss by all
his audience, transform'd with himself also suddenly into
Serpents, according to his doom giv'n in Paradise; then deluded with a
shew of the forbidden Tree springing up before them, they greedily
reaching to taste of the Fruit, chew dust and bitter ashes. The
proceedings of Sin and Death; God foretels the final Victory of his

Son over them, and the renewing of all things; but for the present
commands his Angels to make several alterations in the Heavens
and Elements. Adam *more and more perceiving his fall'n condition*
heavily bewailes, rejects the condolement of Eve; *she persists and at*
length appeases him: Then to evade the Curse likely to fall on thir   25
Ofspring, proposes to Adam *violent wayes which he approves not,*
but conceiving better hope, puts her in mind of the late Promise made
them, that her Seed should be reveng'd on the Serpent, and exhorts
her with him to seek Peace of the offended Deity, by repentance and   30
supplication.

Of the
TENTH BOOK[.]

THe Son of God presents to his Father the Prayers of our first
Parents now repenting, and intercedes for them: God accepts
them, but declares that they must no longer abide in Paradise;
sends Michael with a Band of Cherubim to dispossess them; but first
to reveal to Adam future things: Michaels coming down. Adam shews to
Eve certain ominous signs; he discerns Michaels approach, goes
out to meet him: the Angel denounces thir departure. Eve's Lamentation.
Adam pleads, but submits: The Angel leads him up to a high Hill, sets
before him in vision what shall happ'n till the Flood; thence from the
Flood relates, and by degrees explains, who that Seed of the Woman shall
be; his Incarnation, Death[,] Resurrection, and Ascension; the state
of the Church till his second Coming. Adam greatly satisfied and
recomforted by these Relations and Promises descends the Hill with
Michael; wakens Eve, who all this while had slept, but with gentle
dreams compos'd to quietness of mind and submission. Michael in
either hand leads them out of Paradise, the fiery Sword waving behind
them, and the Cherubim taking thir Stations to guard the Place.

Emendations to the Arguments

Corrections made in second printing of Arguments in 1669[2]:
3. head: period added
3.24: ? > ;
10. head: period added
10.11: comma added

THE VERSE

THe Measure is *English* Heroic Verse without Rime, as that of
Homer in *Greek,* and of *Virgil* in *Latin;* Rime being no necessary
Adjunct or true Ornament of Poem or good Verse, in longer Works
especially, but the Invention of a barbarous Age, to set off wretched
matter and lame Meeter; grac't indeed since by the use of some   5
famous modern Poets, carried away by Custom, but much to thir
own vexation, hindrance, and constraint to express many things
otherwise, and for the most part worse then else they would have
exprest them. Not without cause therefore some both *Italian* and
Spanish Poets of prime note have rejected Rime both in longer and   10
shorter Works, as have also long since our best *English* Tragedies,
as a thing of it self, to all judicious eares, triveal and of no true
musical delight; which consists only in apt Numbers, fit quantity of
Syllables, and the sense variously drawn out from one Verse into
another, not in the jingling sound of like endings, a fault avoyded by the   15
learned Ancients both in Poetry and all good Oratory. This neglect
then of Rime so little is to be taken for a defect, though it may seem
so perhaps to vulgar Readers, that it rather is to be esteem'd an
example set, the first in *English,* of ancient liberty recover'd to
Heroic Poem from the troublesom and modern bondage of Rimeing.   20

ERRATA

LIb. 1. Vers. 25. for *th' Eternal,* Read *Eternal.*
Lib. 1. V. 409. for *Heronaim,* r. *Horonaim.*
Lib. 1. V. 758. for *and Band* r. *Band and.*
Lib. 1. V. 760. for *hundreds* r. *hunderds.*
Lib. 2. V. 414. for *we* r. *wee.*
Lib. 2. V. 881. for *great* r. *grate.*
Lib. 3. V. 760. for *with* r. *in.*
Lib. 5. V. 193. for *breath* r. *breathe.*
Lib. 5. V. 598. for *whoseop* r. *whose top.*
Lib. 5. V. 656. for *more Heaven* r. *more in Heaven.*
Lib. 6. V. 184. for *blessed* r. *blest.*
Lib. 6. V. 215. for *sounder* r. *so under.*
Lib. 10. V. 575. for *lost* r. *last.*

Other literal faults the Reader of himself may Correct.

Discussion of Added Preliminary Material

"Printer to the Reader"

The difference between the two versions (four-line or six-line) is that "is procured." (found in issues 4, 5) was replaced by "I have procur'd it, and withall a reason of that which stumbled many others, why the Poem Rimes not." (also found in copies of issues 4, 5). Reference, of course, is to the statement on "The Verse." The catchword "THE" on a3r (half of the argument for book 10 appears above this) shows that "The Verse" existed and was printed when the four-line version of the printer's statement was written and printed, not created as an afterthought. The four-line version is recorded by Fletcher in six copies of 1668[2] and nine copies of 1669[1]. His statement (2.177) accounts for this otherwise strange continuance of the earlier, incomplete version in issue 5: "The 1669[1] title page is frequently found tipped on to the stub left by cutting off the 1668[2] title page"; that is, the nine copies noted would seem to be 1668[2] copies (issue 4) with a replaced title page (issue 5). The six-line version is recorded by Fletcher in 28 copies of 1668[2] and 45 copies of 1669[1]. All copies of 1669[2] omit the printer's statement. UK copies of issues 4 and 5 both have the six-line version; UK issue 6 omits it. The Huntington Library copy of issue 4 has the six-line version, issue 5 the four-line version, and issue 6 omits it.

Fletcher's information concerning copies used for collation (2.3–5) is confusing and incomplete. Numbering is not chronological, and various numbers for copies are not used (55–60, 73–75, 87–90, 100–105, 128–30, 165–80). According to his statement on 2.3, the numerical gaps exist to correspond roughly "to about the number of remaining copies that might be found still in existence."

Nonetheless, he does cite copy 176 in textual notes but there is no identification of such a copy. While he correctly reports that copy no. 1, 1667^1, has "No preliminary leaves," he also says that copies no. 2, 1667^2, and no. 3, 1668^1 lack the "Printer to the Reader" (his meaning of "Arg.3," which he attaches to these copies and which in itself is confusing since he uses that abbreviation only for the printer's remark and does not use it with the Arguments). Of course, 1667^1, 1667^2, and 1668^1 do not include the preliminary leaves (including "The Printer to the Reader"), but Fletcher's notation for copies no. 2 and no. 3 implies that, although they omit the statement, they include the rest of the preliminary leaves. If indeed the copies reported do include the remaining preliminary leaves—and similar notations on other copies of various issues also have confusing and imply possibly inaccurate information—those leaves must have been inserted, using the second printing of the preliminary leaves reset for 1669^2 (since the printer's remark is omitted), sometime after 1669. No preliminary leaves should have been included in the second and third issues. Similarly, a copy with the third title page of 1668^1 owned by UK (1669x) is apparently the 1669^1 issue of text with leaves from 1668^2 and 1669^2, and includes the second printing of this introductory material.

According to Fletcher's listings some copies of earlier issues have the preliminary sheets bound in. See nos. 79, 81, 86, all given as 1667^2, which are cited as having the six-line "Printer to the Reader," in turn implying that they evidence all the preliminary leaves. Likewise his information records that nos. 53, 94, 98, all given as 1668^1 or 1668^{1A}, have the six-line statement (and implying also the remainder of the preliminary leaves). No. 49, a copy of 1668^2, has no preliminary leaves (various reasons for this may appertain); and no. 140, a copy of 1669^1, has no preliminary leaves but evidences the reset Vv signature of 1669^2, suggesting that the title page for an alleged copy of issue 5 was used in a copy of issue 6. These anomalous copies may owe their existence to much later booksellers who created them to complete a copy or to create a marketable book.

Fletcher does not record a variant in the First Argument between its appearance in the four-line version and the six-line version, although his facsimile clearly shows the difference. In line 11 the four-line version reproduced (unidentified as to copy) has "Chaos:" while the six-line version has "Chaos." (also unidentified as to copy). (The second printing of the preliminary material gives "Chaos:" as well.) Other copies of the six-line version that we have checked print the colon.

The Arguments

The resetting and second printing of these preliminary materials in 1669² resulted in the following alterations (aside from spacings, linage, and nonsignificant type or font changes). These alterations provide repeated proof that the compositor of the second printing of the preliminary leaves was different from the first and was reflecting his own mechanics and his own inaccurate understanding of the text. Nothing in the variants of the second printing suggests that they be adopted except for correction of the first compositor's errors, such as omission of periods after "Argument" and "Book" (but see the note on "entertain'd" in book 9 below). As in standard bibliographic reportage, ∧ indicates a lack of punctuation, and thus emphasizes the point of difference for that variant. When punctuation is not involved in creating a difference, it is omitted from collation. The Scolar facsimile and the UK and HEH 1668² and 1669¹ copies give the first printing; UK and HEH copies of 1669², the second printing. (See also under "Printer to the Reader" above the comment on "Chaos" in line 11 of the first argument.)

Book 1

heading ARGUMENT: / ARGUMENT. [period in middle of type]

1.6: *Deep* / *deep*
1.8: describ'd / described
1.11: *dark-* | *nesse* / *dark* | *ness* [the hyphen does not always print]
1.16: *chief* / *cheif*
1.18: *adjoyning. To* / *adjoyning, to*
1.18: *Speech* / *speech*

1.19: *hope / hopes*
1.20: *World*∧ */ World,*
1.21: [first] *Prophesie*∧ */ Prophesie,*
1.23: *determin / determine*
1.24: *Councell / Councel*
1.25: *Palace / Pallace*
1.26: *Counsel / Councel*

As will be observed, the changes in the second printing are frequently wrong (such as "hopes") and at times alter Miltonic spelling
(which would be "determin").

Book 2

2.2: *Battel / Battle*
2.2: *hazarded / hazzarded*
2.7: *shall / should*
2.8: *honourd / honoured*
2.9: *wayes / ways*
2.11: *Journey / journey*
2.13: *op'nd / open'd*
2.13: *Gulf / gulf*

Fletcher reports that *"and discover"* (line 13) is *"vnd discover"* in
copies 13, 29, 33, 130, all of which are the issue of 1669^2. This
implies that all other 1669^2 copies examined have *"and discover"*
correctly. Of further copies examined, UK and HEH copies of 1669^2
(and UK 1669^x) have *"vnd discover."*

Book 3

running head BOOK∧ / BOOK.
3.1: *world / World*
3.2: *his right / the right*
3.2: *hand; foretells / hand, foretells*
3.3: *mankind / Mankind*
3.3: [first] *Justice / justice*
3.4: *VVis- | dom / wis- | dom*

3.4: *imputation, | imputation*∧
3.7: *seduc't | seduc'd*
3.11: *Godhead, | Godhead;*
3.12: *death*∧ *| death,*
3.13: *undergoe | undergo*
3.19: *The Lymbo | the Lymbo*
3.24: *Angel! | Angel;*
3.25: *Creation*∧ *| Creation,*
3.25: *here | there*

Alterations such as "his" to "the" and "here" to "there" suggest that the compositor of the second printing was reading the text and changing it to fit his (inaccurate) reading.

Book 4

4.4: *despare; | despare,*
running head: Argument, / Argument.
4.9: *to work | te work*
4.11: *forbidden | forbiddcn*
4.22: *evill | evil*

The Argument for book 4 is on two pages; thus, the heading, not reproduced here, lies in the midst of its printing.

Book 5

5.7: *appearance | appearing*
5.11: *enemy; | enemy,*
5.13: *thereof; | thereof*∧

The first alteration is particularly interesting in evidencing the compositor's misreading.

Book 6

6.2: *Fight | fight*
6.3: *Pow-* | *ers | pow-* | *ers*
6.3: *Councel, | Councel*∧

6.4: *Fight* / *fight*
6.8: *Hee* / *He*
6.11: *Enemies* / *enemies*

Book 7

7.2: *World* / *world*
7.8: *search* / *seek*
7.12: *solitude* / *sollitude*

Book 8

running head: Argument∧ / Argument.
8.5: *Enemy* / *enemy*
8.11: *human* / *humane*

Book 9

running head: Argument∧ / Argument.
9.4: *Son* / *Angels*
9.4: *descends*∧ / *descends,*
9.7: *sympa-* | *thie* / *sympa-* | *thy*
9.8: *Man* / *man*
9.9: *To make* / *to make*
9.10: *way* / *Way*
9.11: *Track* / *Tract*
9.15: *entertained* / *entertain'd*
9.20: *foretels* / *foretells*
9.23: *condition*∧ / *condition,*
9.24: *rejects* / *rejccts*
9.26: *wayes*∧ / *wayes,*

The inaccurate change from "Son" to "Angels" (as well as "Track" to "Tract") iterates the unacceptability of the second printing of the preliminary leaves. However, the Miltonic spelling of "entertain'd" (or it might have been "entertaind") is noteworthy.

Book 10

running head BOOK∧ / BOOK.
10.1: *Prayers* / *prayers*
10.3: *but* / *and*
10.4: *Cherubim* / *Cherubims*
10.6: *signs;* / *signs,*
10.9: *happ'n* / *happen*
10.10: [second] *Flood* / *flood*
10.10: *degrees* / *degrecs*
10.11: *Death*∧ / *Death,*
10.11: *Ascen-* | *tion;* / *A-* | *scention,*
10.13: *Relati-* | *ons* / *relati-* | *ons*

The subtle alteration of God's feelings with the change in line 3 from "but" to "and" should be noted.

The Verse

Comment is given on each difference recorded in the second printing, with "error" signifying an inaccuracy by the compositor of 1669[2]. As noted above, copies of the fourth and fifth issues examined have state 1 of "The Verse," and only the sixth issue of 1669 has state 2.

2: and of *Virgil* / and *Virgil*
 "of" is not necessary but offers better grammar; the deletion was perhaps made to remove the hyphenation of "*La-* | *tin*".
5: Meeter / Meetet
 error
 running head, a4r: *The Verse.* / The Argument.
 error
12: triveal / trivial
 spelling correction
15: avoyd- | ed / avoided
 change of a Miltonic spelling
19: *English,* / *English*∧
 variant found only in copy 34 [1669[2]]

19: liberty∧ / liberty,
  error
20: troublesom / troublesome
  change of a Miltonic spelling
20: Rimeing / Riming
  spelling correction

In all, the reset second printing of "The Verse" in 1669 represents the compositor's work and mechanics. Although two changes make "corrections," two specifically alter Miltonic spelling to standard form.

Errata

The three changes in the reset second printing are all incorrect: *"Honoraim."* (for *"Horonaim."*), *"bundreds"* (for *"hundreds"*), "Lib. 2." for "Lib. 6." The 13 errata themselves do not include all the many and obvious corrections needed for this very long text, although the sentence "Other literal faults the Reader of himself may Correct" was apparently intended to cover that. Attention to each erratum is instructive. Only one correction (see 3.741) was made in second and third states of the last page of book 3; the erratum is corrected in issues 4, 5, and 6, and is made in states 2 and 3 of the page, but the line reference (which is still inaccurate) is altered only in state 3 of the page. The UK and the HEH copies of 1669[2] both have state 3 of the page. Fletcher's statistics do not indicate the copies (issues) in which these states of this page occur. All but one erratum are made in 1674.

1.25: *th' Eternal > Eternal*
  "th'" appears in the manuscript and was (later?) deleted.
1.409: *Heronaim > Horonaim*
  corrected in agreement with the manuscript.
1.758: *and Band > Band and*
  corrected in agreement with the manuscript except that "band" is lowercase; the capital would thus seem not to be Miltonic but a change by the compositor who also capitalized "Regiment" in the same line.

1.760: *hundreds > hunderds*
> change from the manuscript spelling to Milton's spelling of this word.

2.414: *we > wee*
> either spelling could have been Milton's; this change was not made in 1674.

2.881: *great > grate*
> the verb is correct, otherwise "Harsh Thunder" is nonsyntactic.

3.741 (760): *with > in*
> correction made in states 2 and 3 of the page.

5.193: *breath > breathe*
> correction.

5.598: *whoseop > whose top*
> correction.

5.656: *more Heaven > more in Heaven*
> correction; however, the word is correctly spelled "Heav'n" in the text since it is one syllable. The compositor has erred in recording the erratum.

6.184: *blessed > blest* correction to Miltonic spelling and to one syllable as needed.

6.215: *sounder > so under*
> correction.

10.575 [16.579]: *lost > last*
> apparently a correction in meaning which 1674 also follows.

It would seem that the corrector (proofreader) recognized incidental errors in the text of 1667, the first issue; note the alteration in 3.741 (760), which indicates early recognition of at least this one error. (It is, of course, noted in the Errata as 3.760.) It is difficult to assign these 13 errata to someone other than the compositor doing spot checks rather than to an agent for Milton examining the full text. The proofing would seem to have been based on some reference to the manuscript (note the errata for book 1), but other items correct the compositor's errors (for example in 5.598). The erratum for 2.414 suggests that "we" was the compositor's spelling and "wee" the form in the manuscript. That spelling in the manuscript could represent Milton's spelling or the amanuensis'. The lack of alteration in 1674 suggests that whoever oversaw the revision of its text (and much attention is paid to spelling, implying an informed agent for Milton) knew that Milton usually simplified his spelling of this pronoun in later years to "we," or the compositor of 1674 ignored the erratum or set his own spelling.

Further Changes in the Second Edition, 1674

Aside from revision of books 7 and 10 into two books each and the addition of 15 lines, correction of errata, alteration of spelling, capitalization, and so on throughout the text, the second edition makes some verbal changes, almost all of which are clearly errors. See the following as well as "Textual Errors" in the 1667 text beginning on page 417, which 1674 has corrected. Unless otherwise noted, the citation to the left is from 1667, that to the right from 1674.

1.703: found *MS, 1667* / found out *1674* [a crux]
2.282: where / were [a crux]
2.483: thir / her [error]
2.527: his / this [error]
Argument, book 4: find him out *1668, 1669* / find him *1674* [error?]
4.705: shadier / shadie [error?]
4.928: The / Thy [error]
7.906 [8.269]: as / and [error?]
7.1035 [8.398]: [indented] / [not indented] [is this an error?]
8.213 [9.213]: hear / bear [error]
8.394 [9.394]: Likest / Likeliest [error]
8.922 [9.922]: hast / hath [correction?]
8.1019 [9.1019]: we / me [error]
8.1092 [9.1092]: for / from [error]
8.1093 [9.1093]: from / for [error]
Argument, book 10: meet / met [error in Fletcher's copies 17 and 32]
Argument, book 10: full assembly / full of assembly [error in Fletcher's copies 17 and 32]

Argument, book 10: taste /take [error]
9.58 [10.58]: may / might [error?]
9.397 [10.397]: those / these [error]
9.408 [10.408]: prevaile / prevailes [error]
9.550 [10.550]: fair / [omitted] [error]
10.380 [11.380]: to amplest / to the amplest [error]
10.427 [11.427]: [second] sin / [omitted] [error]
10.647 [11.651]: tacks / makes [a crux]
10.1426 [12.534]: will / well [error]

BIBLIOGRAPHY

Amory, Hugh. "Things Unattempted Yet: A Bibliography of the First Edition of *Paradise Lost.*" *Book Collector* 32 (1983): 41–66.

Anderson, Paul B. "Anonymous Critic of Milton: Richard Leigh? or Samuel Butler?" *Studies in Philology* 44 (1947): 504–18.

Anonymous. *Dr. Bentley's Corrections and Emendations on the Twelve Books of Milton's Paradise Lost.* London: J. and J. Knapton et al., 1732.

———. *Idea of the Perfection of Painting. Translated by J. E., An.* N.p., 1668.

Athenæum, The. No. 2579 (March 31, 1877): 416. "Our Library Table," review.

Beale, John. See von Maltzahn, Nicholas (1992).

Bentley, Richard, editor. *Milton's Paradise Lost. A New Edition.* London: Jacob Tonson, 1732.

Browne, R. C. *English Poems by John Milton. Edited with Life, Introduction, and Selected Notes.* Oxford: Clarendon Press, 1866. 2 vols. Revised by Henry Bradley in 1894.

———. Review. *The Academy* 12 (July 28, 1877): 82–83.

Coleridge, K. A. *A Descriptive Catalogue of the Milton Collection in the Alexander Turnbull Library, Wellington, New Zealand.* Oxford: Oxford University Press, 1980. See Items 90–91, pp. 122–29.

Creaser, John. "Editorial Problems in Milton: Part I." *Review of English Studies* 34 (1983): 279–303.

———. "Editorial Problems in Milton: Part II." *Review of English Studies* 35 (1984): 45–60.

Crump, Galbraith Miller. *The Mystical Design of "Paradise Lost."* Lewisburg, Pa.: Bucknell University Press, 1975.

Darbishire, Helen, ed. *The Manuscript of Milton's "Paradise Lost," Book I.* Oxford: Clarendon Press, 1931.

Dobranski, Stephen B. "Simmons' Shell Games: The Six Title Pages of *Paradise Lost.*" In *"Paradise Lost: A Poem Written in Ten Books": Essays on the 1667 First Edition,* ed. Michael Lieb and John T. Shawcross Pittsburgh: Duquesne University Press, 2007.

Evelyn, John. See von Maltzahn, Nicholas (1992).

Fletcher, Harris Francis. *John Milton's Complete Poetical Works Reproduced in Photographic Facsimile.* Urbana: University of Illinois Press. Vol. 2 (1945): The First Edition of *Paradise Lost,* with the Manuscript of Book I. Vol. 3 (1948): The Second Edition of *Paradise Lost.*

Haak, Theodore, trans. "Das Verlustigte Pardeiss," books 1–3 and beginning of 4. Uncertain date. See Pamela R. Barnett, *Theodore Haak, F. R. S. (1605–1690).* 'S-Gravenhage: Mouton and Co., 1962.

Hale, John K. "*Paradise Lost:* A Poem in Twelve Books, or Ten?" *Philological Quarterly* 74 (1995): 131–49.

———. "The 1668 Argument to *Paradise Lost.*" *Milton Quarterly* 35 (2001): 87–97.

Hobart, Sir John. See Rosenheim, James M. (1978).

Hog, William, trans. *Paraphrasis Poetica in Tria Johannis Miltoni, Viri Clarissimi, Poemata, Viz. Paradisum Amissum, Paradisum Recuperatum, et Samsonem Agonisten.* Londini: Johannis Darby, 1690. Reissued in Rotterdam by Eliam Yvans, 1699. Ten-book version.

Hunter, William B. "The Center of *Paradise Lost.*" *English Language Notes* 7 (1969): 32–34.

Johnson, Samuel. "Life of Milton." *Prefaces, Biographical and Critical to the Works of the English Poets* (1779). Shawcross, John T. ed. *Milton 1732–1801: The Critical Heritage.* London: Routledge & Kegan Paul, 1972.

Leigh, Richard (?), Samuel Parker (?), Samuel Butler (?). *The Transproser Rehears'd: Of the Fifth Act of Mr. Bayes's Play.* Oxford: Printed for Thomas Sawbridge, 1673.

Lieb, Michael. "Encoding the Occult: Milton and the Traditions of *Merkabah* Speculation in the Renaissance." *Milton Studies* 37 (1999): 42–88.

———. "S. B.'s '*In Paradisum Amissam*': Sublime Commentary." *Milton Quarterly* 19 (1985): 71–78.

Lindenbaum, Peter. "Authors and Publishers in Late Seventeenth Century: New Evidence on Their Relations." *The Library* 17 (1995): 250–69.

———. "The Poet in the Marketplace: Milton and Samuel Simmons." In *Of Poetry and Politics: New Essays on Milton and His World,* ed. P. G. Stanwood, 249–62. Binghamton, N.Y.: Medieval and Renaissance Texts and Studies, 1995.

Lowndes, William Thomas. *The Bibliographer's Manual of English Literature.* London: William Pickering, 1834. Rev. ed. Henry G. Bohn, ed. London: George Bell & Sons, 1857–61.

Martz, Louis L. "A Poem Written in Ten Books." *Poet of Exile: A Study of Milton's Poetry.* New Haven: Yale University Press, 1980, chap. 9, 155–68, 326–27.

Marvell, Andrew. "Last Instructions to a Painter." James Osborn Collection, Yale University, MS PB VII/15; Portland MSS, University of Nottingham, MS PwV299; and *The Third Part of the Collection of Poems on Affairs of State* (London, 1689), 1–24.

———. *The Rehearsall Transpros'd: The Second Part*. London: Printed for Nathaniel Ponder, 1673.

Milton, John. *Paradise Lost in Ten Books. The Text Exactly Reproduced from the First Edition of 1667, with an Appendix Containing the Additions Made in later Issues and a Monograph on the Original Publication of the Poem*. London: Basil Montague Pickering, [1873]. Monograph is by R[ichard] H[erne] S[hepherd]. Preliminary leaves in Appendix.

———. *Paradise Lost as Originally Published by John Milton, Being a Facsimile Reproduction of the First Edition. With an Introduction by David Masson*. London: Elliot Stock, 1877. Reprinted, Folcroft, Pa.: Folcroft Library Editions, 1972, 1976; Philadelphia: R. West, 1978. Reviews: *The Athenæum*, March 31, 1877, 416; *The Academy*, July 28, 1877, 82–83 ("Restoration Reprints," by R. C. Browne).

———. *Paradise Lost: 1667. A Scolar Press Facsimile*. Menston, England: The Scolar Press, 1968. Reprinted 1972, 1973. Notice in *Milton Newsletter* 2 (1968): 46–47; review in *Seventeenth-Century News* 28 (1970): 12.

———. *Paradise Lost. A Poem in Twelve Books. The Author John Milton. The Second Edition Revised and Augmented by the same Author*. London: Printed by S. Simmons, 1674. Includes Samuel Barrow's poem "In Paradisum Amissam" and Andrew Marvell's poem "On Paradise Lost."

———. *Paradise Lost. A Poem in Twelve Books. The Authour John Milton. The Fourth Edition. Adorn'd with Sculptures*. London: Printed by Miles Flesher, for Richard Bently and Jacob Tonson, 1688. Two further issues: one for Bently alone and one for Tonson alone. Includes John Dryden's epigram under the Robert White frontispiece portrait.

———. *Paradise Lost*, ed. John T. Shawcross. San Francisco: Andrew Hoyem at The Arion Press, 2002. "A Note on the Text," 391–94.

Milton Newsletter 2 (1968): 46. Review.

Moyles, R. G. *The Text of "Paradise Lost": A Study in Editorial Procedure*. Toronto: University of Toronto Press, 1985.

Parker, Samuel. *A Reproof to The Rehearsal Transprosed, in a Discourse to Its Author*. London: Printed for James Collins, 1673.

Parker, Willliam Riley. *Milton: A Biography*. Oxford: Clarendon Press, 1968. Rev. ed. by Gordon Campbell, 1996.

Phillips, John. *Montelions Predictions; or, The Hogen Mogen Fortuneteller*. London: Printed by S. and B. Griffin, for Thomas Palmer, 1672.

Qvarnström, Gunnar. *The Enchanted Palace: Some Structural Aspects of "Paradise Lost."* Stockholm: Almqvist and Wiksell, 1967.

Rosenheim, James M. "An Early Appreciation of *Paradise Lost." Modern Philology* 75 (1978): 280–82.

Seventeenth-Century News 28 (1970): 12. Review.

Shawcross, John T. "Orthography and the Text of *Paradise Lost."* In *Language and Style in Milton: A Symposium in Honor of the Tercentenary of* Paradise Lost, ed. Ronald David Emma and John T. Shawcross, 120–53. New York: Frederick Ungar, 1967.

———. "The Texts of Milton's Works." In *The Riverside Milton*, ed. Roy Flannagan, xi–xxxii. Boston: Houghton Mifflin, 1998.

———. *With Mortal Voice: The Creation of* Paradise Lost. Lexington: University Press of Kentucky, 1982.

Stevens, David H. *Reference Guide to Milton from 1800 to the Present Day.* Chicago: University of Chicago Press, 1930.

von Maltzahn, Nicholas. "Laureate, Republican, Calvinist: An Early Response to Milton and *Paradise Lost* (1667)." *Milton Studies* 29, ed. Albert C. Labriola (Pittsburgh: University of Pittsburgh Press, 1992), 181–98.

———. "Samuel Butler's Milton." *Studies in Philology* 92 (1995): 482–95.

Whaler, James. *Counterpoint and Symbol: An Inquiry into the Rhythm of Milton's Epic Style.* Cøpenhagen: Rosenkilde and Bagger, 1956.

Wilson, Hugh. "The Publication of *Paradise Lost:* Censorship and Resistance." *Milton Studies* 37, ed. Albert C. Labriola (Pittsburgh: University of Pittsburgh Press, 1999): 18–41.